IMAGES
*of America*

# POESTENKILL

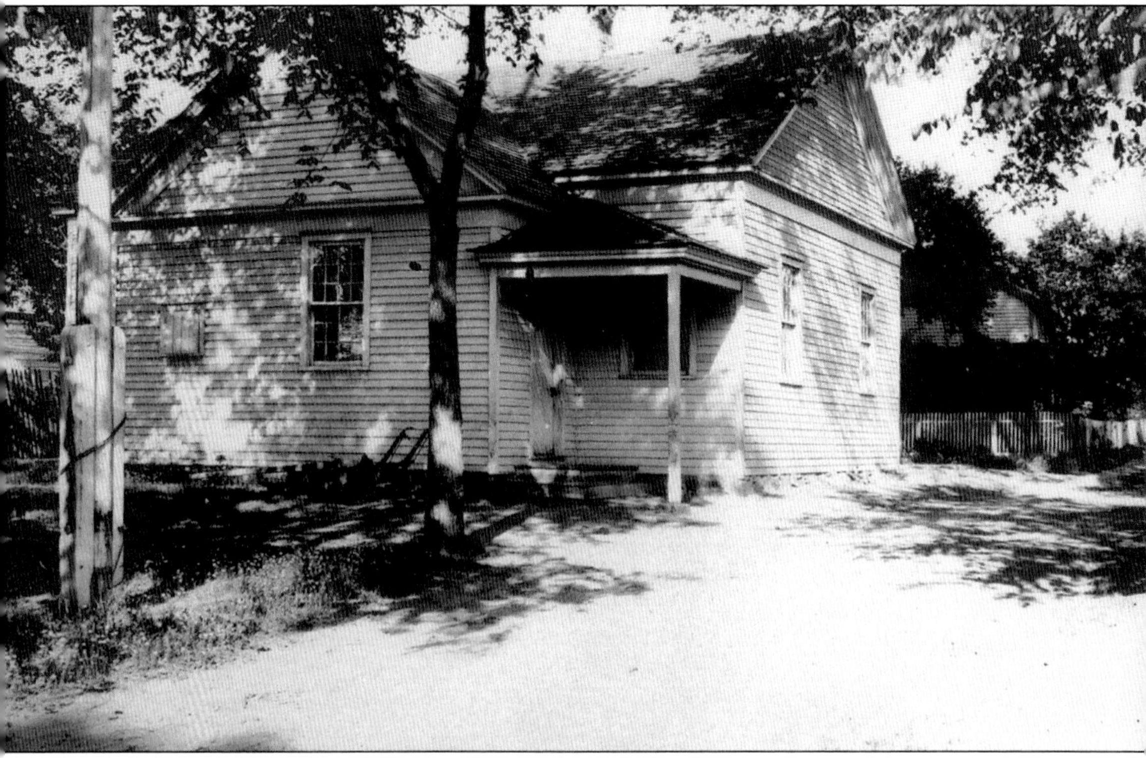

This is a picture of the front of the District No. 3 school, the Village School, which was the only two-room school in Poestenkill. It was behind this school that the students planted a tree on Arbor Day.

*On the cover*: It was Arbor Day, May 5, 1908, when the students and teachers of the District No. 3 school, the Village School, decided to plant a tree in the backyard. Identified here are Marilla Cheesbro, Thelma Whitney, Helen Radz, Ethel Chase, Specky Hull, Harold Radz, James Chase, ? Walsh, John Weinbrecht, LeRoy Castle, Leora Prediger, Waldo Chase, Carrie L. Radz (teacher), and Milton Jones. (Author's collection.)

IMAGES
*of America*

# POESTENKILL

The Poestenkill Historical Society
with Linda Sagendorf

ARCADIA
PUBLISHING

ISBN 978-0-7385-5791-5

Published by Arcadia Publishing
Charleston SC, Chicago IL, Portsmouth NH, San Francisco CA

Printed in the United States of America

Library of Congress Catalog Card Number: 2008923562

For all general information contact Arcadia Publishing at:
Telephone 843-853-2070
Fax 843-853-0044
E-mail sales@arcadiapublishing.com
For customer service and orders:
Toll-Free 1-888-313-2665

Visit us on the Internet at www.arcadiapublishing.com

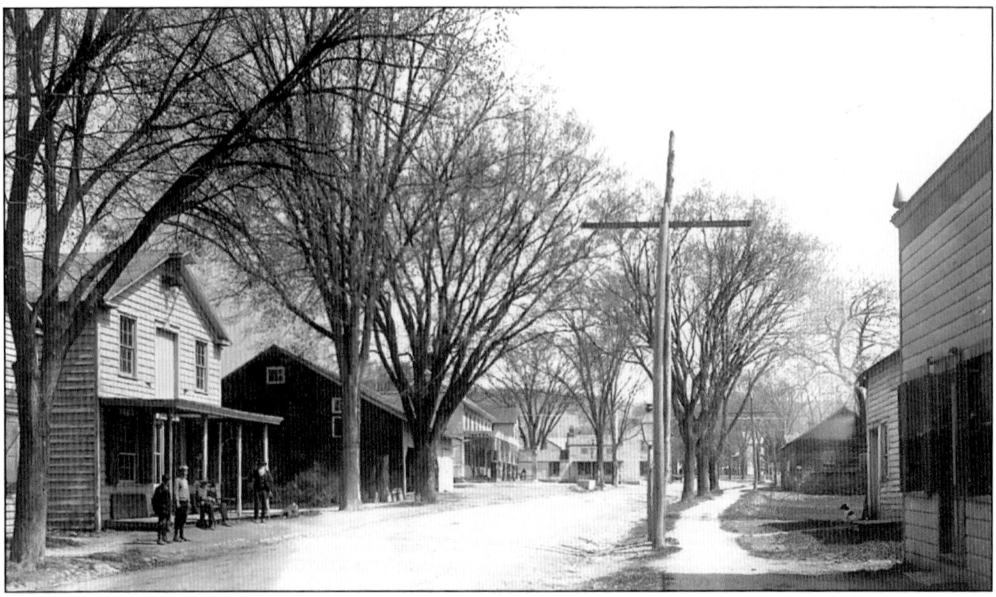

On the far left is the original Bubie's General Store, followed by the sheds used for the neighboring Woodbine Hotel. Union Hall (center) was the home of Fred and Irma Fisher as well as a store and post office, and a large room on the second floor used for public affairs. The first building on the right was a barbershop. The farthest building was the old wooden blacksmith shop. The elm trees lining the street were uprooted during a 1928 storm that produced very high winds.

# Contents

# ACKNOWLEDGMENTS

The Poestenkill Historical Society has been in existence since being granted a charter by the education department of the University of the State of New York on May 1, 1959, for the purposes of promoting interest in the history of the community and collecting and preserving information and objects related to this history. Members of the first board of trustees were Eva G. Hall, Cora Irene Kropp, William L. Millard, Roland H. Trathen, and Rogers B. Finch.

Poestenkill's only pictorial history book was published in 1975 to commemorate our nation's bicentennial celebration. Since then, many persons have asked for a reprint or new pictorial history of our town. Arcadia Publishing editor Rebekah Collinsworth gave us the necessary approval and the work began. Special gratitude is expressed to the working committee of Clifford Dunworth and Joan Zweig. Thank you also to Cathy Sagendorf for her patience in guiding me through the computer aspect of scanning and saving our precious photographs.

I gratefully acknowledge the persons and organizations that made photographs and information available to us. These people are, in alphabetical order, Virginia Swankey Bailey, Charles L. Ballard, Timothy Brod, Charles Bubie, John Bubie, Roger Bubie, Lori Bulson, Alice Castagnier, Alma Clement, Sandra Grunge DeFilippis, Joyce Dickinson, Mary Dzembo, Samuel Dzembo, Eva Gemmill, Lillian Catlin Gooley, Kenneth Gypson, Clarita Mango, Bruce Moody, Margaret Ryan, Linda Sagendorf, Mary Ann Walsh, and Joan and John Zweig, as well as those who previously donated valuable photographs to our archival collection.

—Linda Sagendorf, Town of Poestenkill Historian

# Introduction

This publication highlights the early days of Poestenkill. In a little more than a century, the town's history moved from a virtually self-sufficient population to residents with a sort of suburban dependency on nearby Troy and Albany. But vestiges of the past cling to the 21st century through Poestenkill's elders, its fine old homes, its churches, its library, and its historical society.

The images that follow depict resourceful families who lived in the rural community of Poestenkill. From the early days of photography through the 1950s, these scenes show Poestenkill folks pursuing their daily activities, as well as enjoying special events. Some of the photographs verify the town's extraordinary natural beauty. Its rolling bottomlands and forested mountains supported two major occupations of earlier generations, farming and lumbering, while the Poesten Kill, the important stream that runs through town, powered sawmills, flouring mills, and major industrial sites in Brunswick and Troy.

Very likely those self-sufficient residents from the 1800s, when the population hovered around 1,000, would be strangers in today's relatively fast-paced bedroom community of more than 4,000. Today's town government, in which local residents participate, includes many layers added in recent decades, such as planning and zoning boards, a conservation commission, and multiple county, state, and federal mandates. Once a man may have built his own home in the village or his farmhouse on the mountain. Today however, multidwelling developments are fast replacing the town's agricultural acres.

The lives of local folks were once defined by toil at farms, shops, and mills. But their days were livened by regular church attendance and occasional homemade entertainments. These latter events tended to be the most photographed. With great good luck, many of those images exist today and will be preserved in this publication.

In the early 1600s, long before the age of photography, the Dutch East India Company granted a vast tract of land in the New World to Killean VanRensselaer. The tract would eventually comprise all of Rensselaer and Albany Counties. Dutch farmers were encouraged to immigrate to the VanRensselaer grant and rent farmland from the patroon. This same feudal system continued to control development as well as the lives of local families, until it was abolished by the New York State legislature in the mid-19th century. Some local families still treasure their ancestor's contracts with the patroon.

In the late 1700s, when Stephen VanRensselaer came of age, he became the patroon of VanRensselaer holdings on the east side of the Hudson River. This was the East Manor, and it included Poestenkill. Stephen was called the "good patroon" because—to the consternation of his heirs—he temporarily forgave rents to his tenants. He also started Rensselaer Polytechnic Institute in Troy, was a U.S. congressman, promoted the Erie Canal, and gave lands to East Manor towns, including Poestenkill, for public elementary schools.

Within the lifetime of Stephen, a hamlet named Poestenkill existed beside the Poesten Kill (*kill* being Dutch for creek). That hamlet was then in the town of Sand Lake. On March 2, 1848, for reasons unknown today, the New York State legislature separated approximately 32.5 square miles from the town of Sand Lake and named the town Poestenkill, for the stream that ran through it.

Soon other hamlets, each with a distinct character, sprang up within the new town, although parts of the area were already populated by farms leased from Stephen VanRensselaer, principally by Germans and by Yankees in their epic westward migration. East Poestenkill claimed the mountains to the east, with its own post office, hotel, smithy, school, three churches, and commercial establishments. In Barberville, there was Betsy Barber's store, Henry Moon's hotel, a shoe shop and tinsmith, and, across the road, the Poesten Kill's mighty 100-foot falls. Ives Corners amenities included a large hotel and store, a smithy, and the Ives Corners school. Down the mountain, Poestenkill village boasted two each of hotels, churches, and schools and other numerous industries. The hamlets were centers of population and trade, and farms were scattered throughout the town, even in the mountainous areas. Town fathers established eight school districts throughout the community.

Differences in time and major changes in society have evolved since long-ago cameras snapped the scenes that follow. But somehow, the rugged beautiful terrain transmits strength to today's residents. They continue to build off the heritage of the German, Dutch, and Yankee forefathers—and foremothers—who settled their town. Today Poestenkill maintains its appeal.

—Eva Gemmill

# *One*

# LIFE IN THE COUNTRY

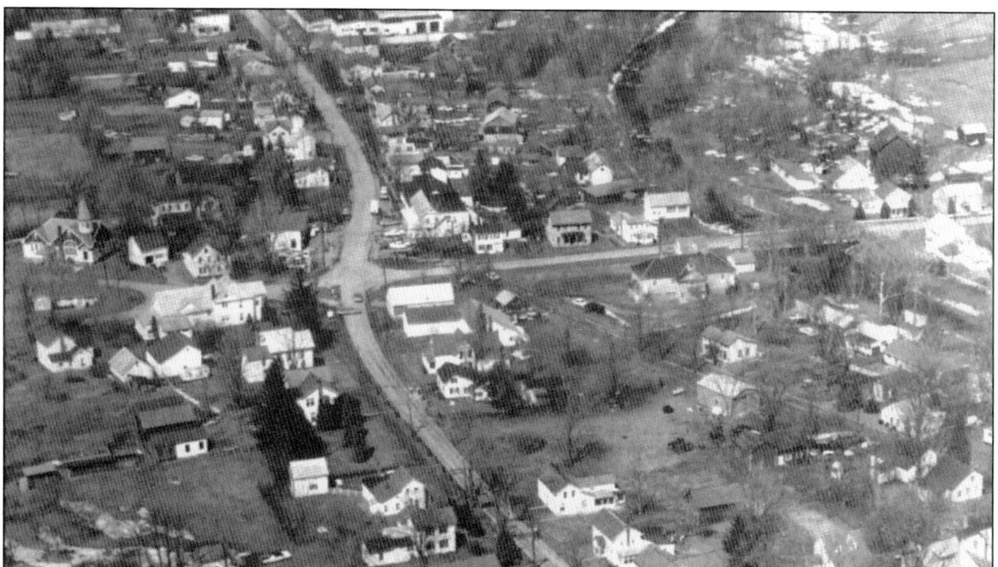

This is a bird's-eye view of Poestenkill from around 1969. This photograph was used on the cover of several issues of the local newspaper *Snake Hill Sun*, published in the 1960s and early 1970s.

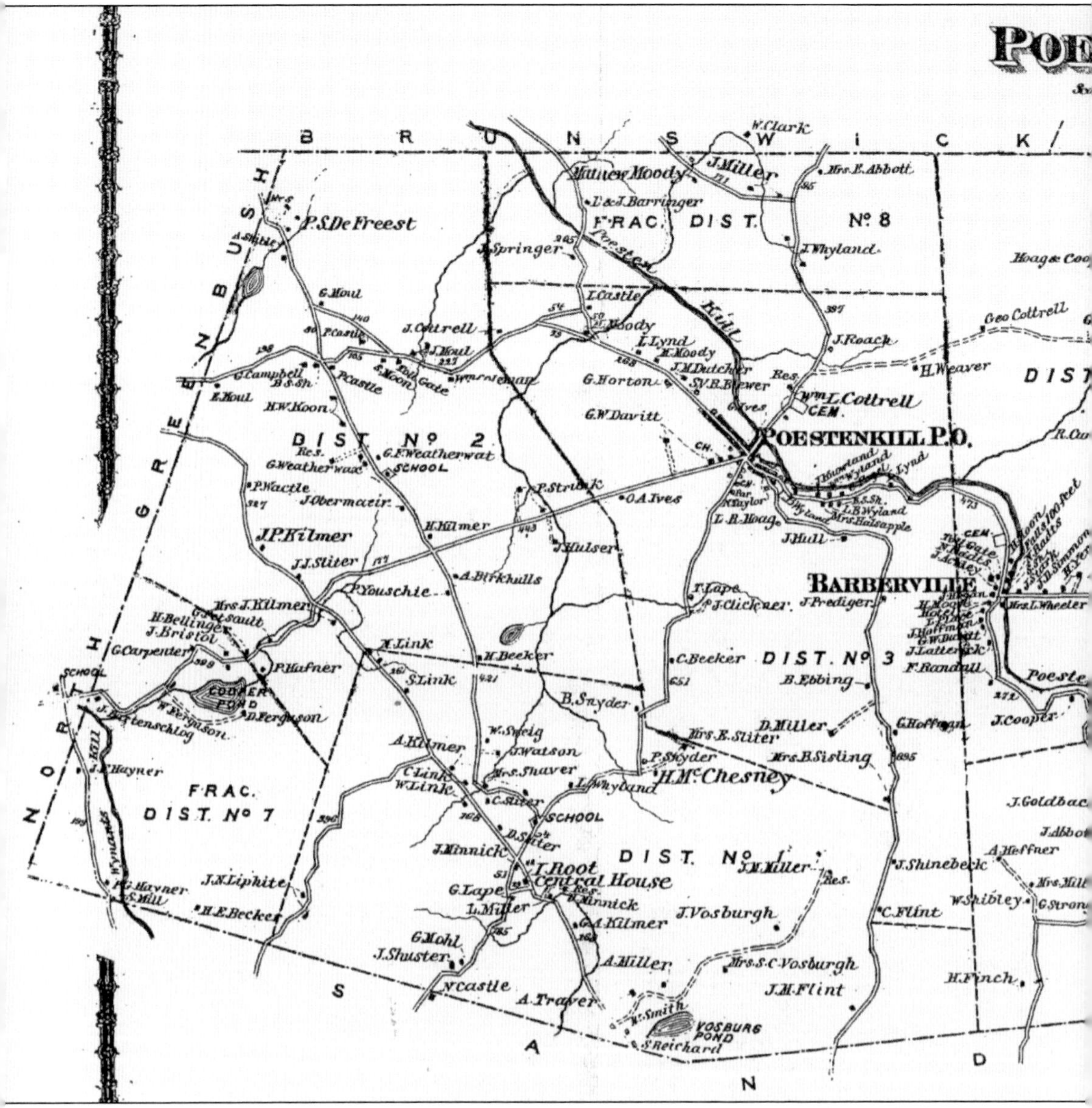


Seen here is a map of the town of Poestenkill. The map shows the town borders and school districts

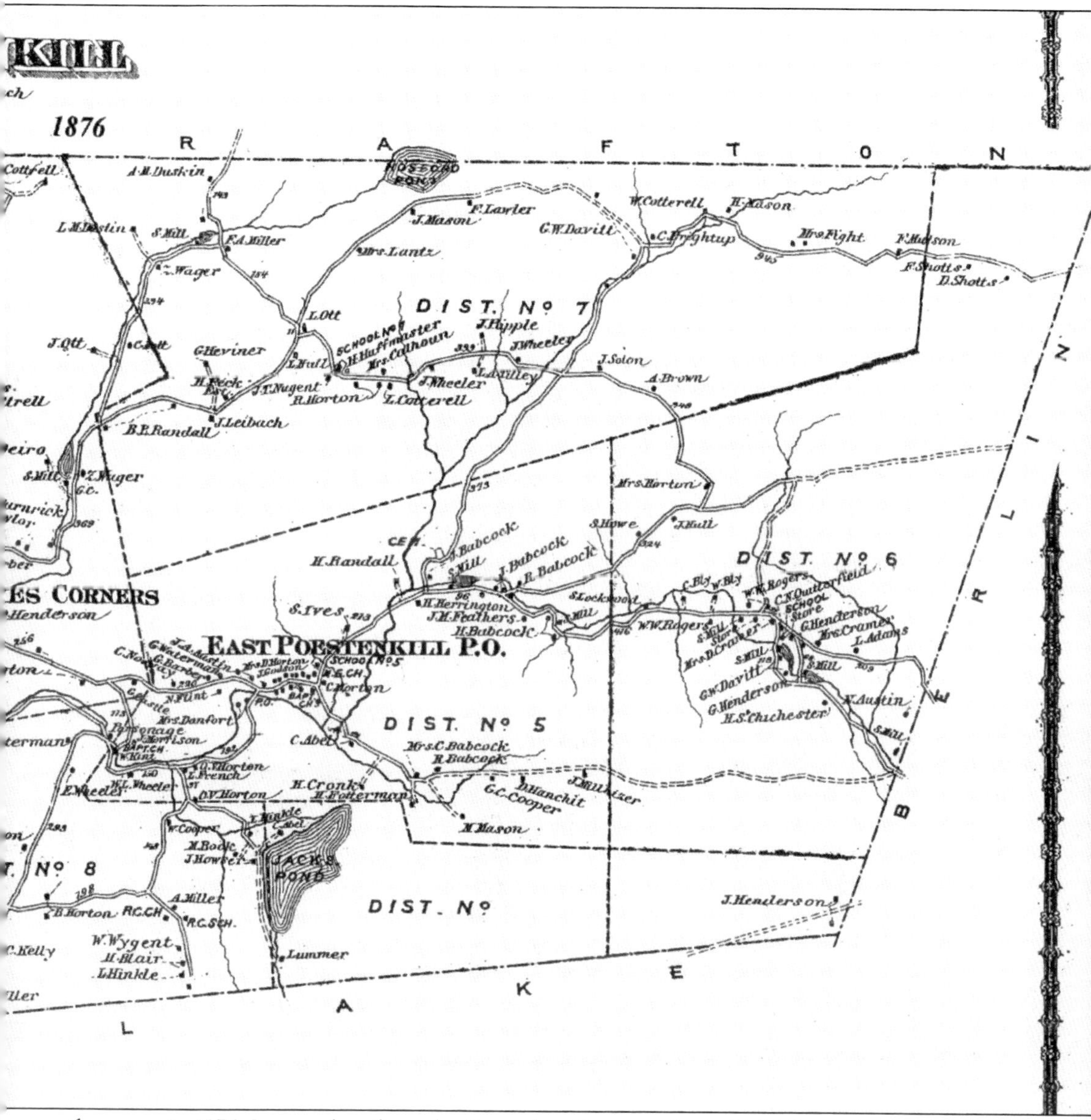


as they were in 1876. It was taken from the Rensselaer County atlas by F. W. Beers from 1876.

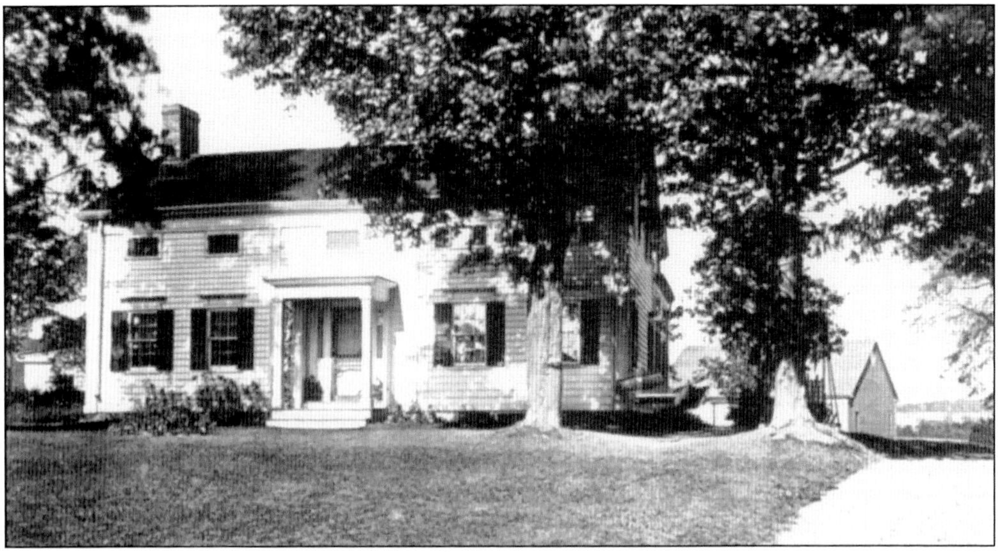

These photographs are of what is now Lochvue Apartments on Spring Avenue Extension. The main house above was built around 1911. Below is the original smaller home, from around 1902, which is still located on the property. The land was conveyed by Stephen VanRensselaer to John DeFreest on June 11, 1805.

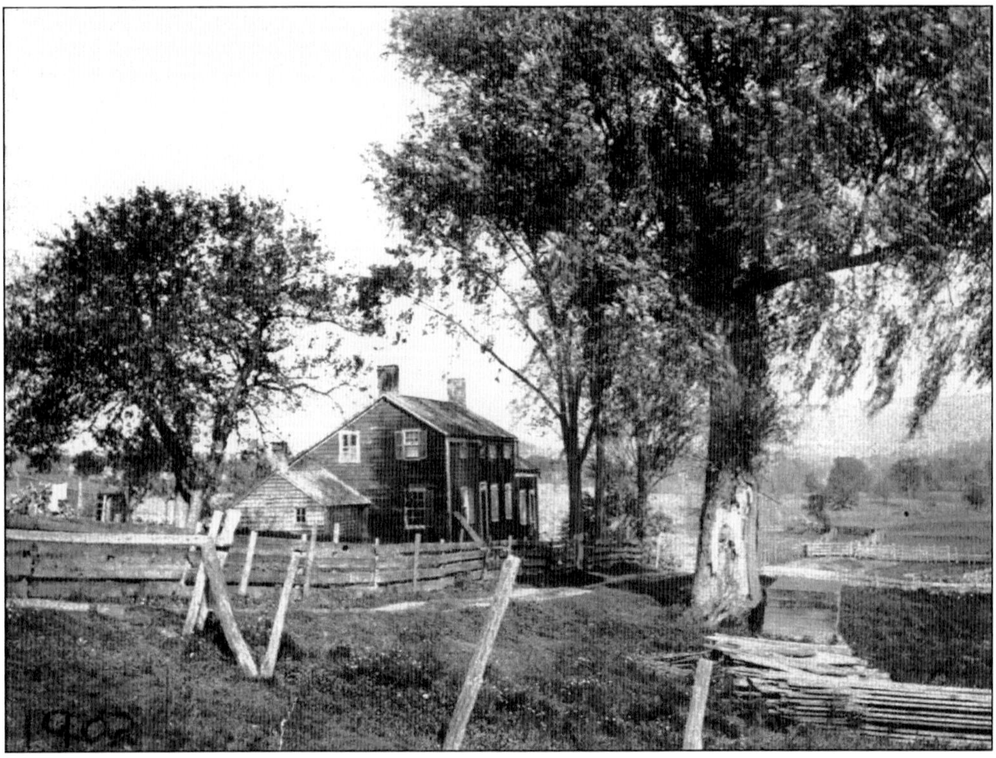

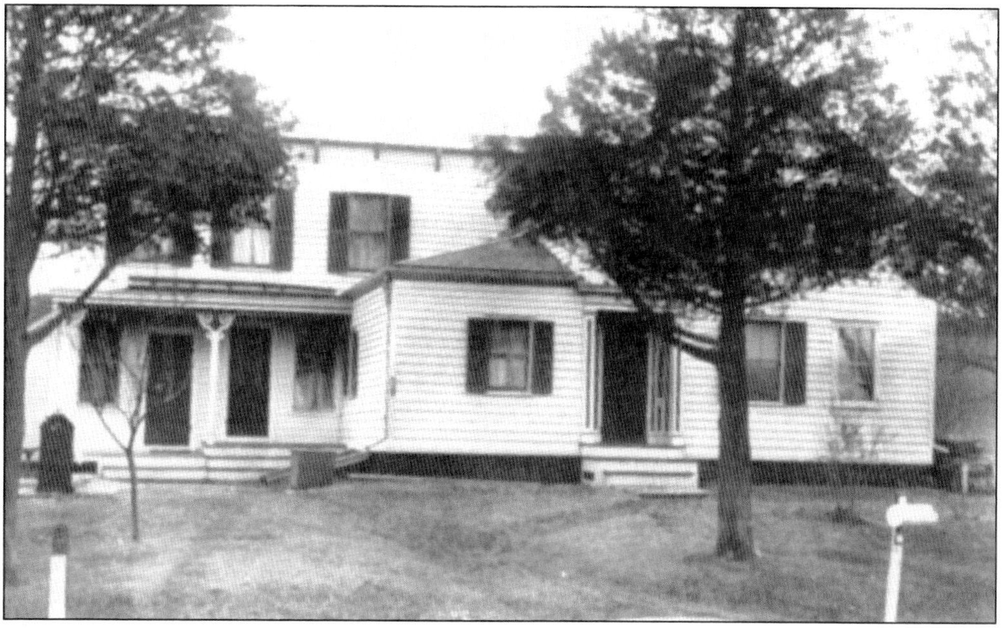

This stately home on Spring Avenue Extension, from around 1908, was owned by the Colehammer family. It was demolished in the late 1950s at the request of the last remaining relatives.

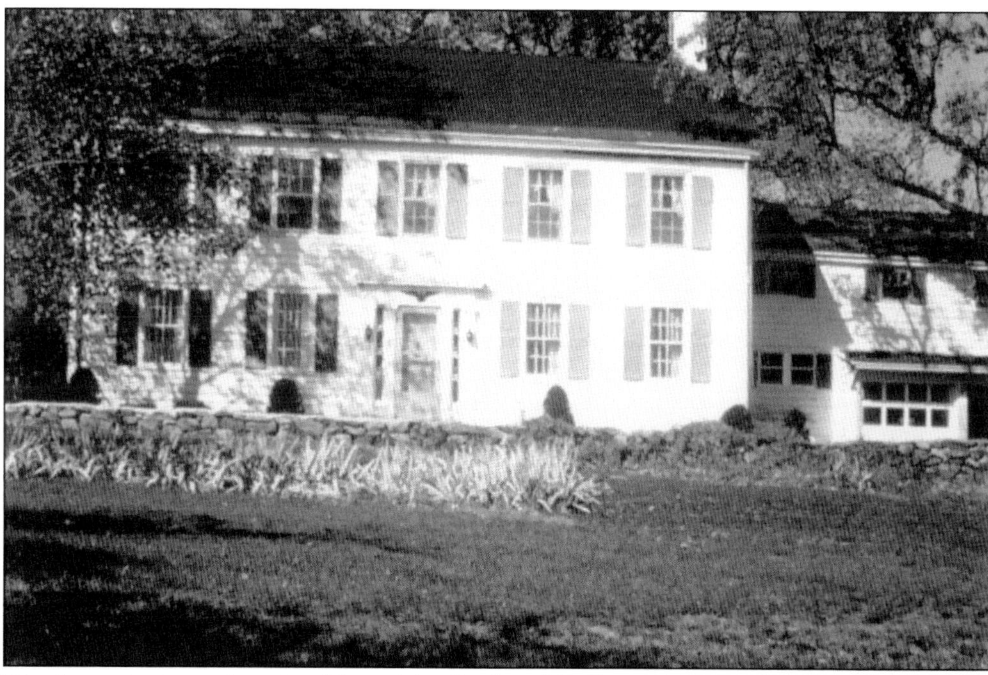

The home is situated on land leased by Stephen VanRensselaer to Christeyean Cooper on June 24, 1790, subject to payment of "one bushel fifty-eight pounds of wheat yearly and three fowls and one load of wood every sixth year." The original house burned, and the present structure was built in 1849.

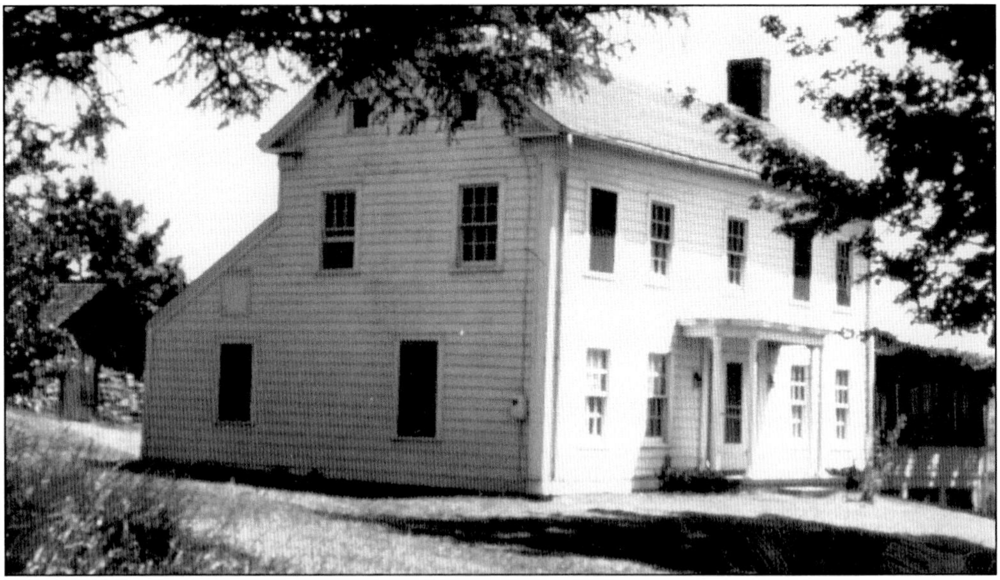

Although 1790 is the date of the first deed known on the Kilmer farm, which the Ryan property is now part of, the William Kilmer family leased the land from Stephen VanRensselaer's East Manor some years previously. Peter Kilmer is believed to have built the main portion of the existing home in the early 1800s as the main dwelling for a farm on 222 acres. At that time, it was surrounded by several large sheds and a white picket fence with two large barns across the road. At the rear of the house stood the stone smokehouse and the family cemetery.

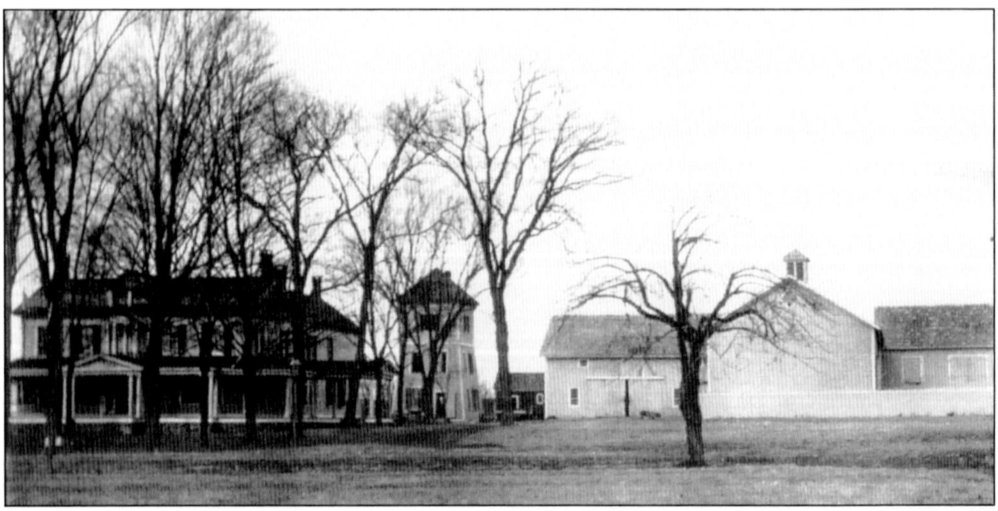

This stately home was built by the Lynd family, one of the earliest families to settle in Poestenkill. In 1904, the property was conveyed to the Holser family. It stayed in that family for three generations.

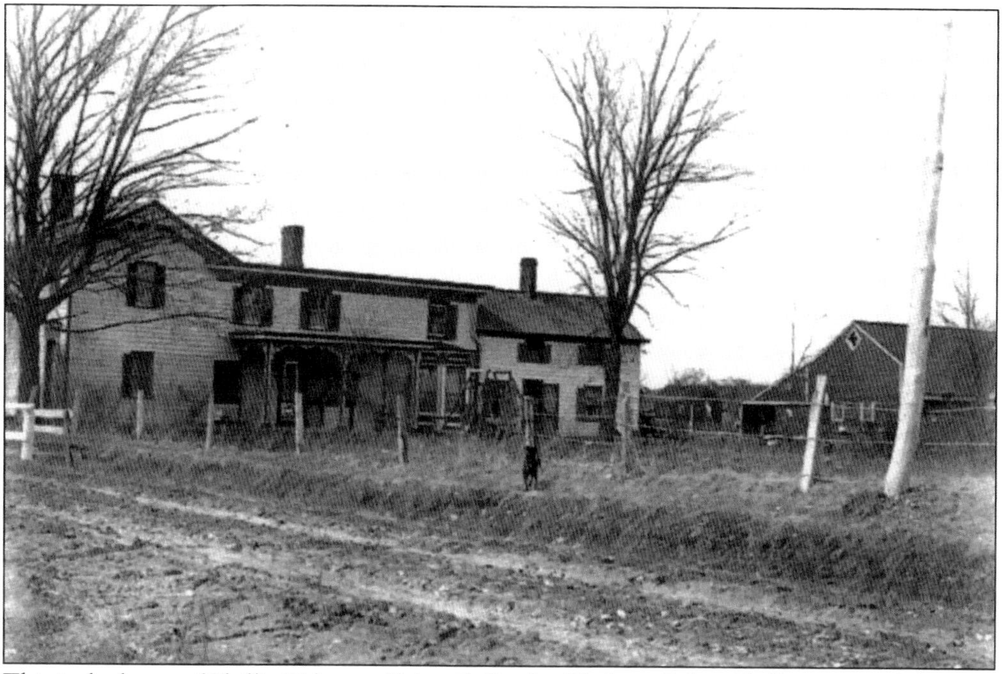

This is the home of Phillip Fisher and his wife Bertha Clickner Fisher. Phillip operated the True Elgin Creamery, located a quarter mile west of the home. Today this house has been transformed into apartments.

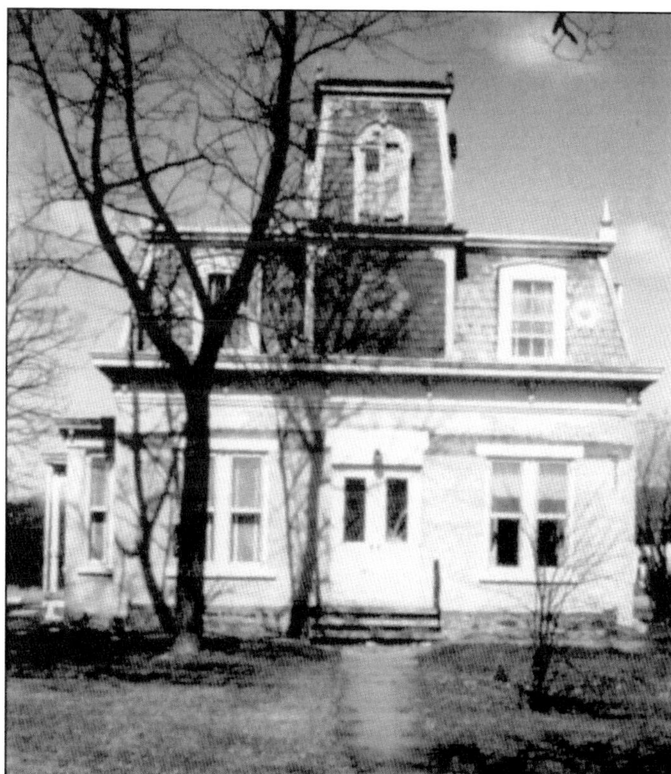

The Daley House was built in 1863. This picture was taken after extensive restoration. The home was built by the Dutcher family and later owned by the Cottrells, and then the Whylands. It is a polychrome, brick-and-slate Victorian with a cupola on the roof.

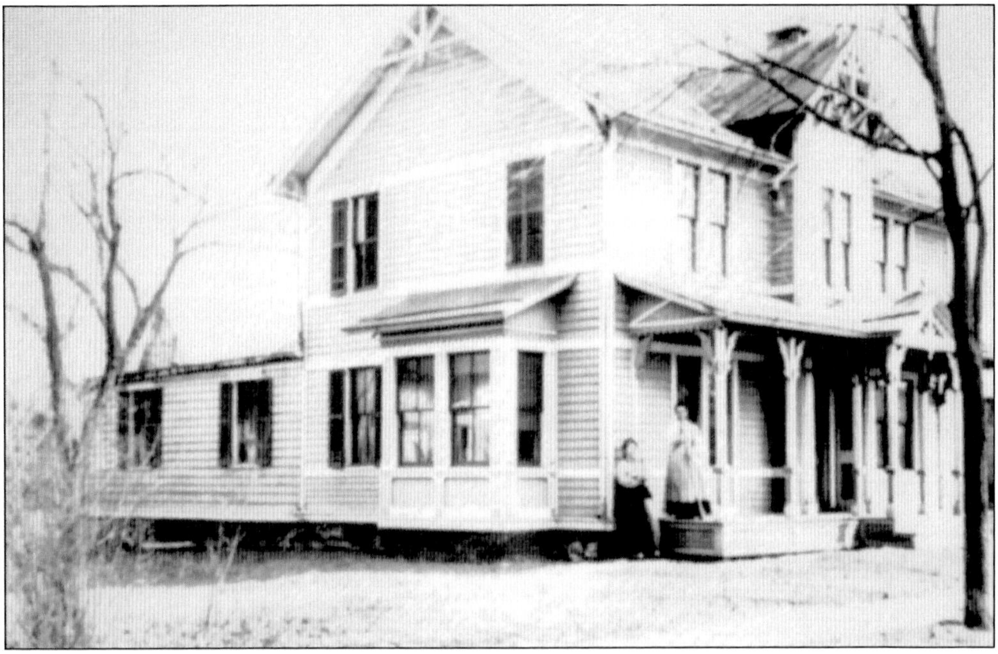

This was the home of the widow Barringer, mother of Charles and grandmother of Aretta and Ethel. It was later the home of Frank Clickner.

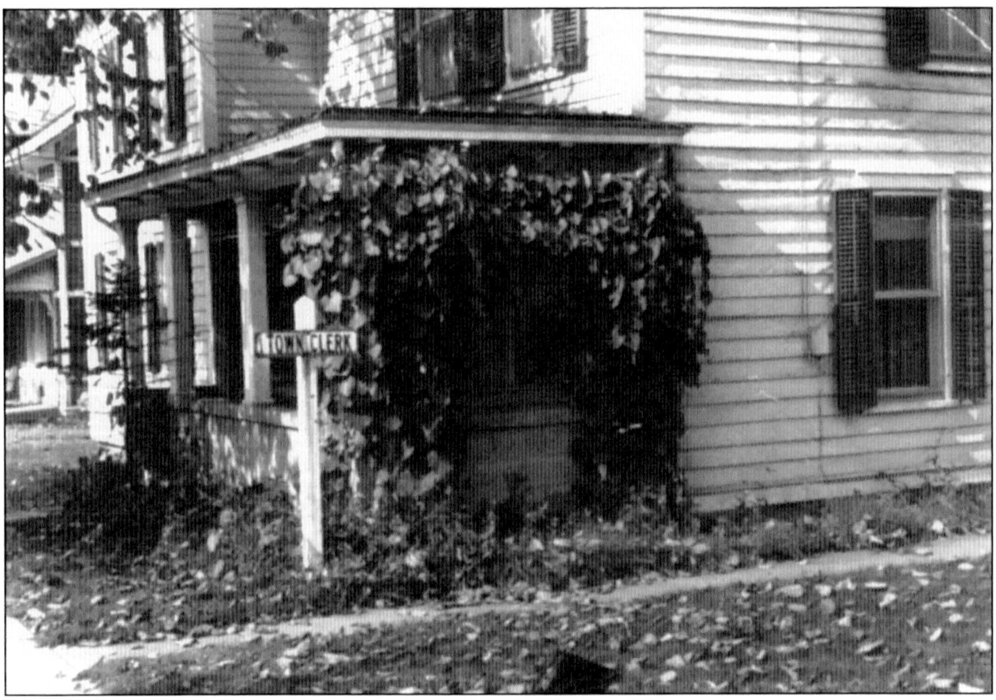


Just east of his mother's home is the home of Charles Barringer and his family. His daughter Aretta lived there until her death. She had the office of the town clerk in the back of her home, as she held that position for over 50 years. The west side of the home was once an old schoolhouse with the upstairs being the living quarters for the teacher. The house was built in 1855.

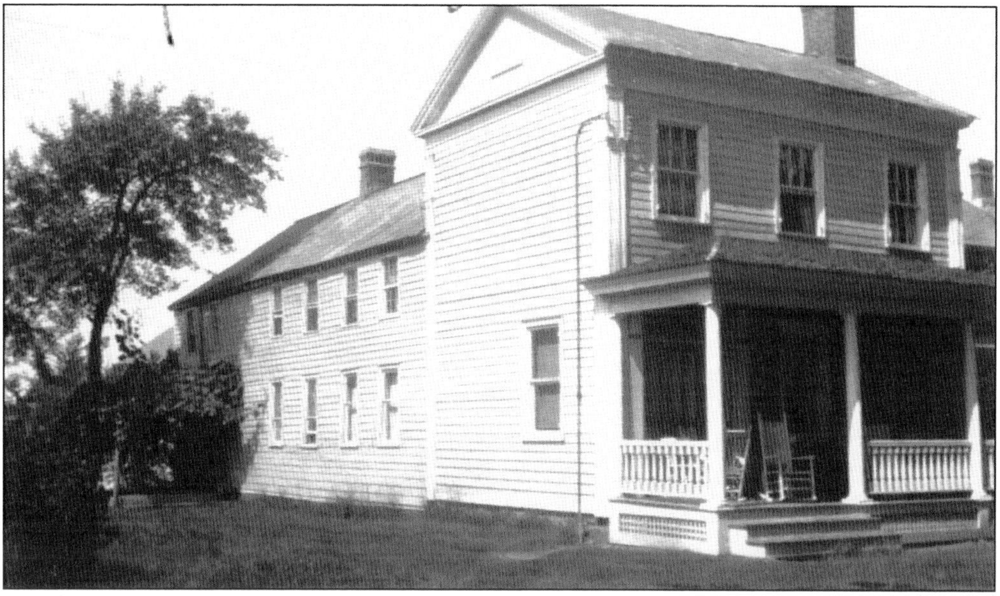

This home was once used as a boardinghouse for students attending the Poestenkill Academy. It is currently a private residence and used as a single-family home.

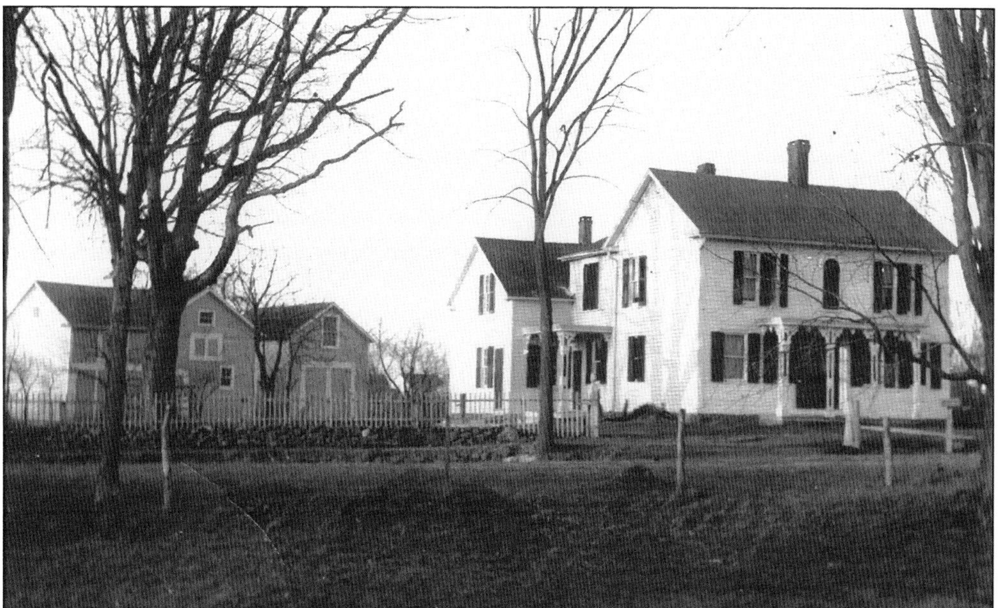

This was the Clint homestead, about 1908, on Snyders Corners Road and is now owned by Joseph and Lois Vartigan.

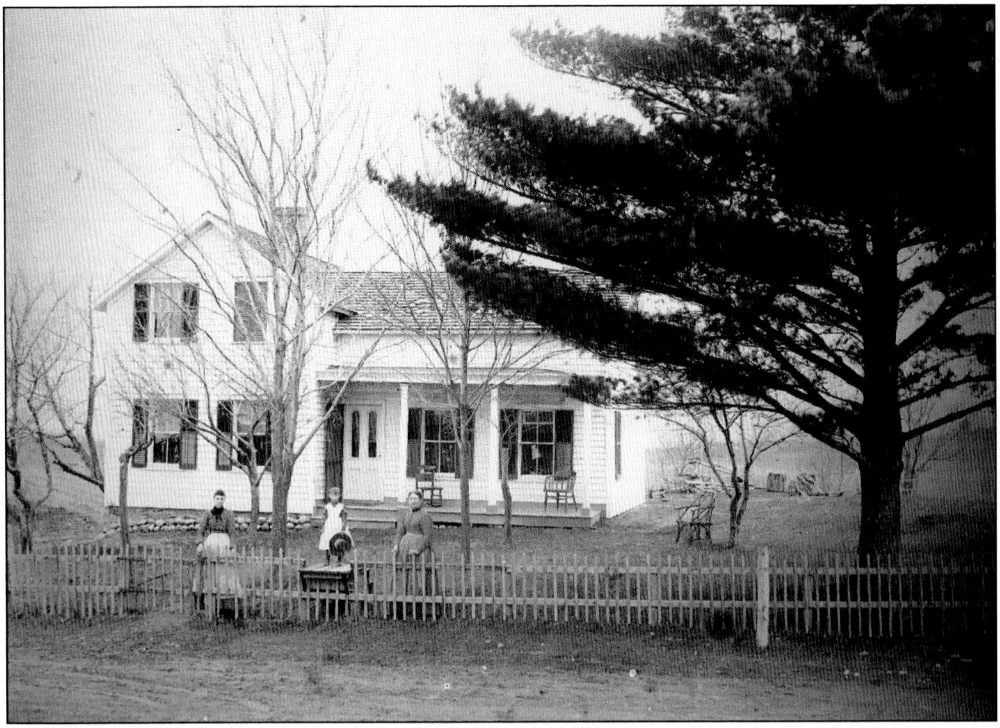

The Zweig homestead on Route 66 across from Algonquin School is seen here. In the foreground are, from left to right, Lilly Sliter, Ila Zweig Reckner, and Melvina Link Sliter.

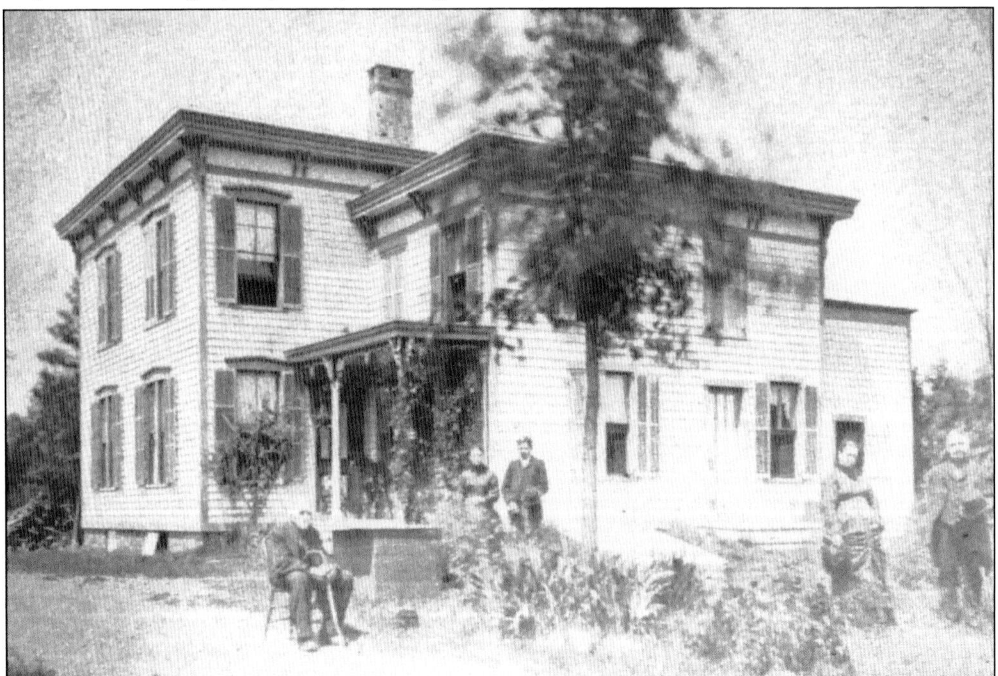

The Devan home is off Round Top Road. It was built by Jacob Clickner and is one of the very few homes in the area built with a flat roof.

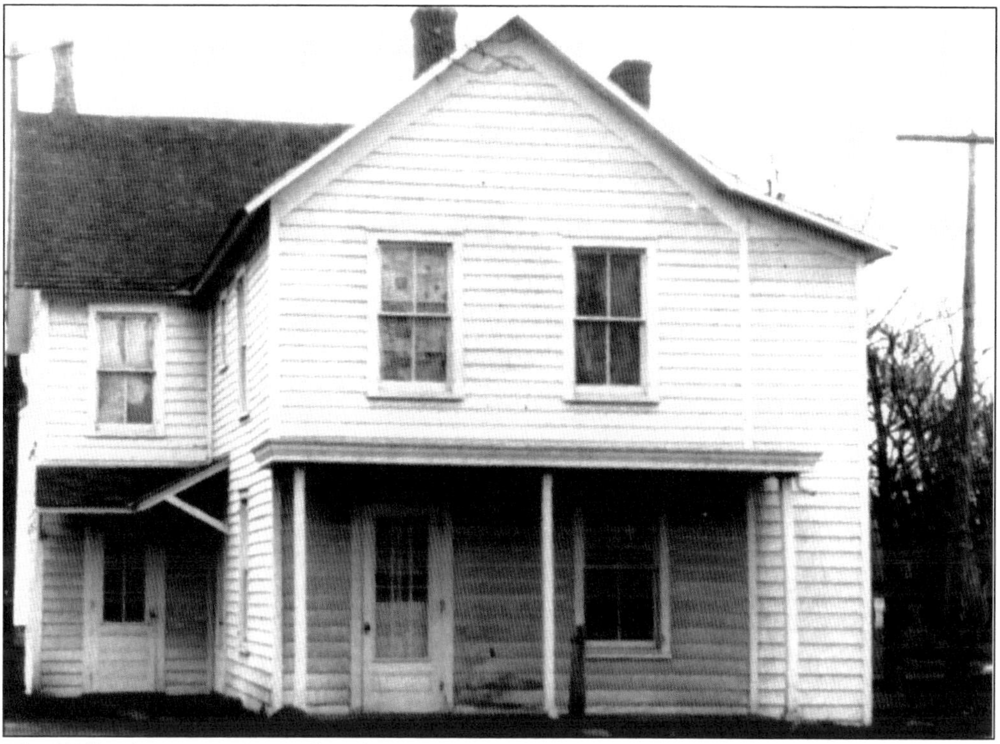

The Wilker home was located at the point where Round Top Road and Snyders Corners Road meet. The home was demolished (below) in the mid-1950s to make way for the new road.

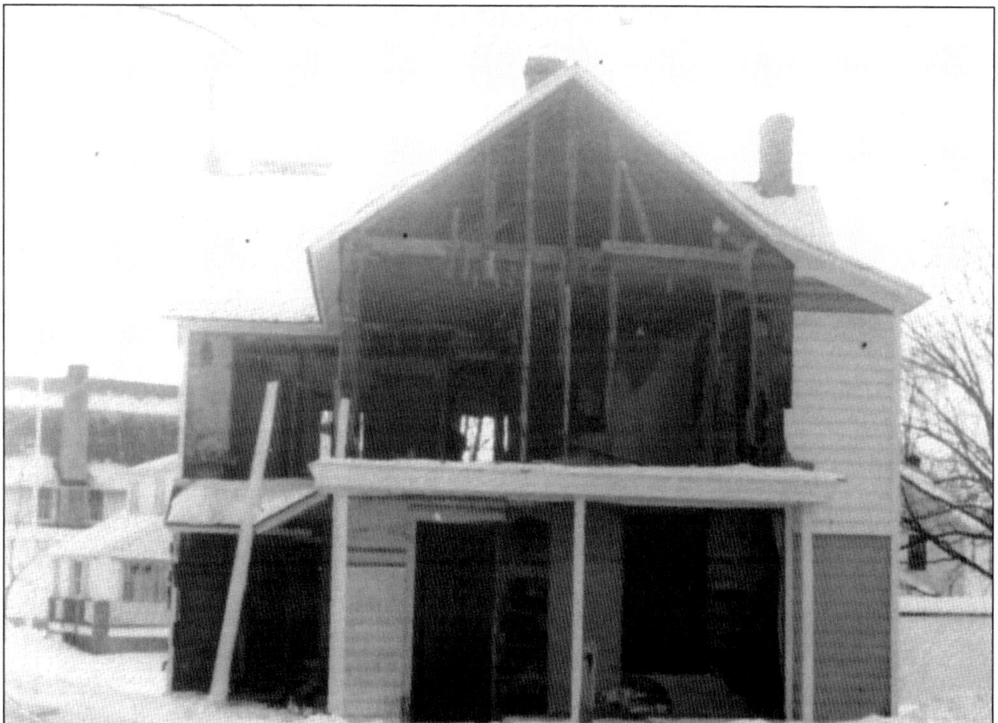

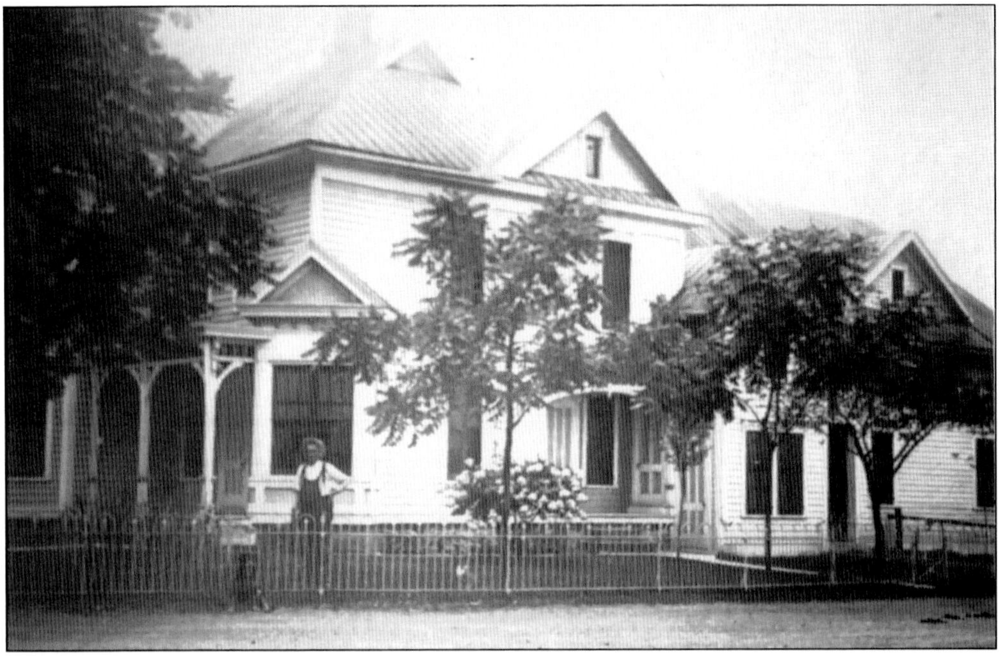

This homestead was built in 1875 by Lysander Clickner and has been in the Clickner/Ives family ever since. It once housed a meat market operated by the Ives family and later Vernon and Arnold Hoffman. The iron fence was removed when the county wanted to widen the road. The barn, now a garage, housed horse stalls and chicken coops, which still remain.

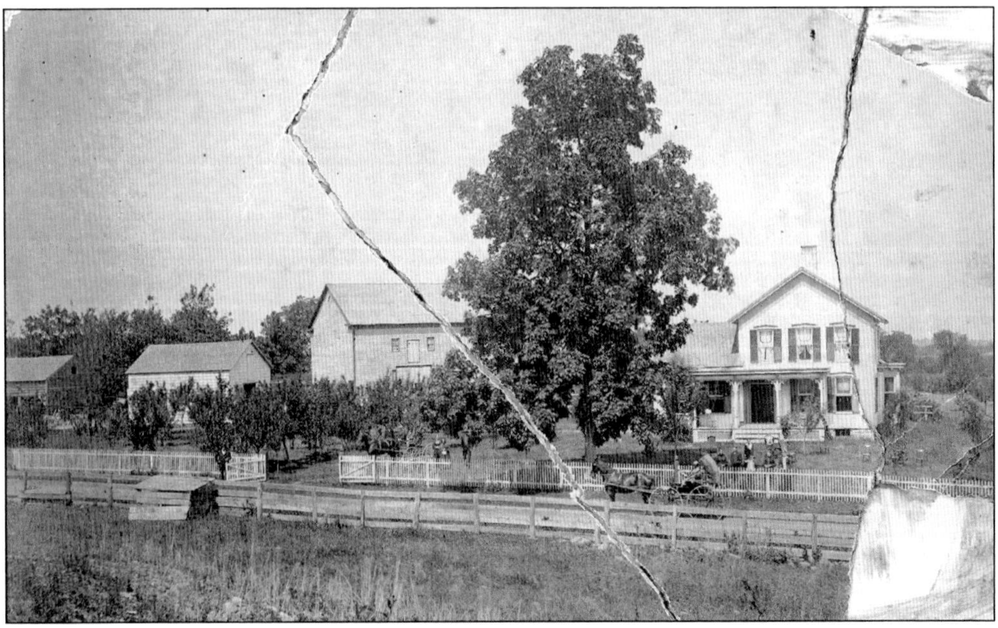

The Brod home is on Farm-to-Market Road just north of the village. This home is still an active small farm and continues to be occupied by the Brod family.

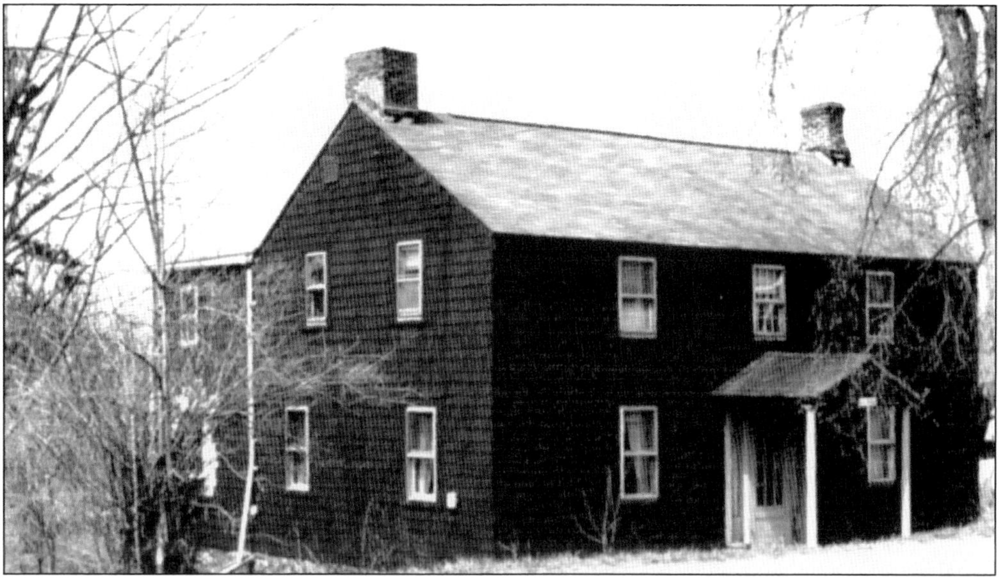

This is the oldest surviving home in the village of Poestenkill. It was built by Archelaus Lynd in the 1750s and boasts three adobe clay-and-brick fireplaces and the remains of a beehive fireplace in the basement.

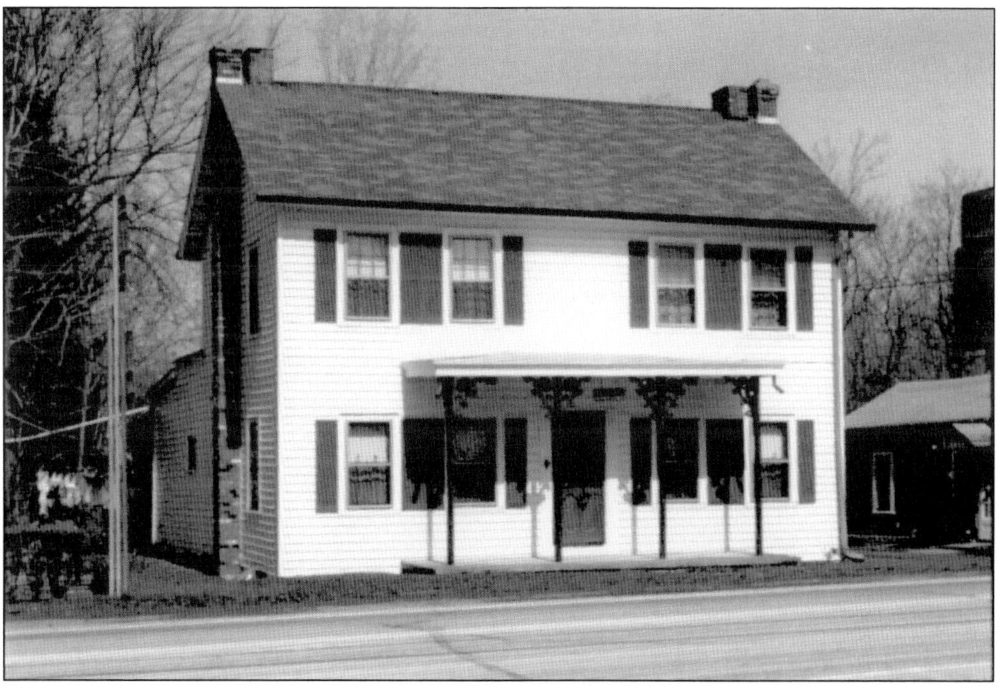

Built around 1850, this is the residence of Alfred Horton. The inside of the home has been modernized but the outside has remained relatively unchanged since it was built.

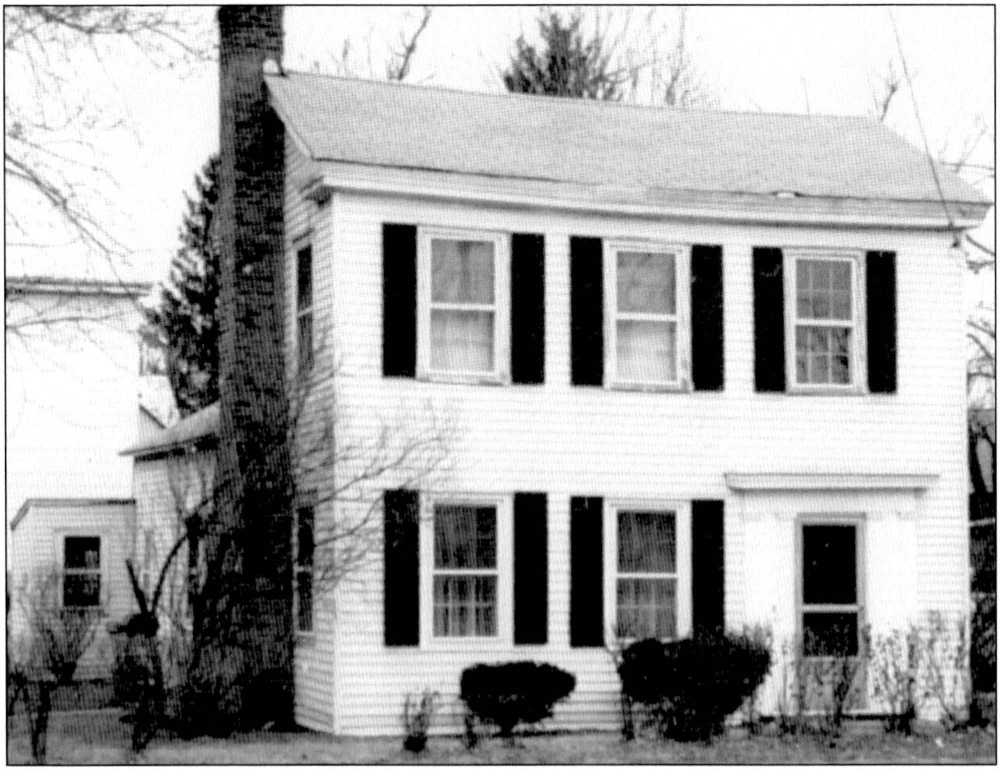

This is the home of Ivan Hall, who operated a general store and post office from a building attached to the south side of the home around 1850. The home was recently demolished, and a new general store/snack bar has been built in its place.

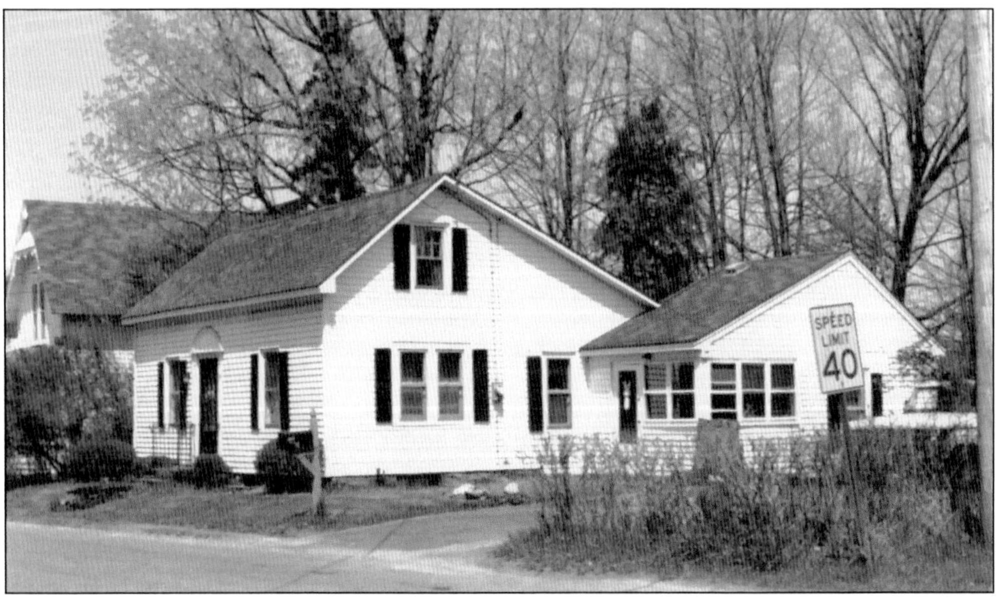


This home on Plank Road is one of the earliest homes built in the village. It was built by Archelaus Lynd and given to his daughter as a wedding gift.

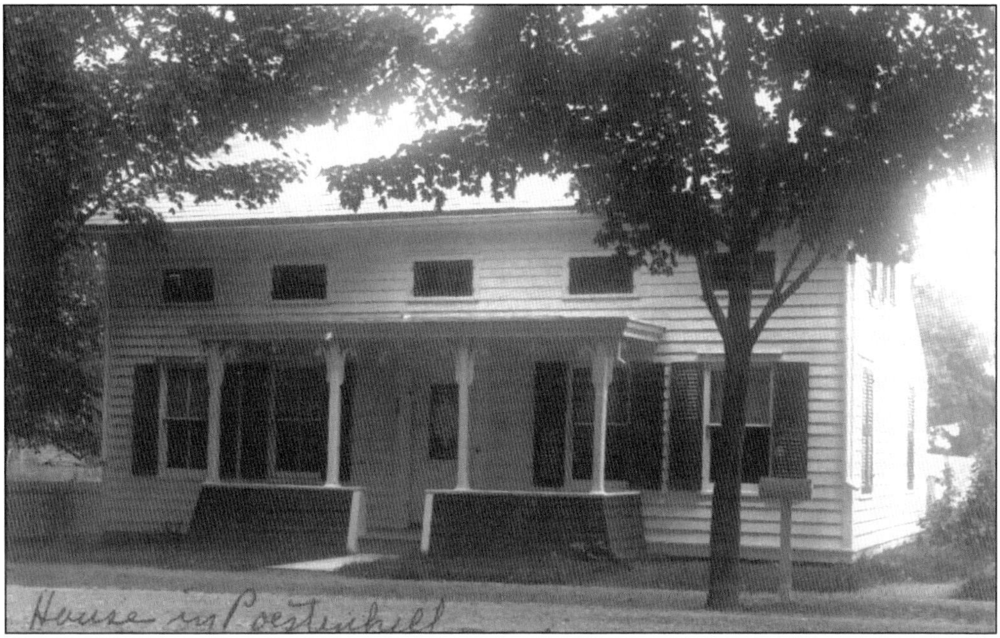


The home shown here was built by Arch McCllen and later owned by the Veith family. It is due east of the current post office.

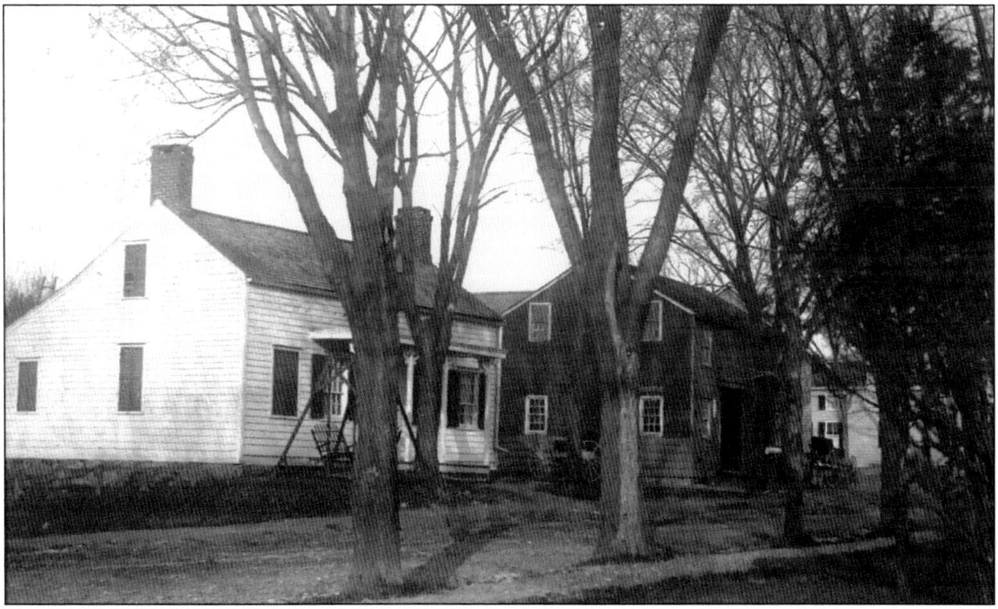

This home and blacksmith shop appear in Joseph Henry Hidley's paintings of Poestenkill in 1852. They were the home and shop of Peter Bosch and located on Plank Road.

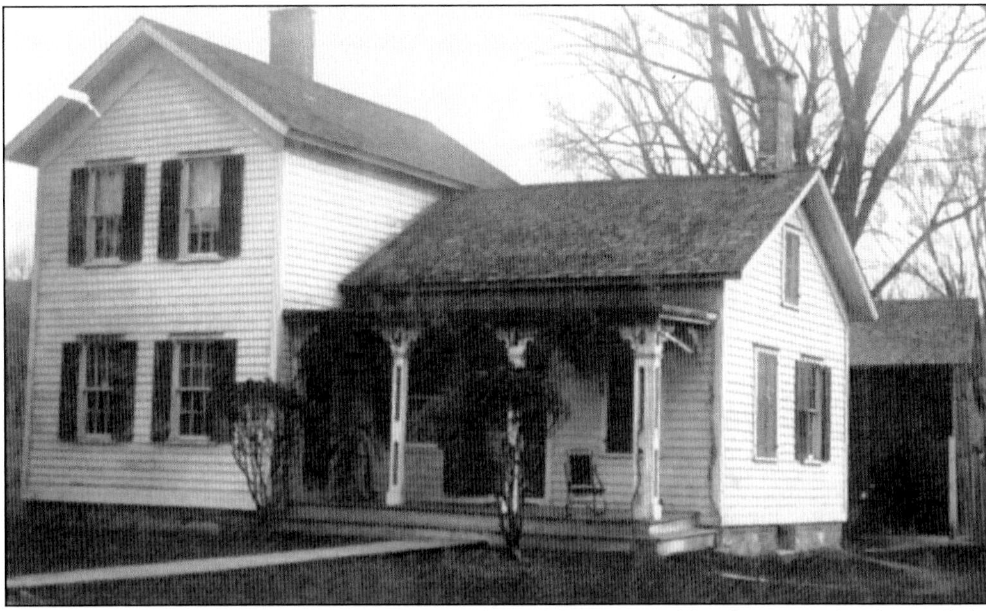

This home was built in 1865 by the Ives family and later owned by the Dater family until the 1960s. John Dater was a local businessman, an accomplished musician, and at one time, town clerk. The building in the back (below) was called the Shop and was where Dater made shirts.

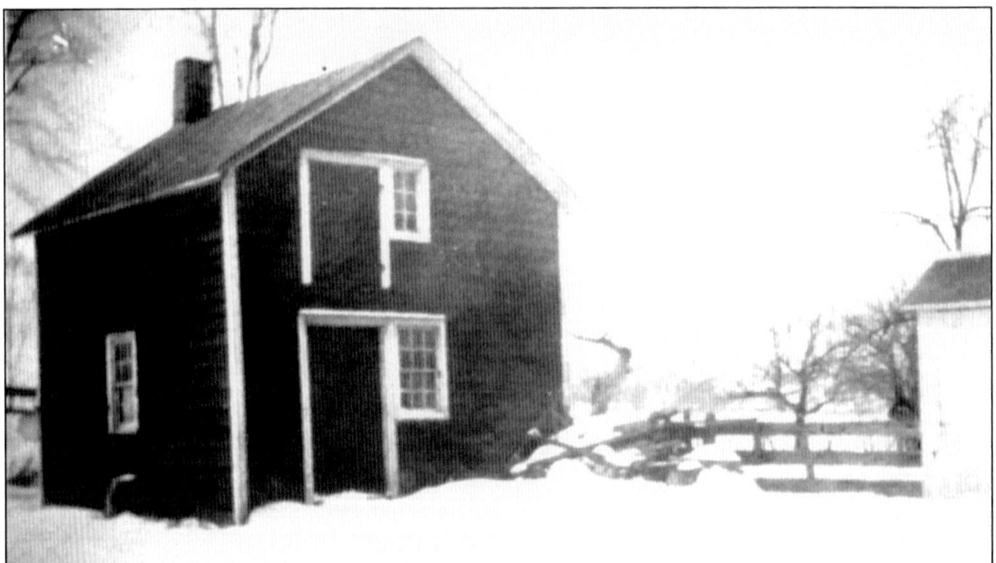

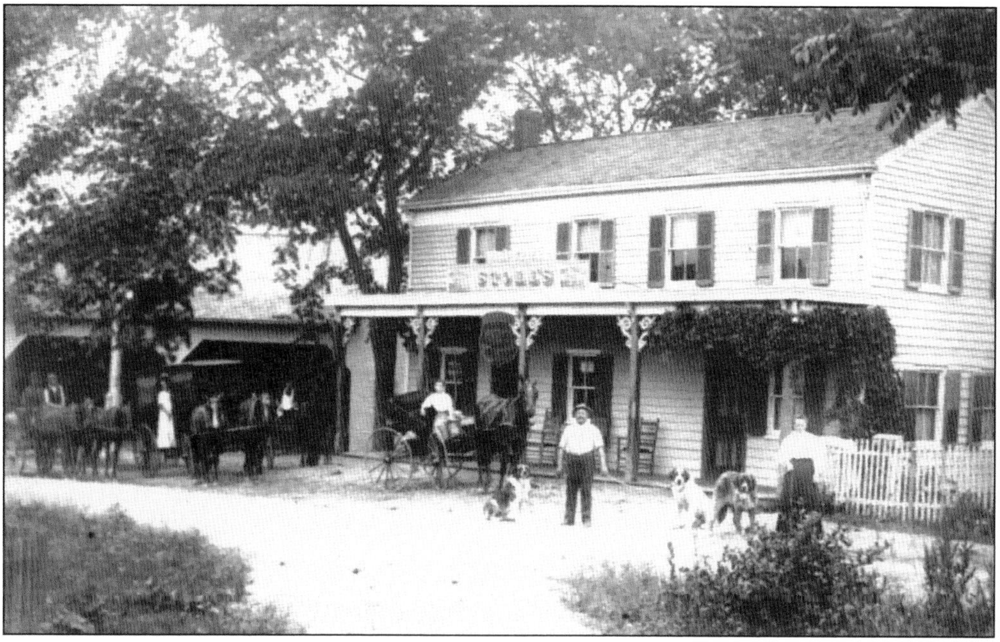

The Eagle Hotel is seen above in its heyday. The sheds at the left were later converted into a home (below).

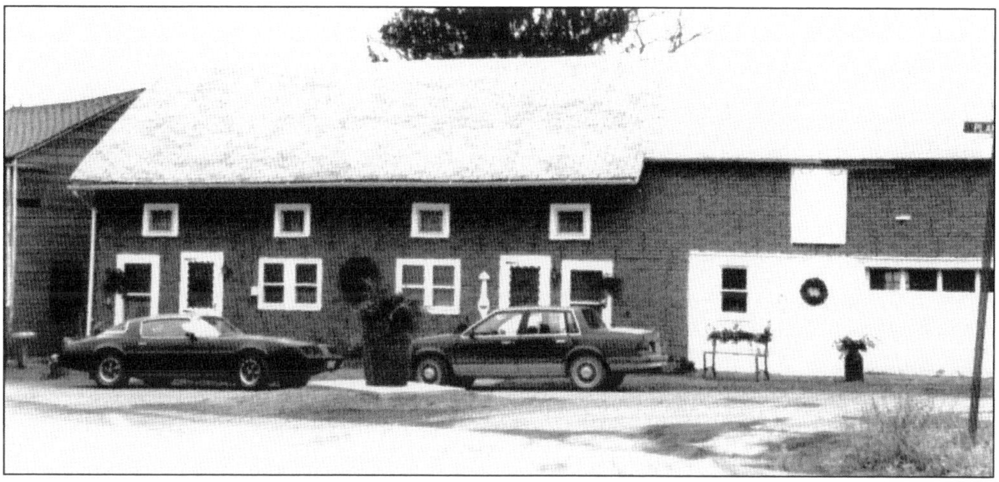

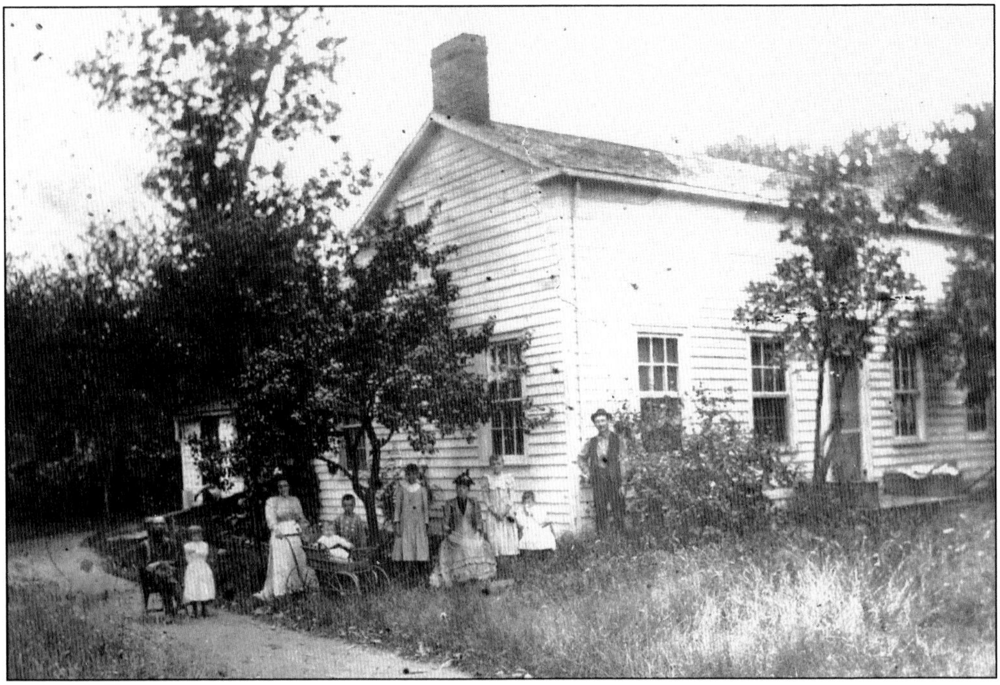

Seen here are Edgar Hull and family at their home on Snake Hill Road. This later became the Forebellar farmhouse around the 1890s.

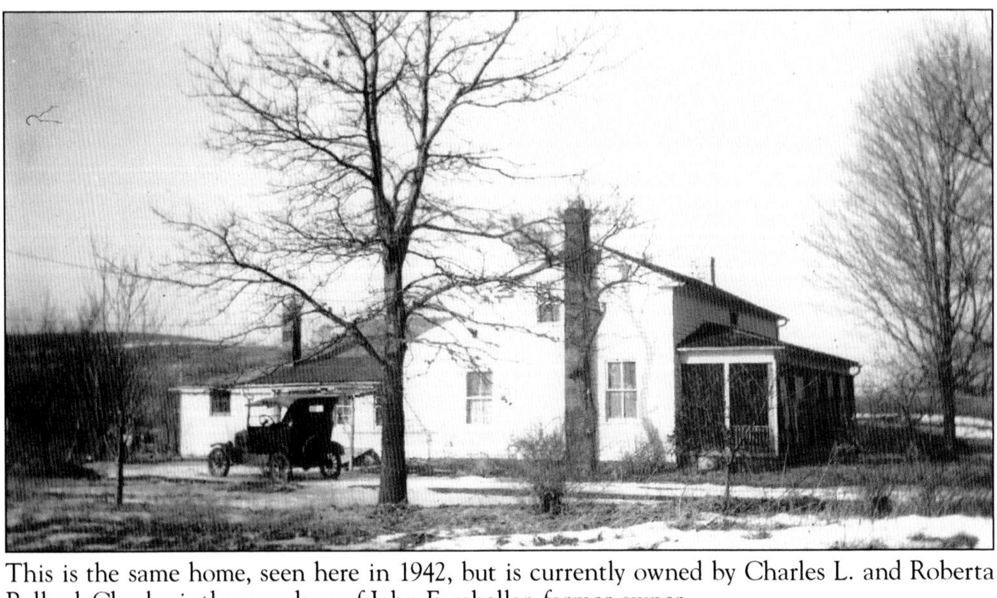

This is the same home, seen here in 1942, but is currently owned by Charles L. and Roberta Ballard. Charles is the grandson of John Forebellar, former owner.

The Whyland home sits on a hill in Barberville. There was a shunpike in the front of the house where people drove their teams around the tollbooth in the road to avoid paying the toll.

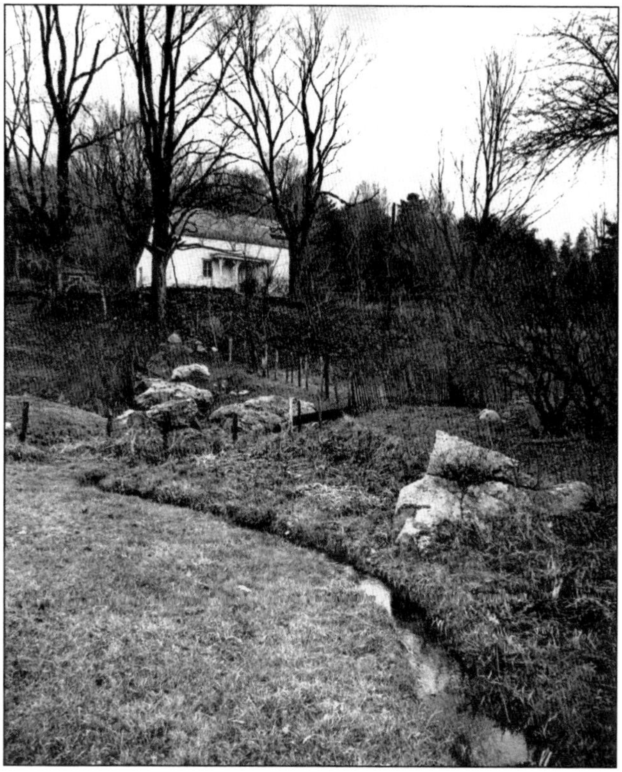

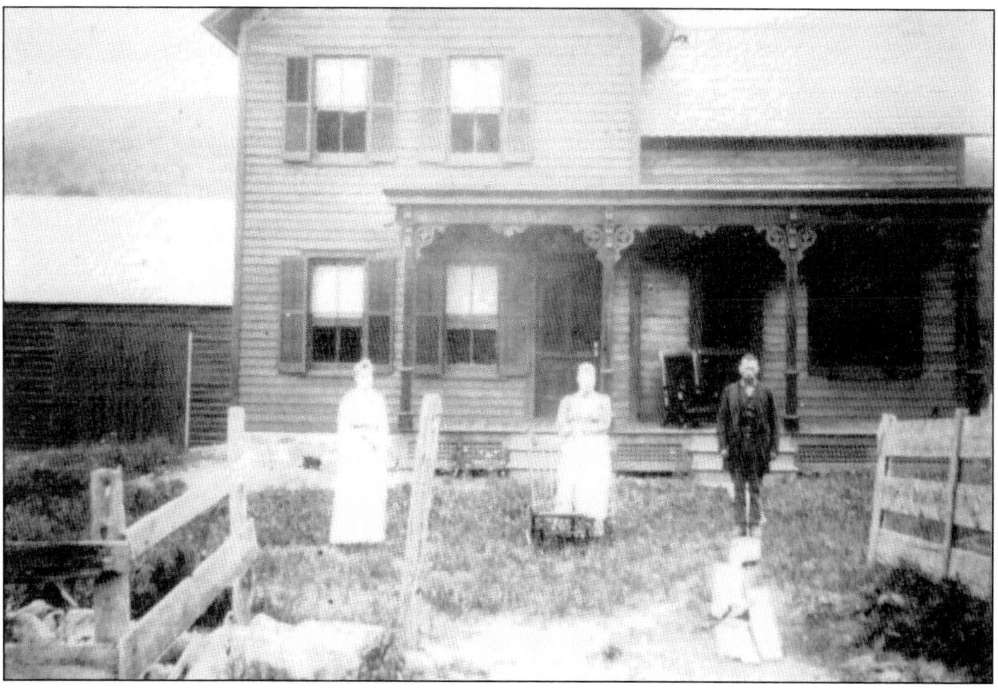

This is the home of Nicholas Radz, who at one time was said to have had the largest barn in town. Radz gave a plot of land to the Hamlet of Barberville for the purpose of a cemetery, which is now known as Brookside Cemetery.

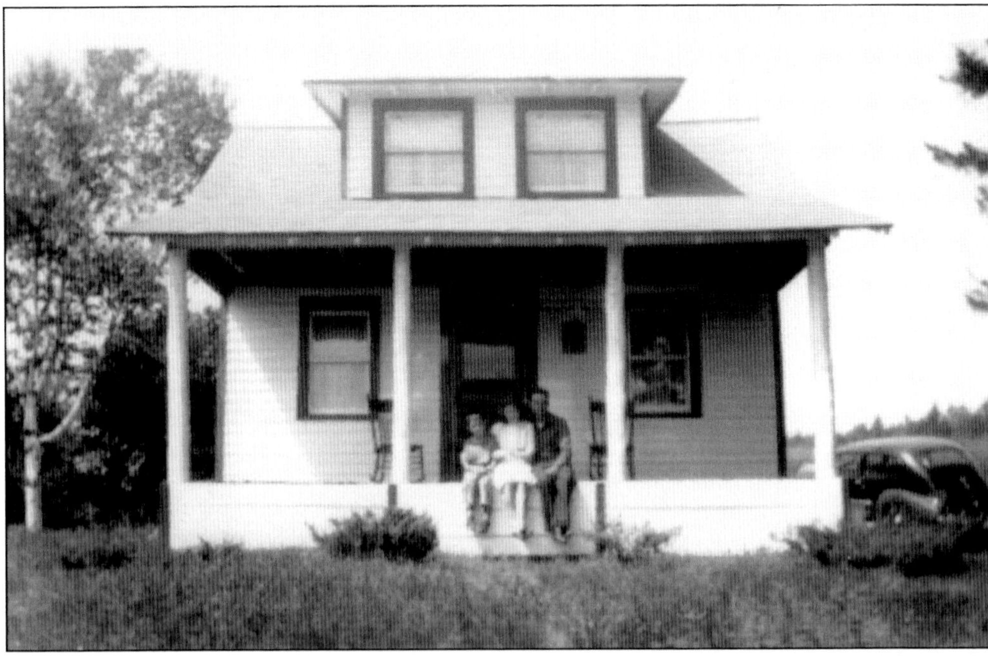

Here is the home of Frank Harold Dustin and his wife, Eva Ward Dustin, located on Blue Factory Road. Frank and Eva had three children, Donald, Helen, and Harold.

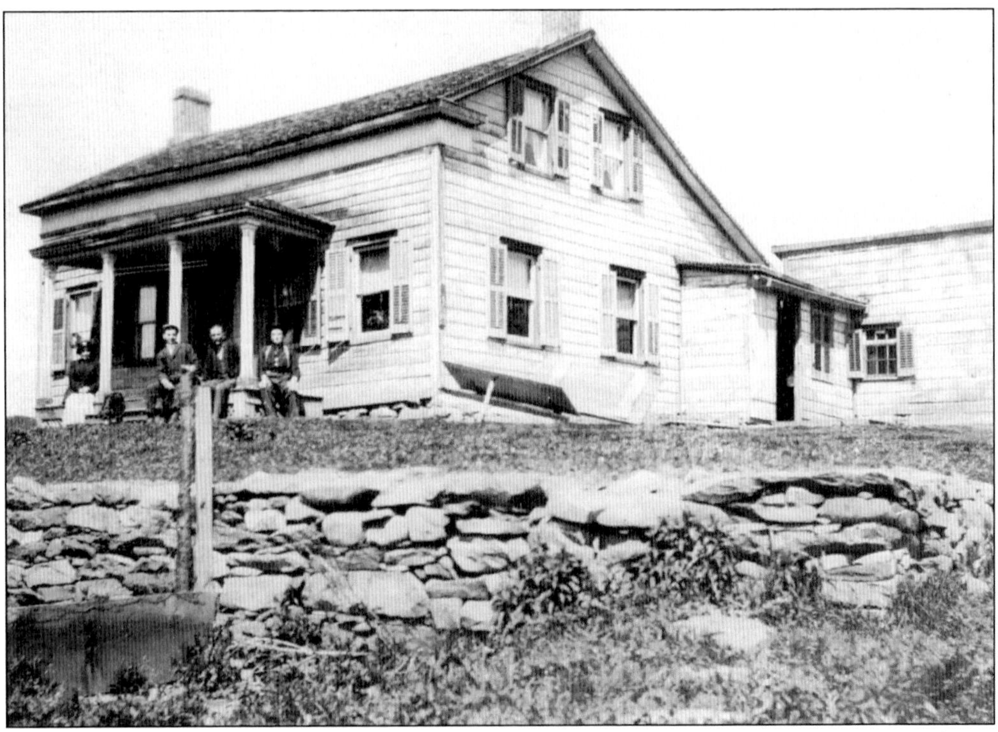

This was the home of Joseph Legenbauer and Nicholas Legenbauer around 1916. Ellen Legenbauer Dzembo was born in this home.

# *Two*

# FARMING OF YESTERYEAR

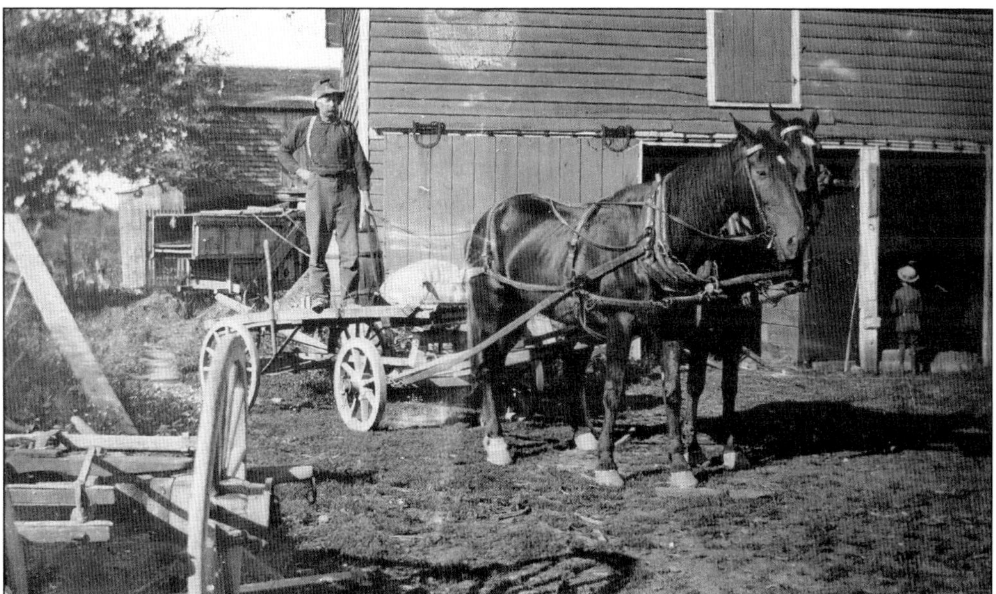

Edward Miller is standing in front of his barns getting ready for the day's work. Miller used his threshing machine to thresh grains for neighboring farmers. His 1890s account book lists the names of farmers, grain threshed, and amount of bushels received, mostly oats and rye.

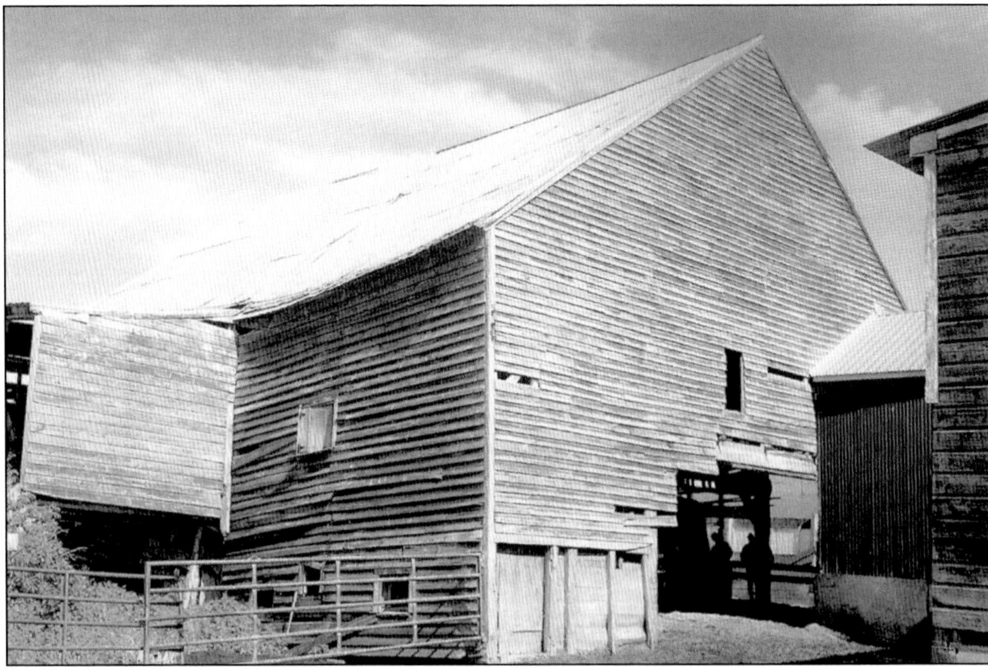

The Wagners owned a large farm on Garfield Road where they grew potatoes that were sold around the area. Today the farm is still in use as a dairy farm, and the milk is sold to local dairies. The original area was leased from Stephen VanRensselaer by the Muller family. A Dutch barn (above), with 1774 incised on one of the anchor beams, was recently moved to Weston, Vermont, where it was reconstructed for the Weston Playhouse.

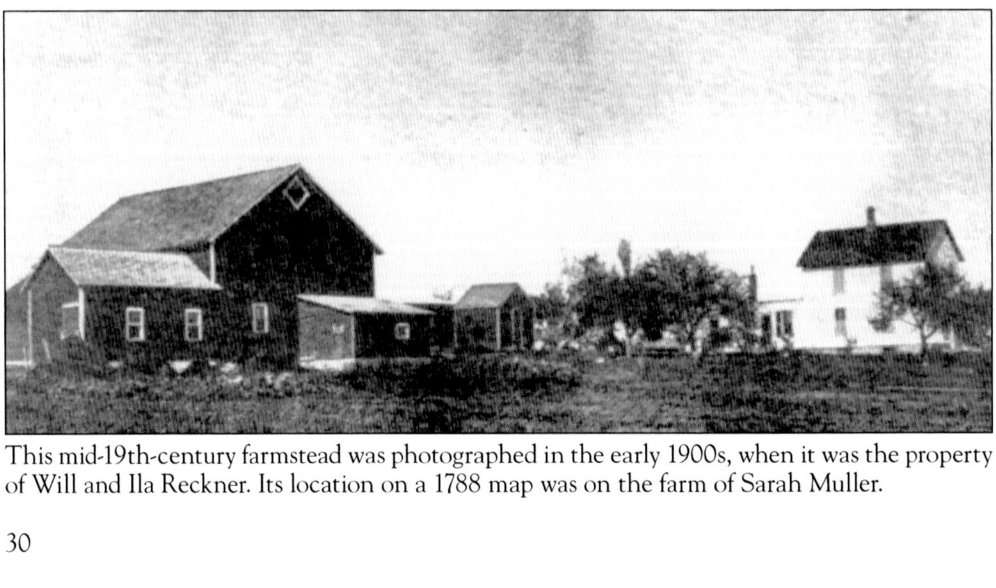

This mid-19th-century farmstead was photographed in the early 1900s, when it was the property of Will and Ila Reckner. Its location on a 1788 map was on the farm of Sarah Muller.

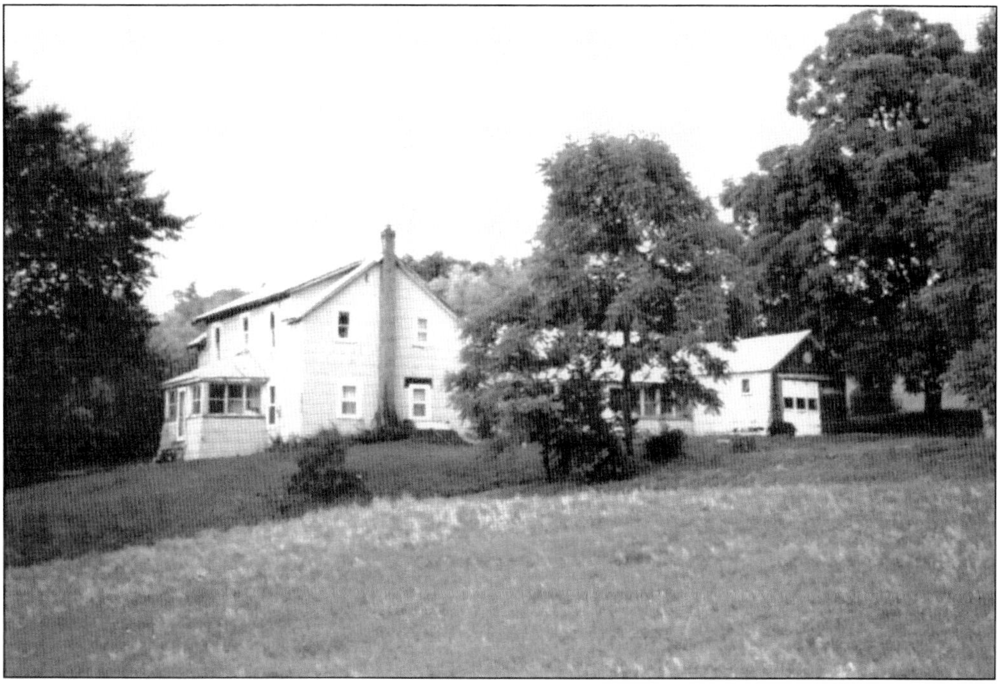

The Walsh farm is one of the old farms located on Farm-to-Market Road (White Church Road). The home (above) shows some of the attached outbuildings. The barns (below) sprawl out on the landscape in the field.

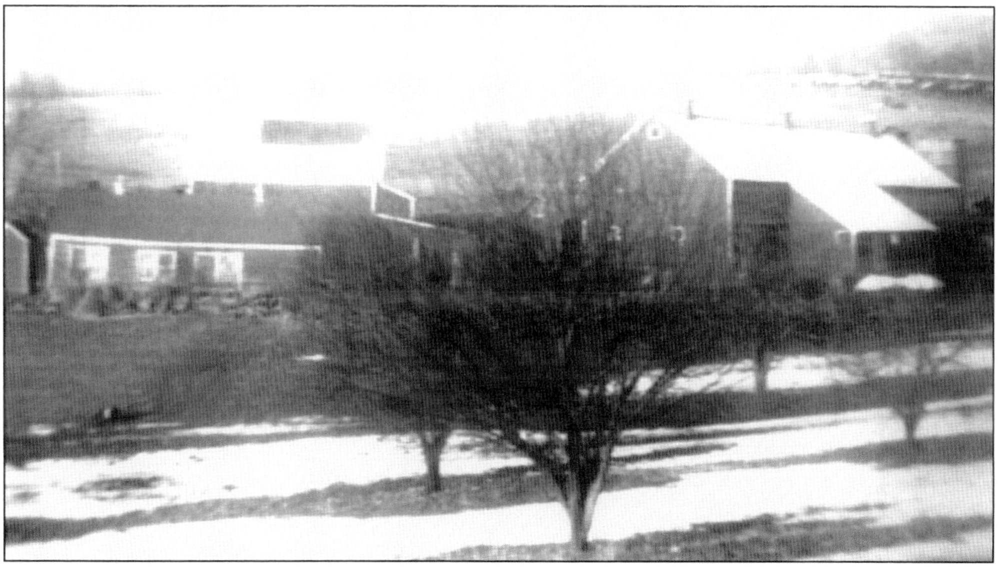

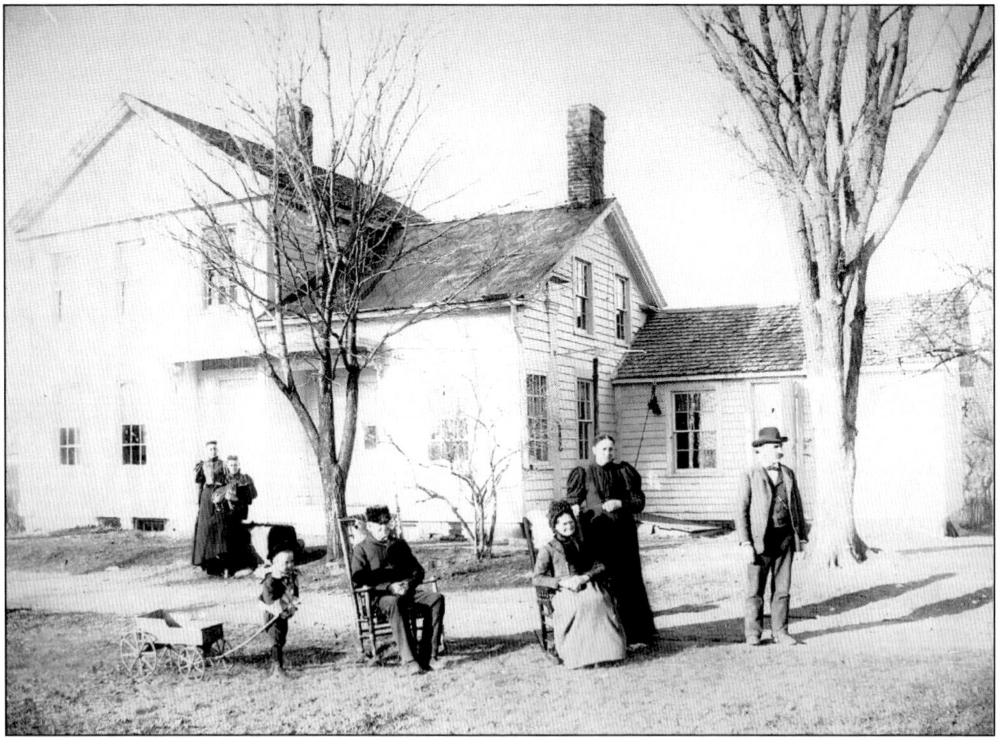

George Ives and wife Sarah Feathers had this house built. In 1882, the Iveses and the Reichard family from Averill Park swapped homes. Henry Reichard and wife Kate then lived here and raised their family. The window over the cellar door is where they dipped snow into reservoirs during the blizzard of 1888. This was their kitchen.

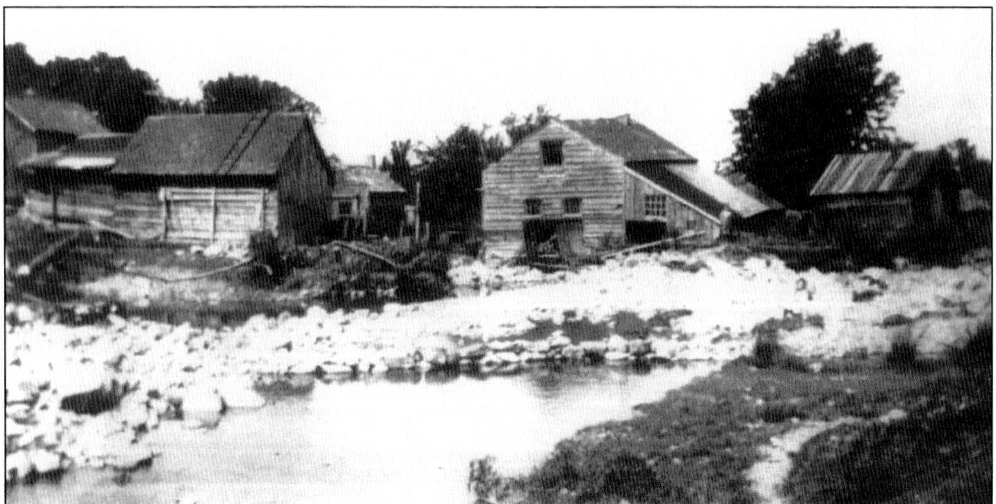

These are the farm buildings as they were after the flood of 1921. Starting at the left is the barn, then a storage shed, the blacksmith shop, the workshop with a spillway and waterway, and finally the icehouse. The farm's shop was where whiffletrees were made and repaired, along with the repairs to harnesses, and the horses were shod.

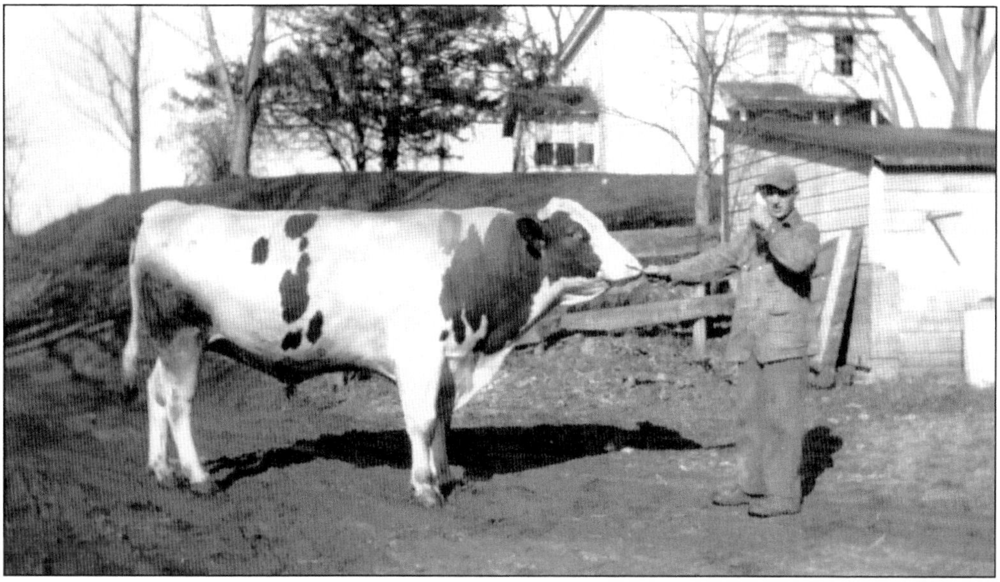

Here are images of the Moody farm. The original lease between Stephen VanRensselaer and David Barringer gave him the use of the land for an annual fee of "fifteen bushels of good merchantable winter wheat, four fat fowl, and one day's service with carriage." Shortly before 1820, a Dutch-style barn was built on the property. The site of the house was thought to be a Native American burial mound but in fact is a glacial landform. However, Native Americans once dwelled there on the banks of the Poesten Kill. Above shows the home in the background as Floyd Moody shows off his sore thumb. Below, in 1949, are Paul Fisher Sr. (in the back), Doris Moody (left), and Donald Moody with barns on the Moody farm in the background.

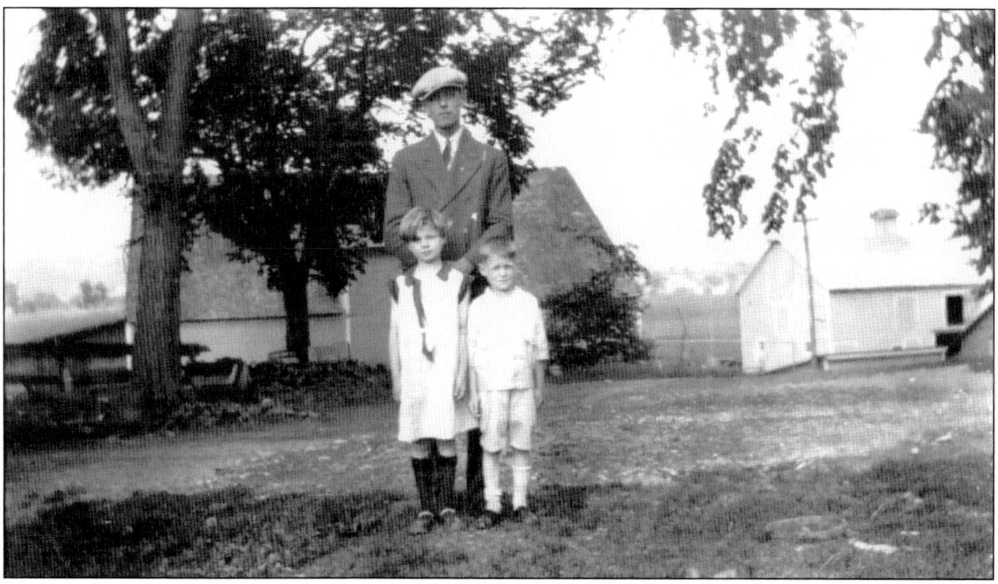

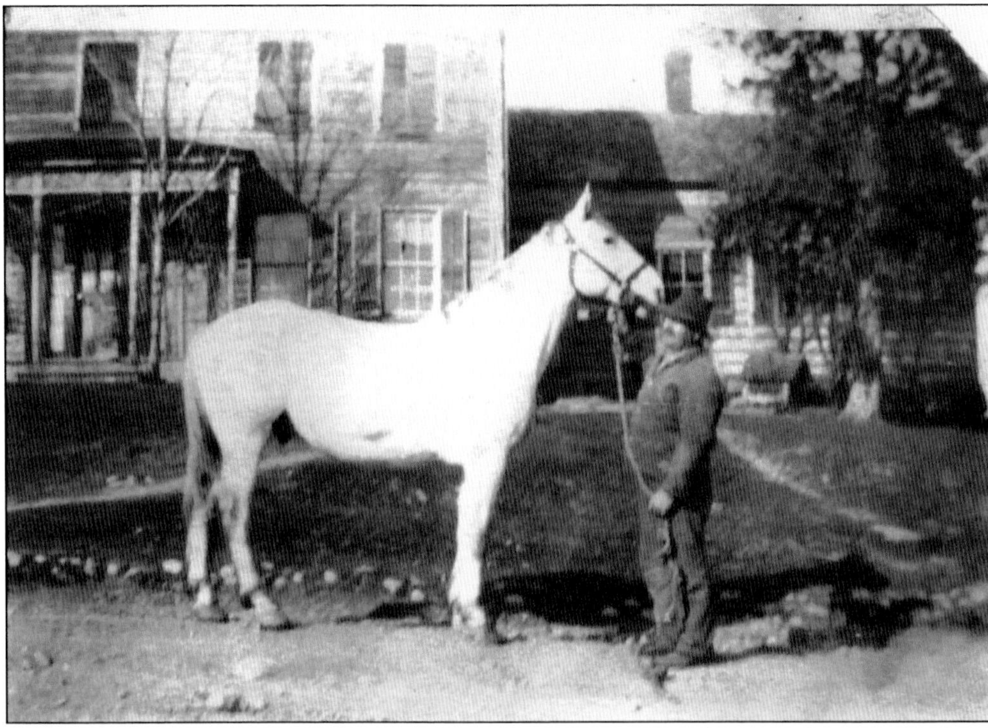

The Heaver/Ryan farm is located at the corner of Weatherwax Road and Snyders Corners Road. The home dates back to 1755. Deeds show the farm being purchased by Peter Kilmer. Above, standing in front of the house, are James Heaver and his horse Billy in 1930. Below, in 1926, Bill Ryan stands in the doorway of the barn.

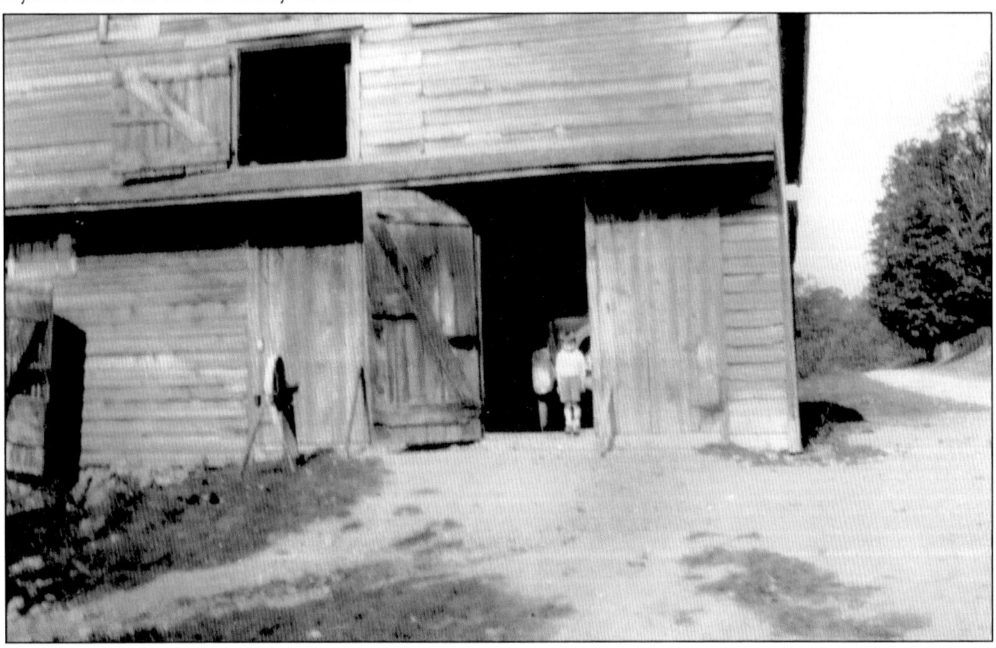

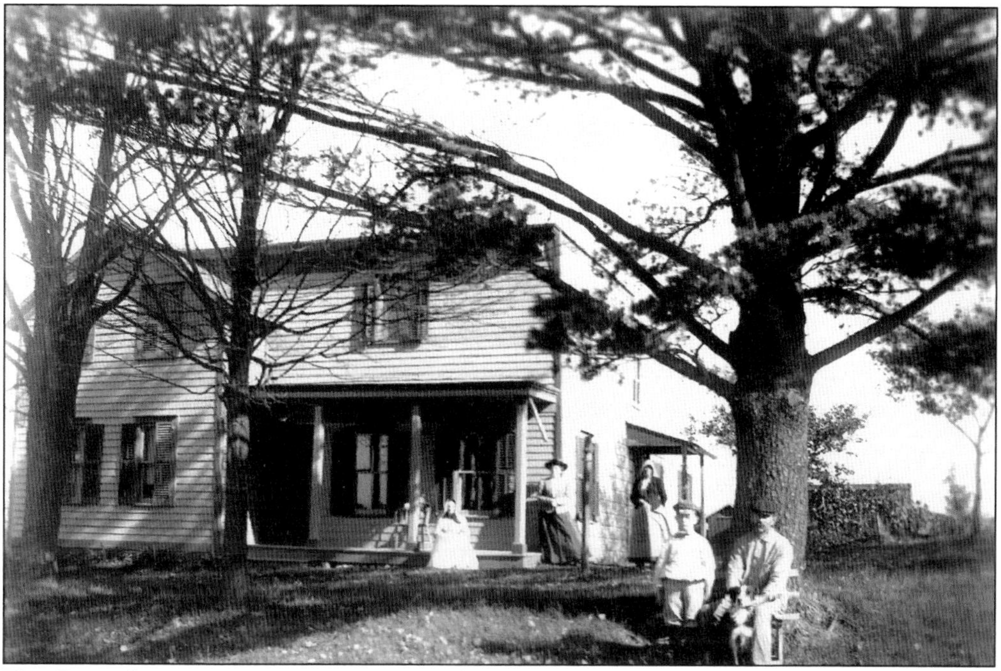

The Zweig farm was on Route 66, across from the Algonquin School. This photograph was taken about 1915. In front are Merrill Zweig with his father, Edward. Standing on the side porch is Lillie Slyter Zweig, and seated on the front porch is Melvina Link Slyter.

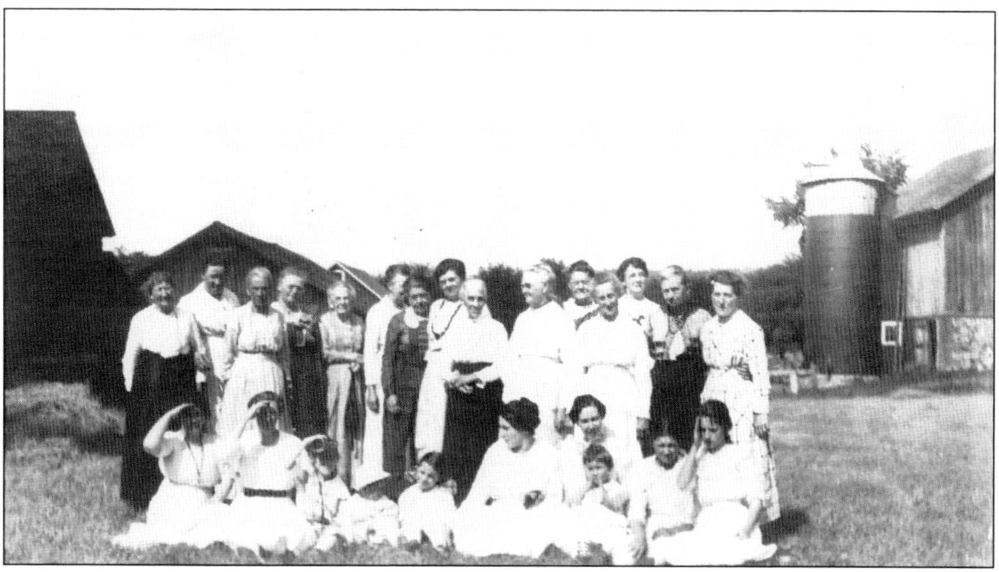

In front of the Sicley barns are the ladies of the women's group of the Lutheran church in Poestenkill at their annual summer picnic gathering.

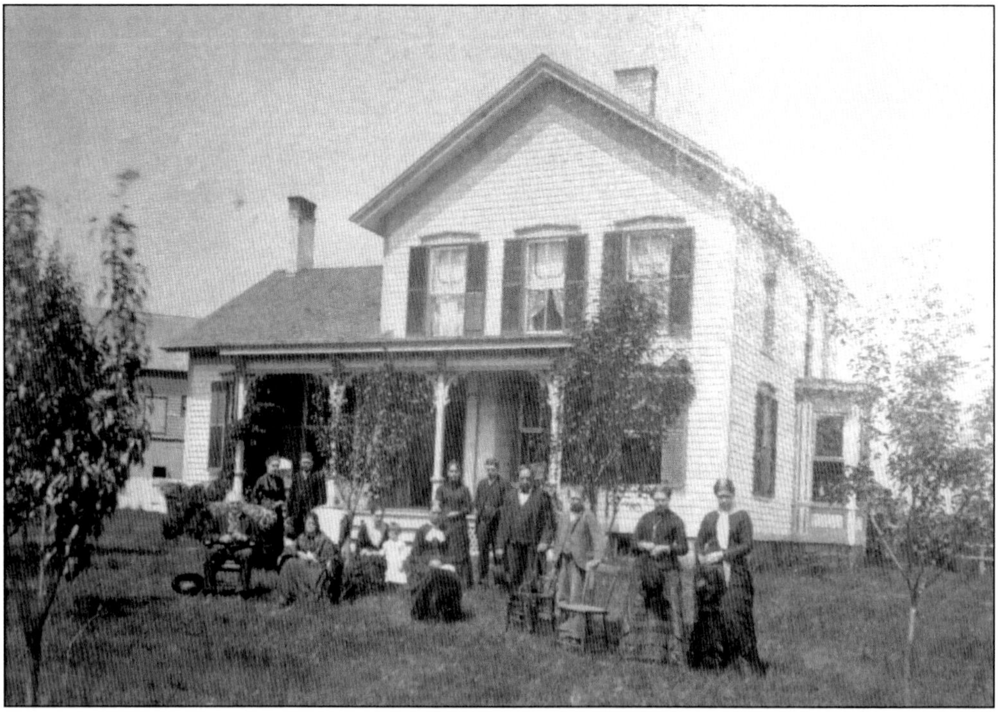

The Clickner farm was on Round Top Road just south of the village. It was the dairy farm of Ward Clickner and his wife, Eva Ives Clickner. The barn has hand-hewn beams. The home dates back over 150 years, boasting of the original woodwork, wide floorboards, and lath-and-horsehair plaster.

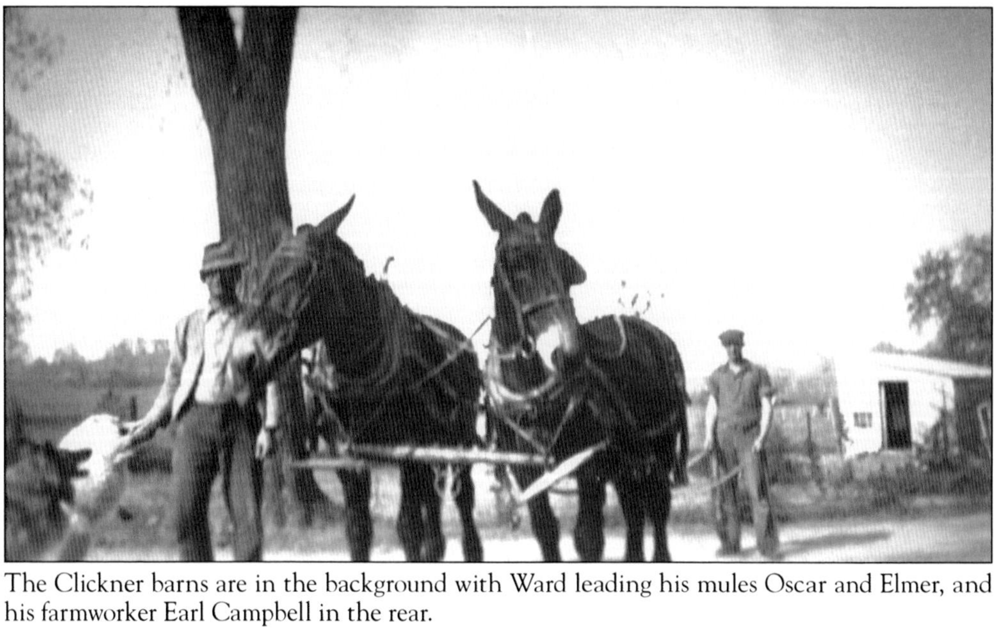

The Clickner barns are in the background with Ward leading his mules Oscar and Elmer, and his farmworker Earl Campbell in the rear.

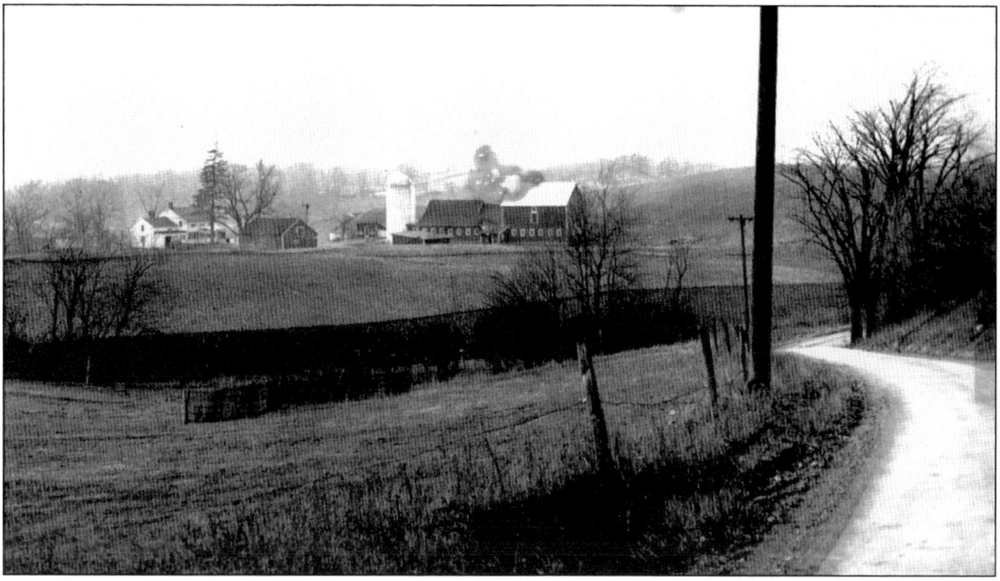

The Hammond farm on Weatherwax Road is sometimes referred to as the Barney Weatherwax farm. William Cooper leased 254 acres from Stephen VanRensselaer in 1790 and thereafter sold 50 acres each to Christian, Frederick, and William Cooper in 1826 and leased another 88 acres to Barney Weatherwax. The Bulson family purchased the farm in 1950. Note the dirt road and no developments.

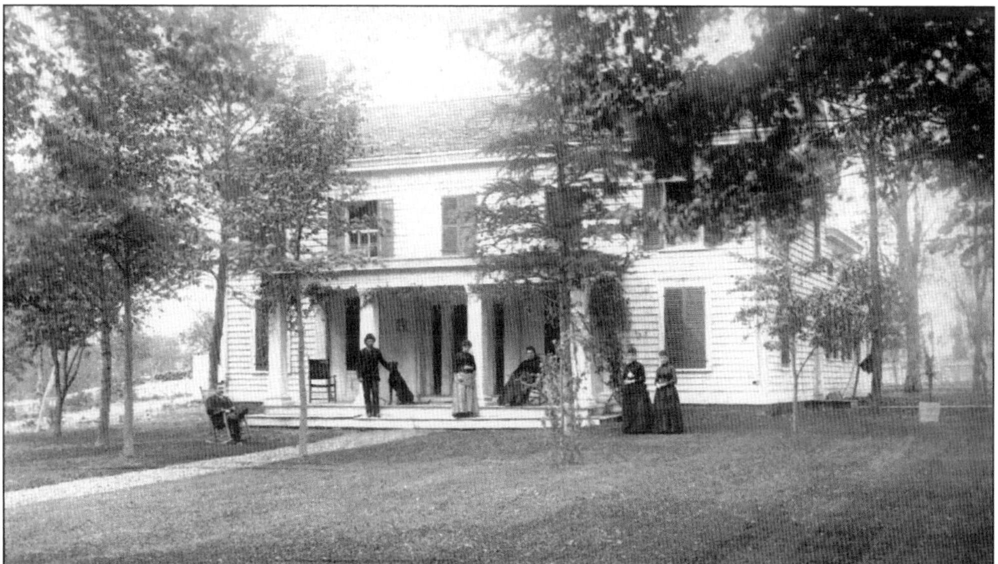

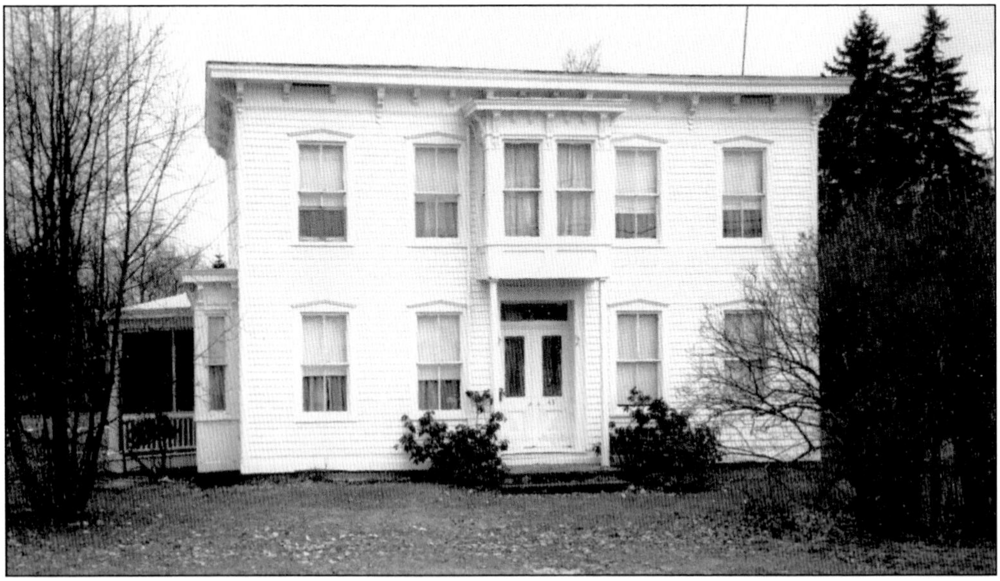

The Davitt farm was located in the village between Main Street and Snyders Corners Road. Above is the original home of the Davitt family. Below shows the family getting a load of hay down the hill, not an easy feat in those days.

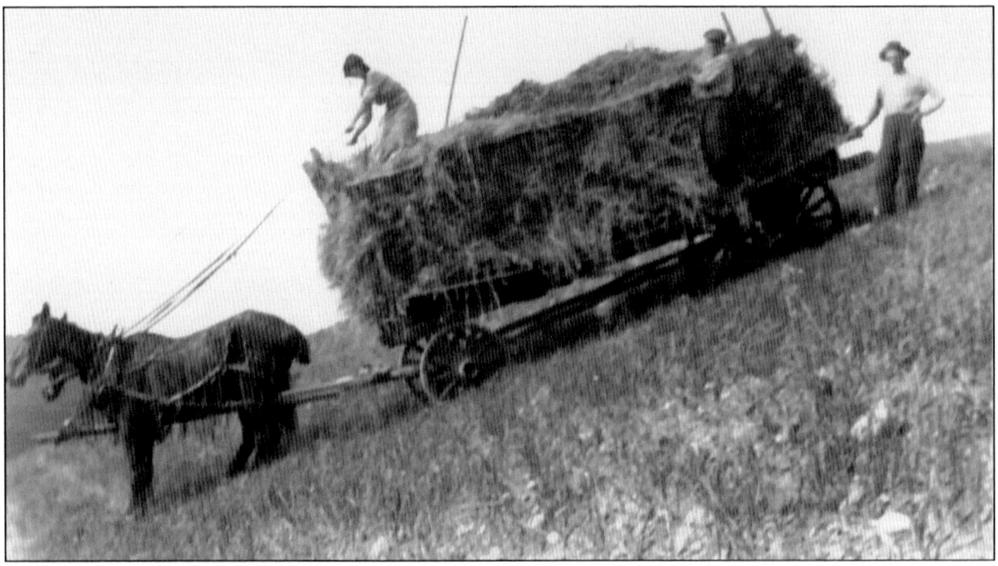

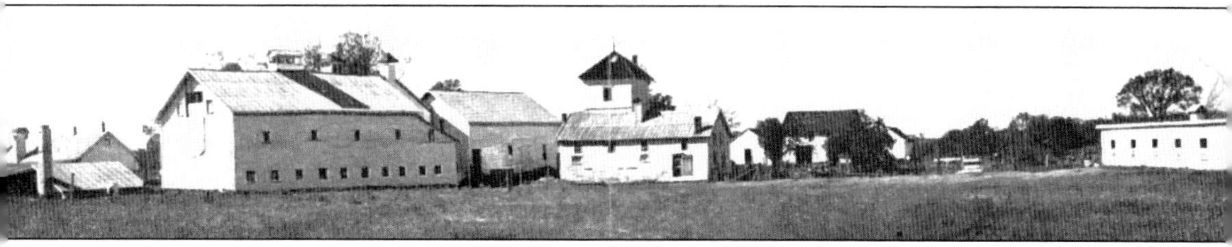

Originally built by the Lynd family, this farm was passed through three generations of Holsers. Here pedigreed leghorns and registered Holsteins were bred, raised and sold in 1942. Among the many buildings was the tank house, which was a three-story building where women were hired to make collars for the shirts. The third floor housed the large water tanks that powered the sewing machines located on the lower floors.

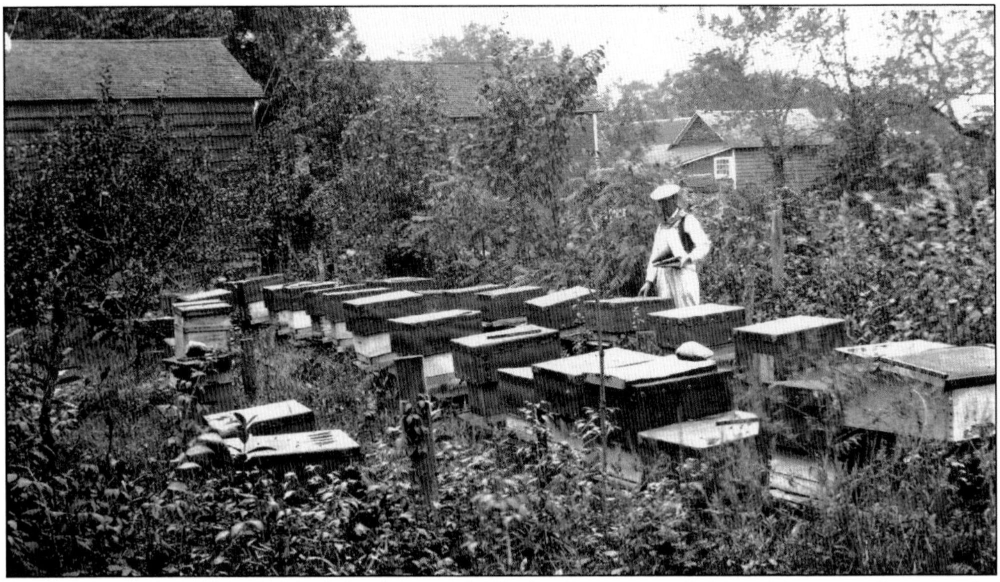

This picture was taken behind the home of Charles Barringer, father of Aretta, who was the town clerk for more than 50 years. Charles kept bees and collected the honey to sell to the local people.

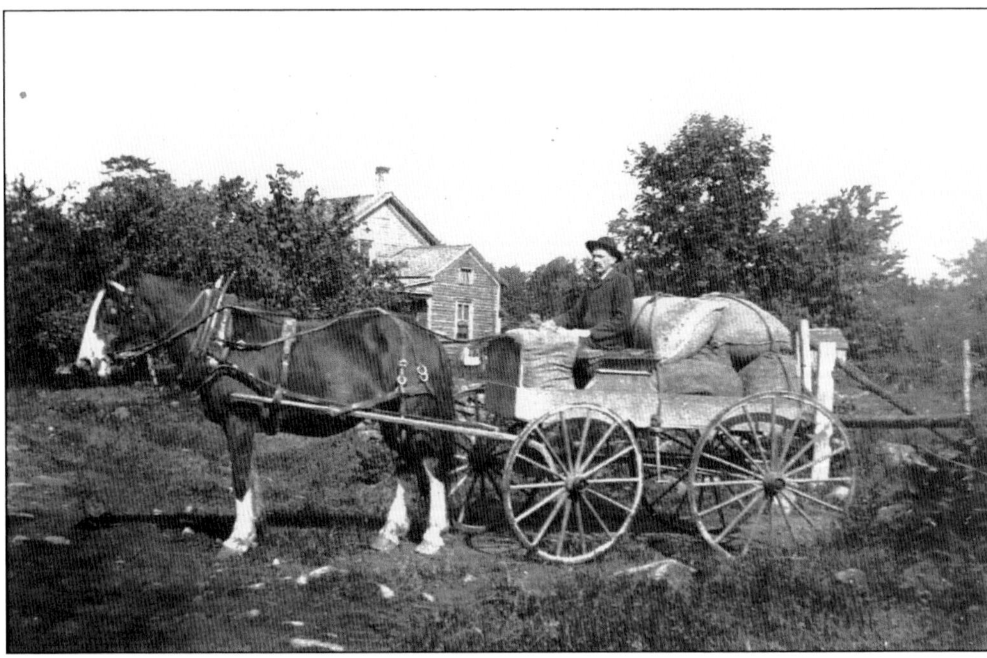

Fred Schroeder is seen around 1909 on his wagon with a load of grain that he is taking to the local gristmill at the foot of Snake Hill Road.

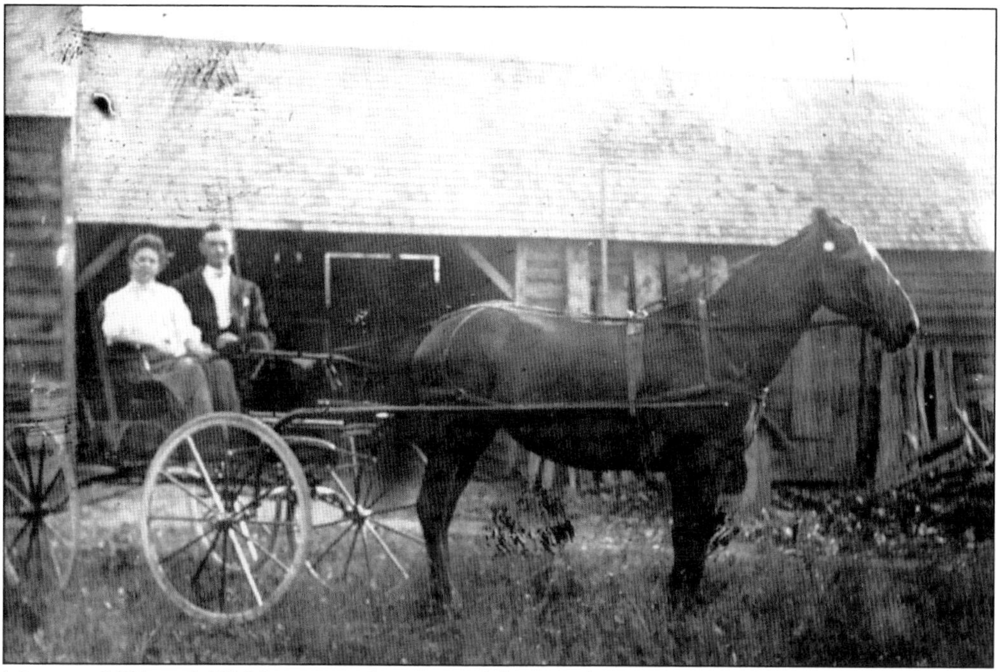

Mary and Edward Walsh are ready to travel home after visiting with their friends on the Strittsman farm on Snyders Corners Road around 1920. Some of the barns on the farm can be seen in the background. This farm is no longer used as a truck farm.

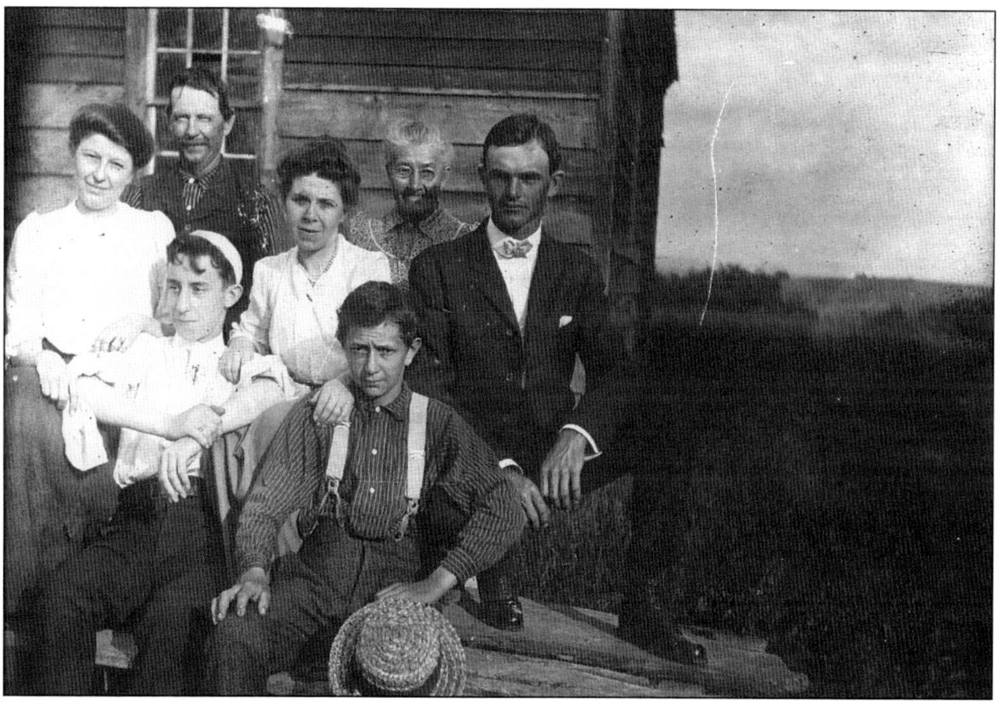

In the back, Mr. and Mrs. Jacob Albert stand in front of one of the barns on the Albert-Strittsman farm around 1920, along with, in the second row, from left to right, Mamie Albert and Mary and Edward Walsh. In the front are Ernest (left) and Andrew Albert.

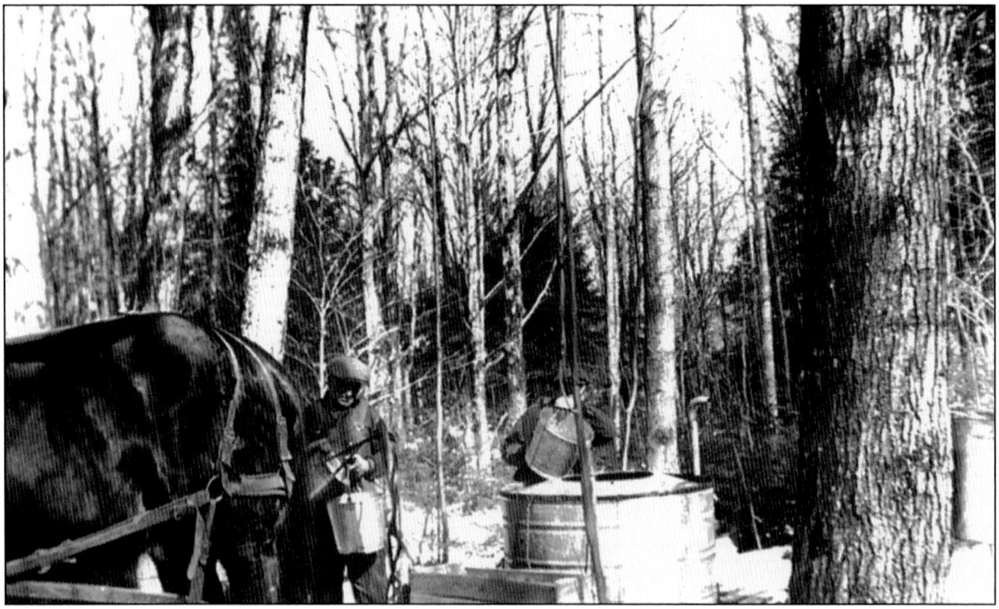

An early product made and sold by some farmers was maple syrup. Here Alvin Catlin takes the sap from the tree to pour into carrying tanks on the sled pulled by horses.

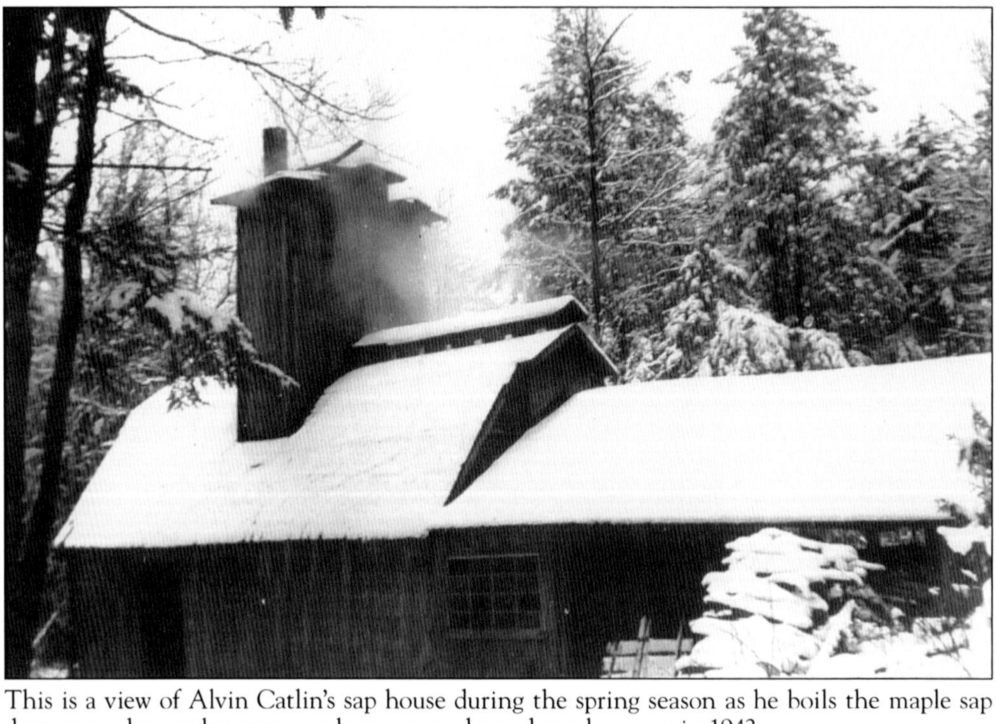

This is a view of Alvin Catlin's sap house during the spring season as he boils the maple sap down to make maple syrup, maple sugar candy, and maple cream in 1942.

# *Three*

# BUSINESS AND INDUSTRY

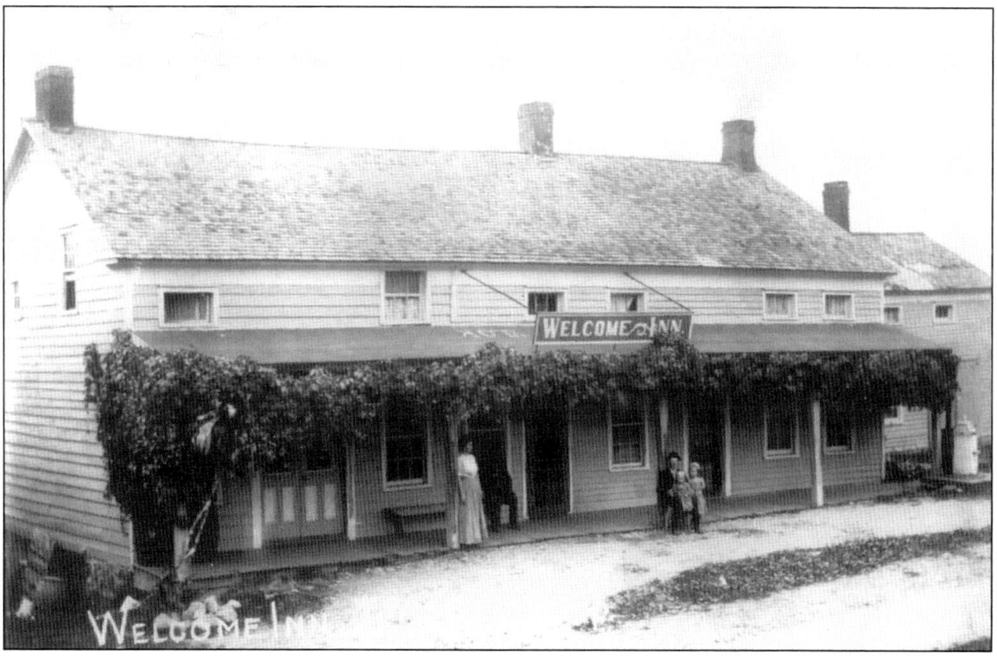


Welcome Inn in East Poestenkill was originally owned by Anna and Henry Milhizer around 1900. This building was later taken over by Eva Flint and became a local general store for the hamlet.

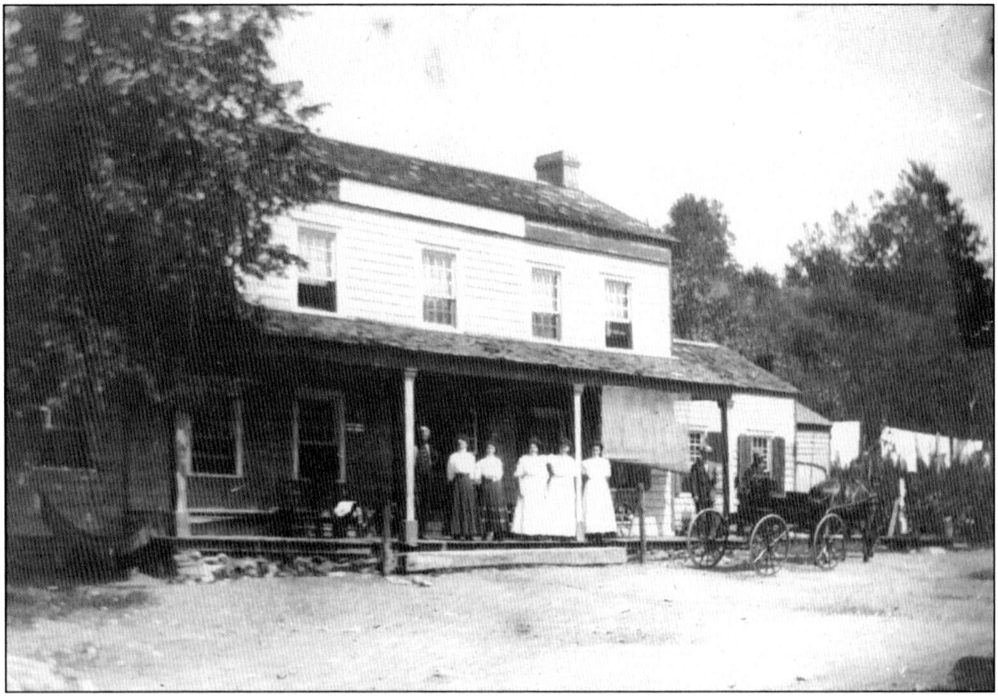

Henry Moon's inn on Plank Road in Barberville is seen here. This was a favorite stopping place for the stage on its trip from Troy to Berlin. The building currently houses apartments.

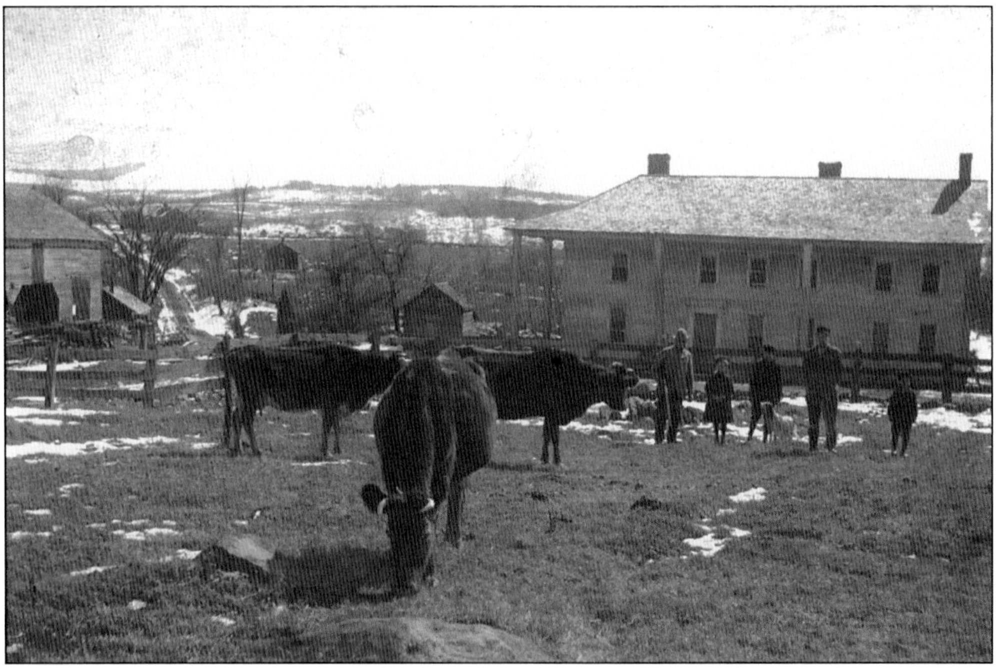

A portion of the old Ives Corners Hotel was built before 1800. James Ives built additions in the early 1800s. Ives's 1828 account book shows services of the rural innkeeper from shoeing horses to selling household staples. He also provided a warm stop for farmers and charcoal manufacturers when taking their products to market. The upstairs ballroom was used for public gatherings.

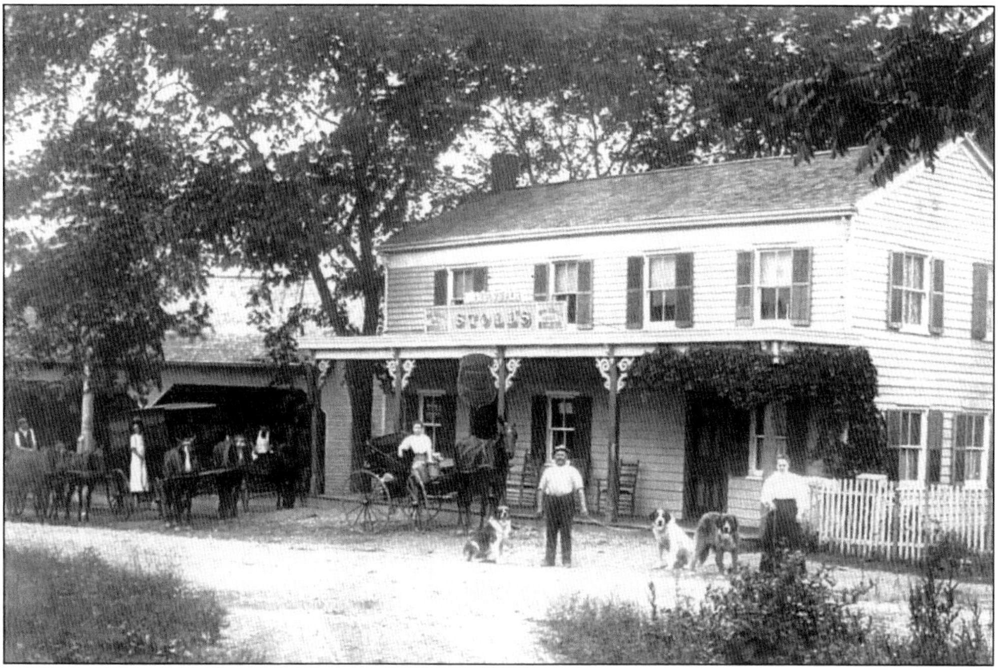

The Eagle Hotel, at the corner of Plank Road and Davis Drive, was a popular site. The sheds were at the left. In the middle wagon is Martin Hunt; Florence Moore is in the carriage in front of the hotel; Jacob Veith stands holding his dogs, one of which was named Bruno; and Mrs. Veith stands at the far right.

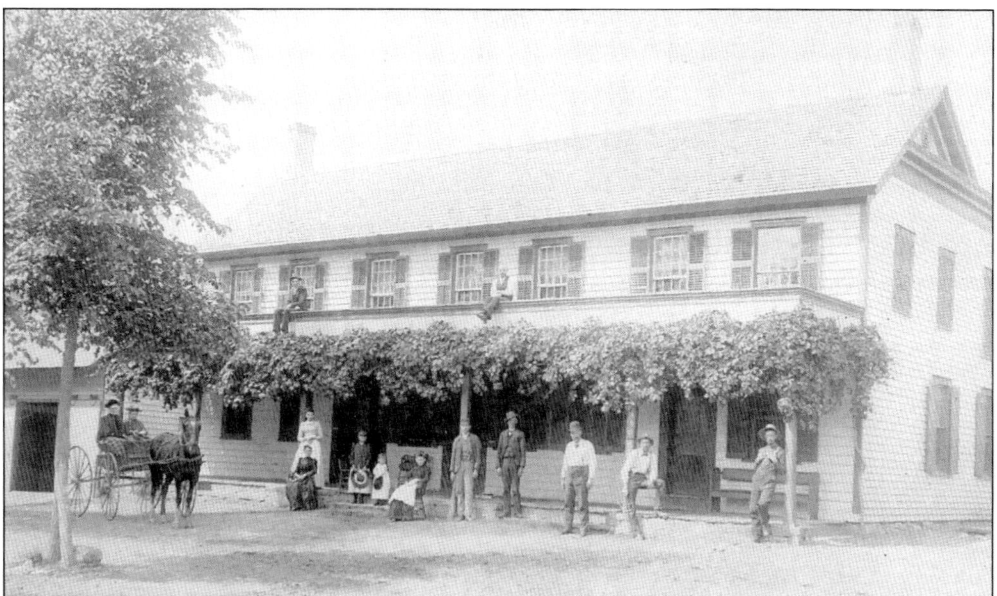

Seen here is Woodbine Hotel in 1892. Seated on the roof, from left to right, are George Myers and George Peck. In the buggy are Em Downey and Blanche Morris, while on the front porch are Carrie Downey, Hattie Newcomb Downey, Erma Downey Fisher, Mousa Riad, Cora Bred, William Abbott, and William Downey.

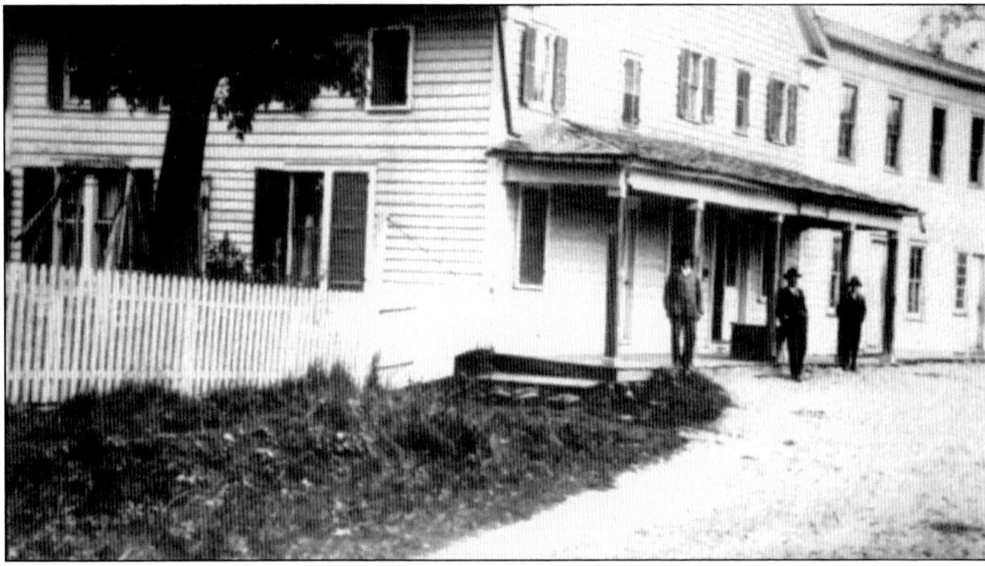

This building was George Barber's store and post office in East Poestenkill, a small hamlet east of the main village of Poestenkill. A substation of the village fire company now stands on this site. This photograph was taken in 1910.

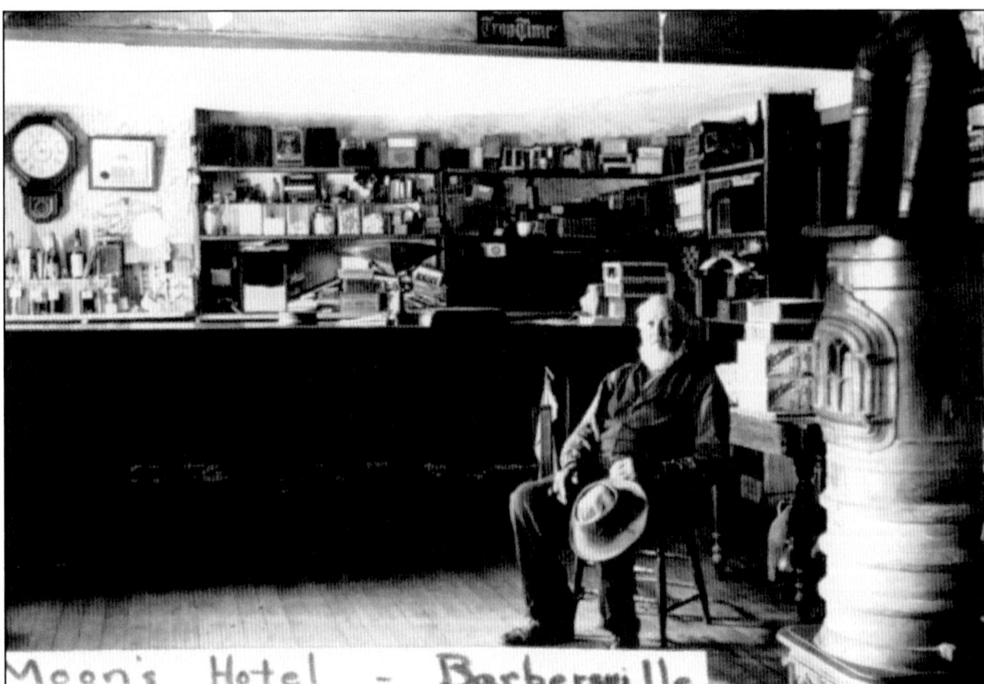


This 1893 photograph shows the inside of Henry Moon's store located in the Moon Inn, across from the head of the Barberville Falls on Blue Factory Road.

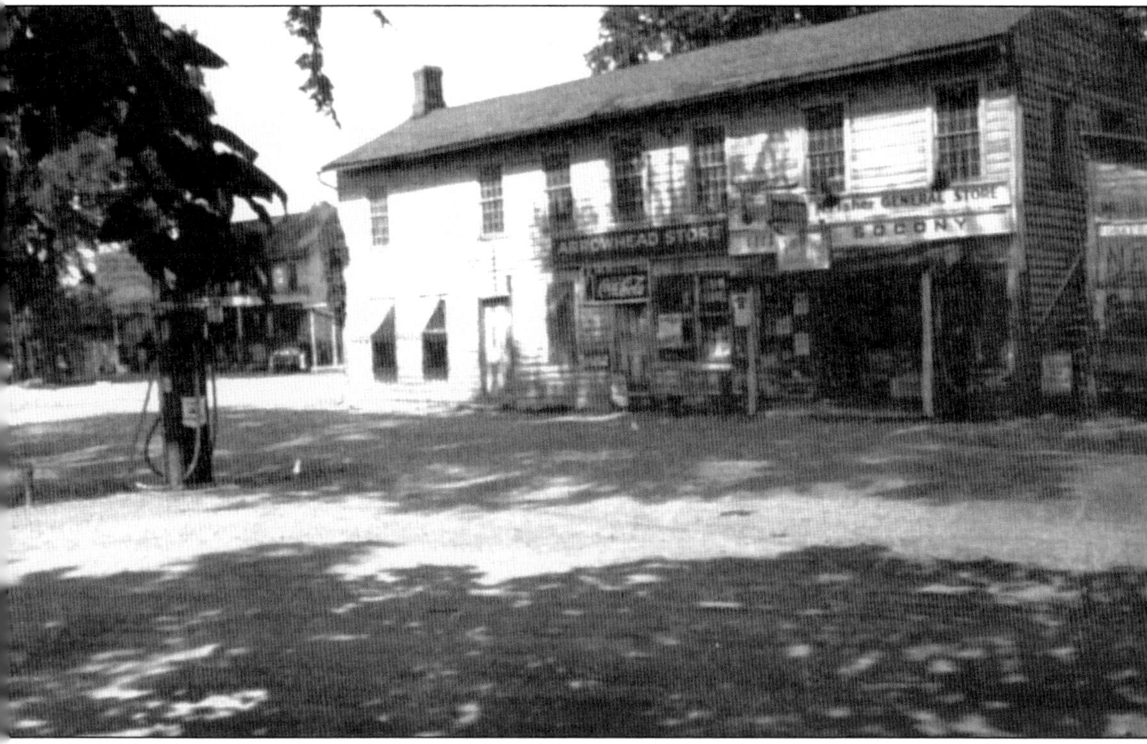


This is the outside view of Union Hall where Nelson Fisher operated a store and later incorporated the post office in one side. The huge ballroom on the second floor was the scene of many civic affairs, lectures, and dances as well as penmanship classes given by Pres. James A. Garfield when he visited Poestenkill during his schooling at Williams College. Garfield held classes and preached sermons to earn money for tuition.

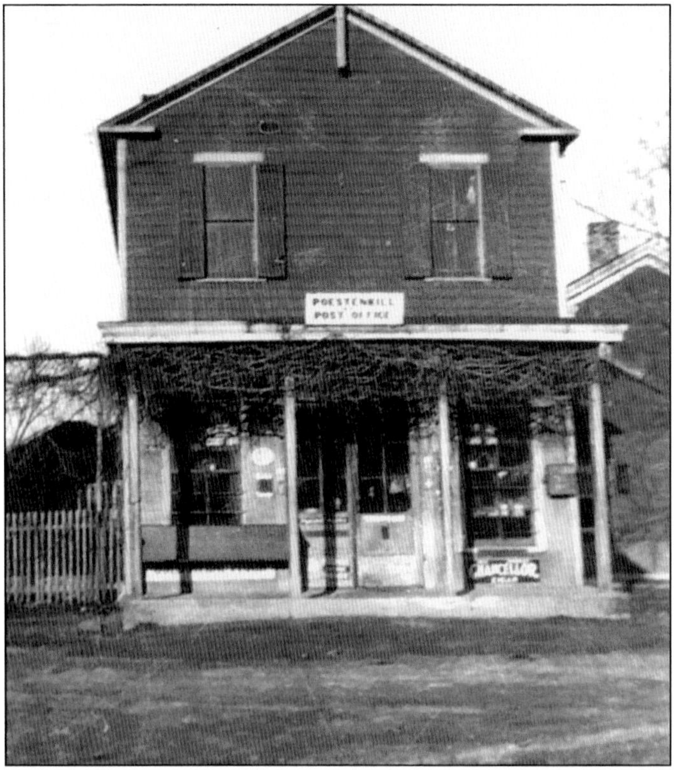


Ivan Hall's store and post office was on the corner of Main Street and Farm-to-Market Road. Hall attached the store to his home in the back so he could easily go from one to the other. Bags of grain, flour, and feed were on the second floor, where they were thrown out a side door into customers' wagons. To the left of Hall's store is the Woodbine Hotel, which was later purchased by John Bubie and converted into a general store.

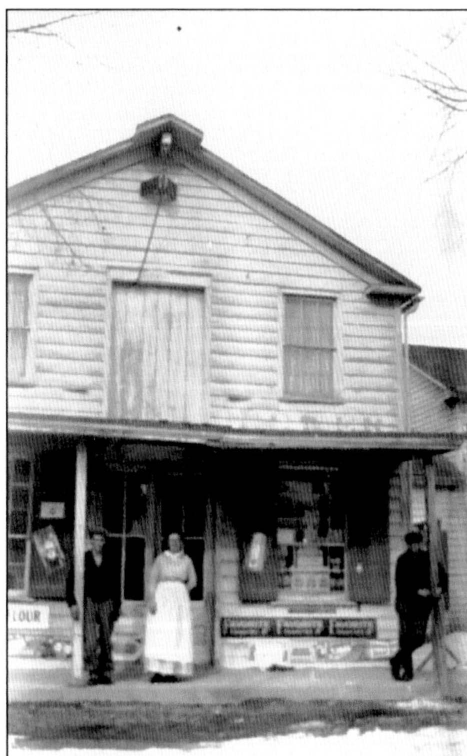

Seen here is John Bubie's store with Helen Chesbrough Herrington standing in front. Once the store moved east a couple buildings, this building was made into an automobile parts store operated by Robert Bubie and now run by his sons, Roger and Richard.

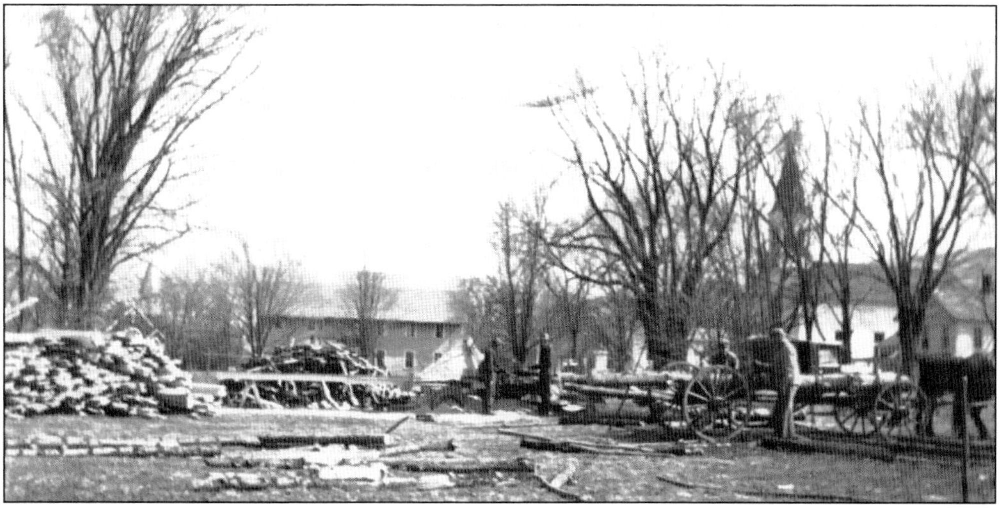

Ward Clickner and Lewis Miller's logging enterprise and sawmill on Round Top Road is seen here in 1939. Note the old firehouse in the background.

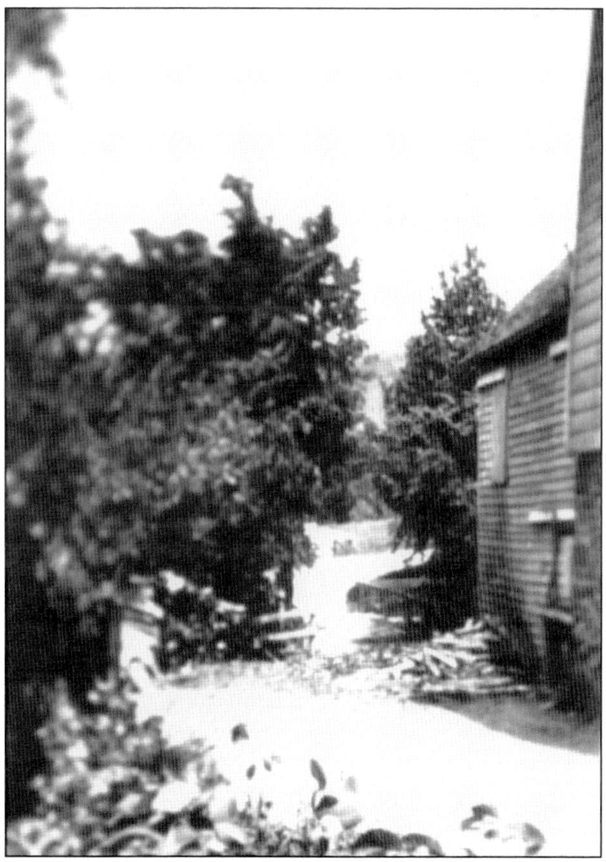

This sawmill was probably run by waterpower from the Poesten Kill. It was run by Charles Heffner and was located on Davis Drive. This photograph is from 1918.

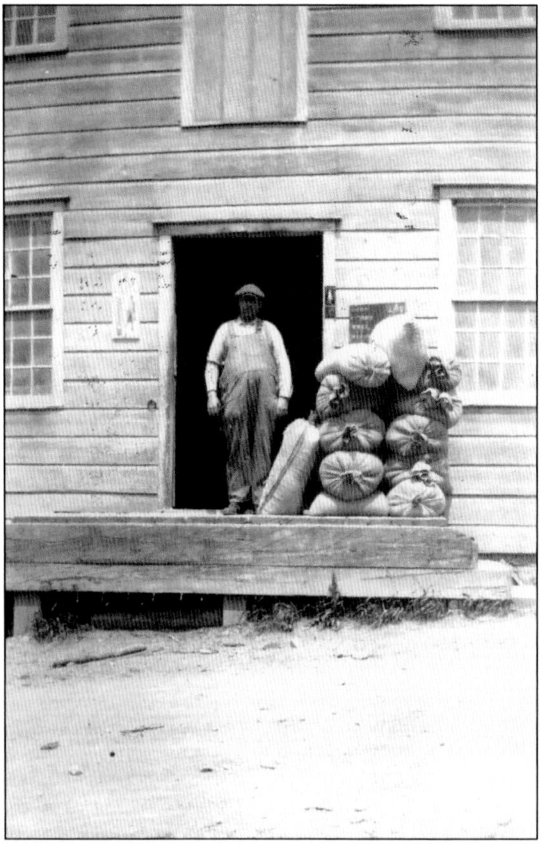

Seen at left is the gristmill where farmers brought their wheat, oats, and rye to be ground into flour. Clarence Miller is standing in the door of the mill. During the spring months, the mill (below) was used as a sawmill. The 1908 photograph shows, from left to right, Harrison Hoag, John Weinbrecht, and John Holser Sr.

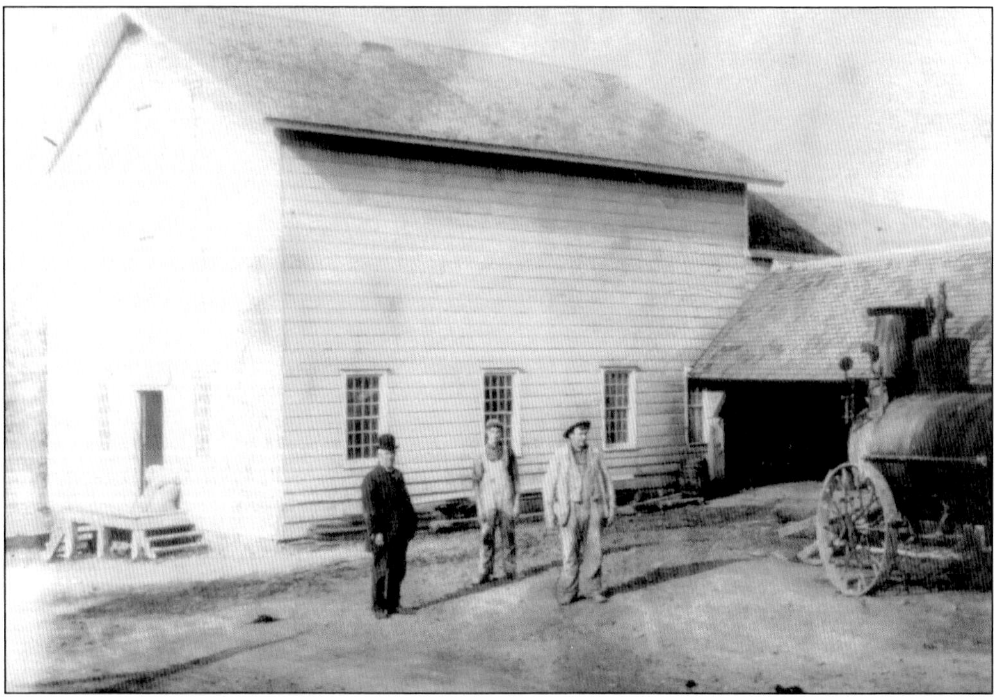

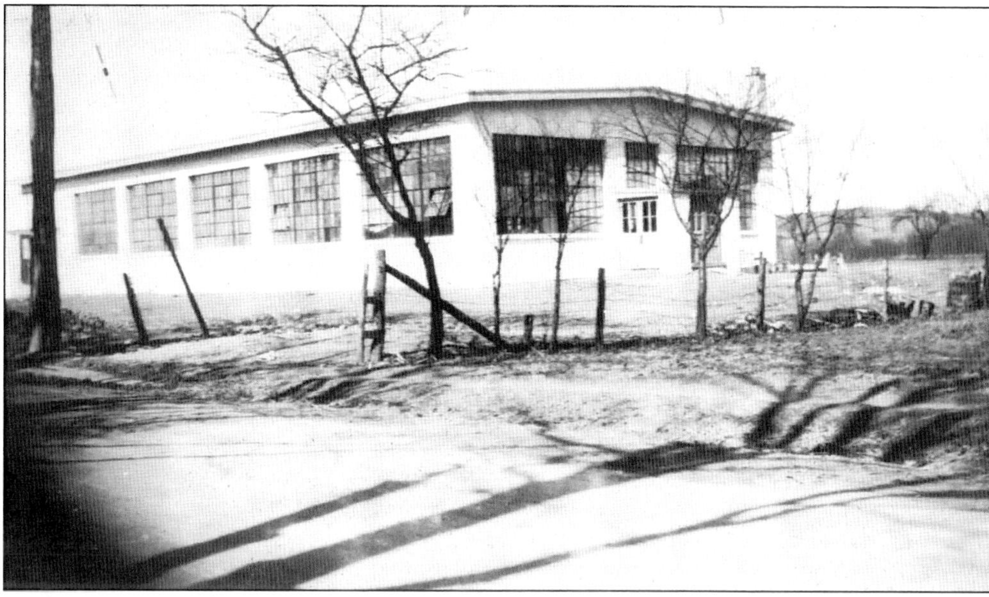

In the years immediately following World War I, the town's economy was given a boost by big business. The mill seen above, around 1920, was a branch of the Swans Down Mills of Hudson and manufactured men's knickers and brown knit jackets, carrying the trade name Thermo-Sweaters. It closed in 1927. Several years later, the 7UP bottling plant moved in and brought electricity to town. Later businesses were the Ebert Box Company and Interstate Laminate Company, the current tenant. Seen below, from left to right, are a few of the mill girls, Alda French, Marilla Forebellar, and Gretchen Obermier.

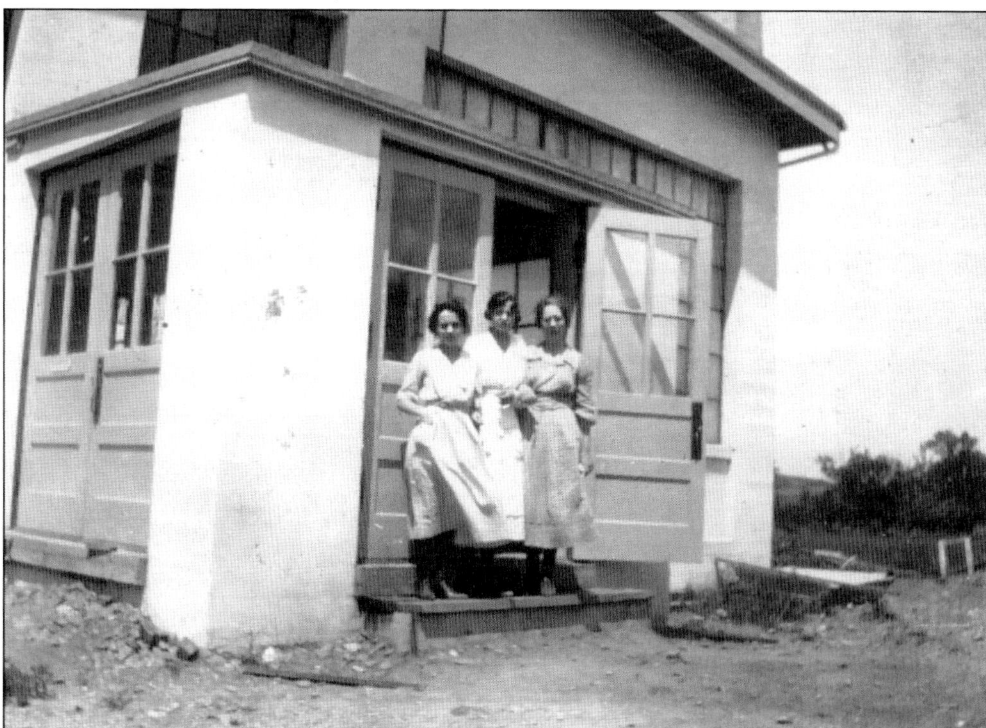

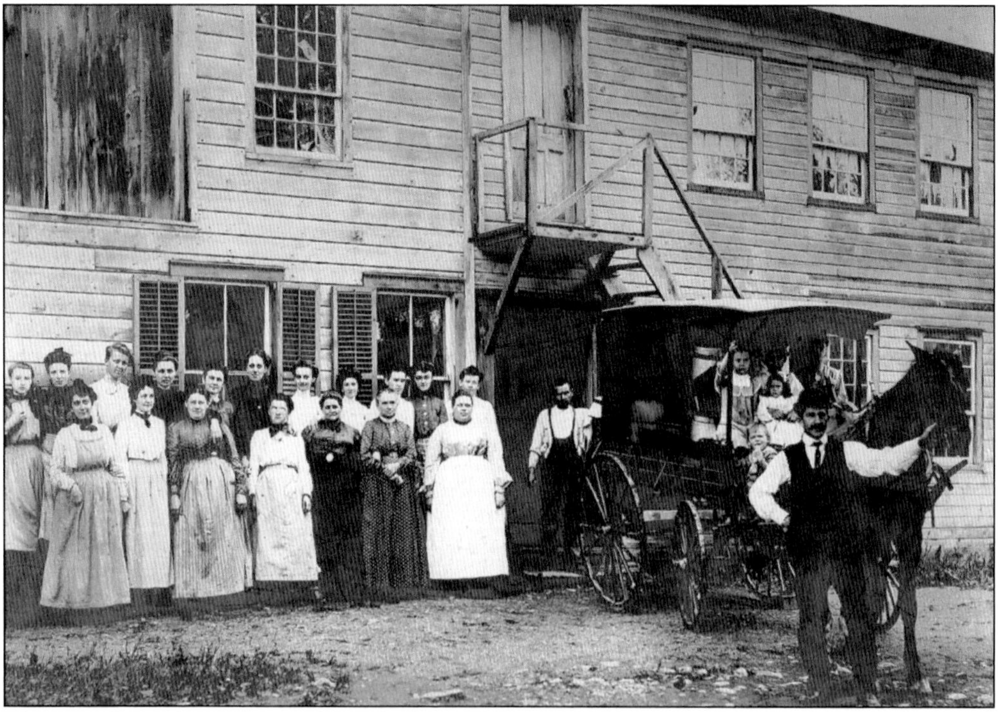

The outside of the wagon maker's shop operated by Lucien Wager, who also operated a shirt and collar factory on the second floor of the building, is seen here. Later William Hoag ran the wagon shop, and John Dater ran the shirt factory. Wager stands in front, holding the horse, while ladies from the factory stand in front of the building.

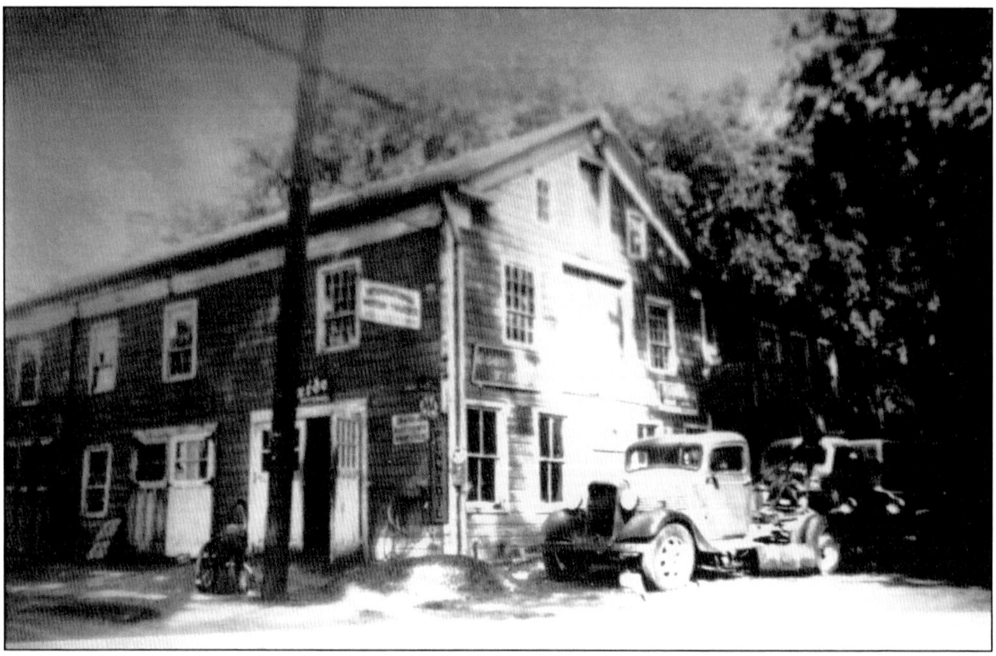

The building was later converted into Walter Forebellar's garage around 1940. The garage was demolished to make way for a new highway.

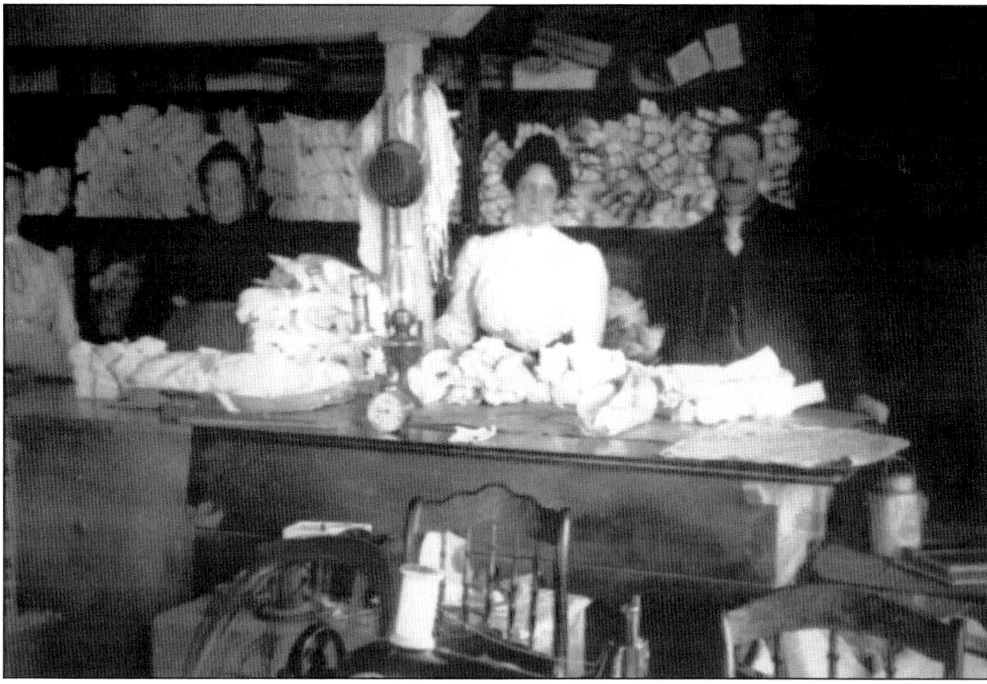

Seen here is the interior of the shirt and collar shop. Above, Organizing and selling collars by size are, from left to right, Ester Hydorn, Lena Schmidt, Bertha Hoag, and Lucien Wager. Identified below on the sewing side of the room are Aretta Barringer, Jennie Prediger, Carrie Wagar, Loiffie Coonrad, ? Lionmo, Lena Bosch, Alice Crouch, Martha Yerdon, Ella Cottrell, ? Prediger, India Cramer, Lena Schmidt, Charles Toussaint, Francis Hydorn, Lucien Wager, Bertha Hoag, and Jennie Horton.

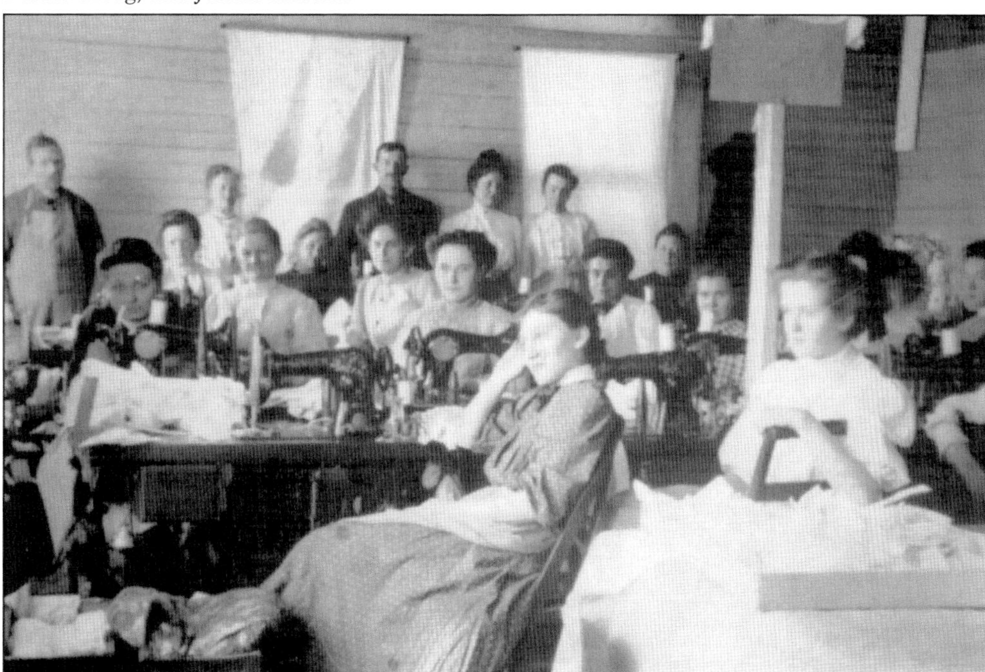

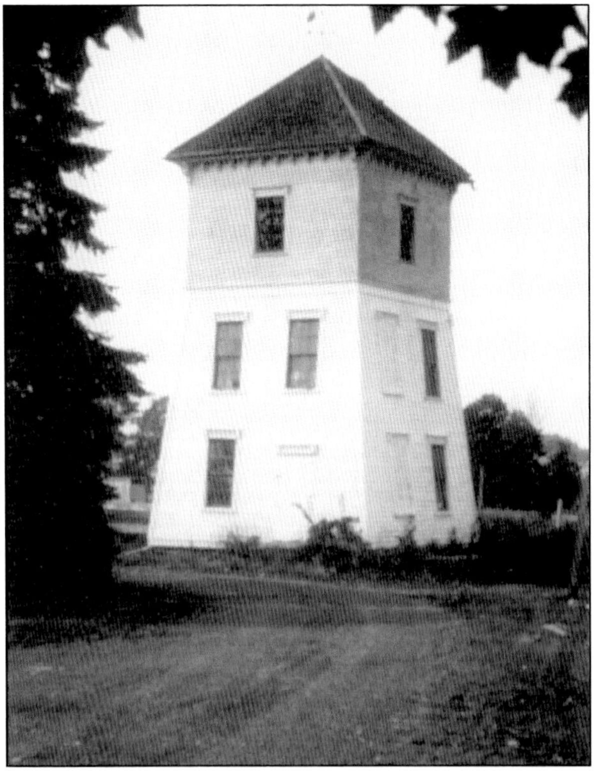

Located on the Lynd farm, later the Holser farm, was the tank house where collars were made. On the top floor were large tanks of water, which operated the sewing machines below. Workers had to rent their machines for 30¢ a week, buy needles to replace broken ones at three packages for 15¢, and buy their own thread.

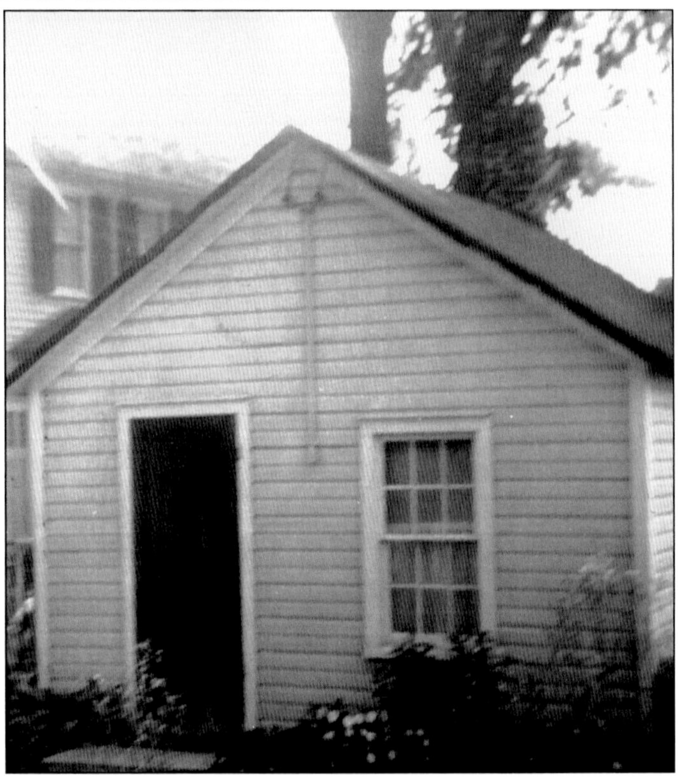

The cobbler shop was located just northeast of the bridge on Farm-to-Market Road. This shop was nicknamed the "10-footer," as it was 10 feet square. Gene Wheeler was the last cobbler to work here.

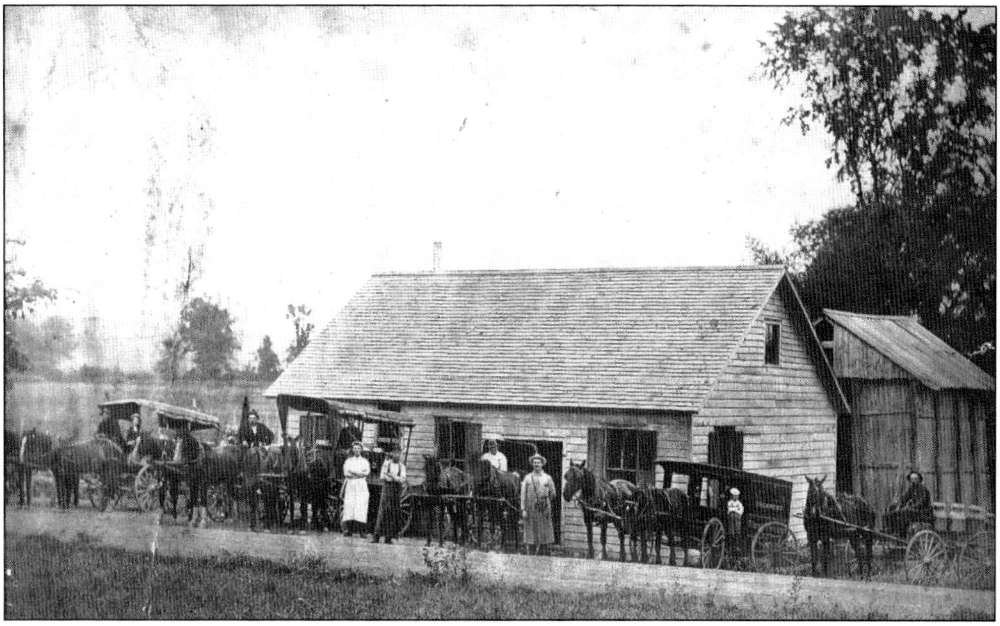

Seen in this 1908 photograph, the True Elgin Creamery was just west of Garfield Road. The creamery was owned and operated by Philip Fisher, standing in front of the door wearing the apron and money pouch. The icehouse stands behind the creamery. Local farmers hauled their raw milk to this creamery, and dairy products were then peddled in town as well as in Troy. Philip's brother Fred was listed as a butter maker.

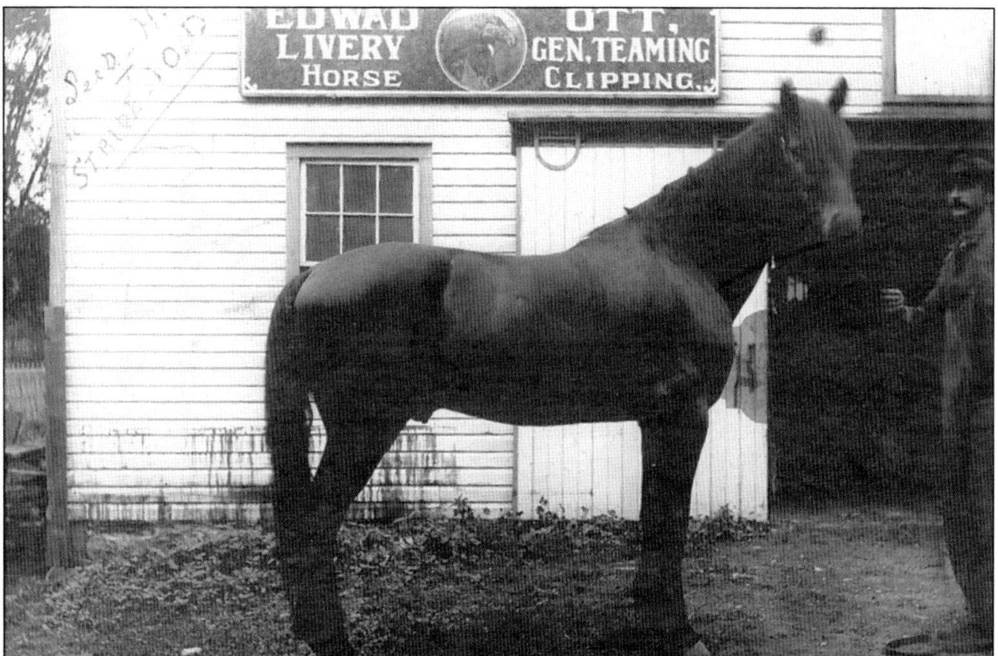


Ed Ott ran this livery stable. Ott is seen here with a horse named Stride Bold. In the front of the barn was a large scale used to weigh hay and crushed stone.

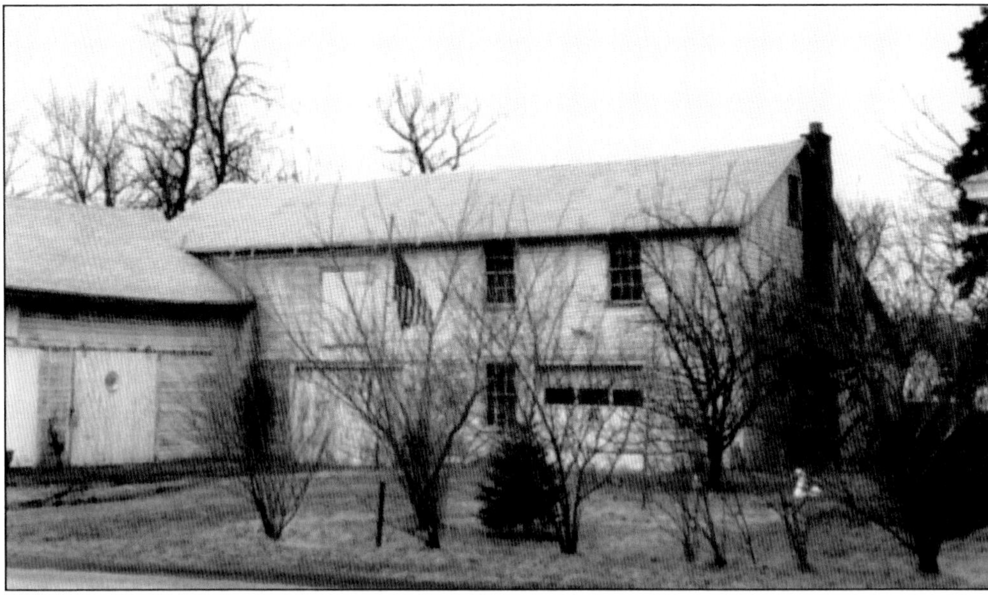

Ed Ott's barns were in the village. One of the barns was used as a voting place for the male citizens in the early days. Due to deterioration of the structures, the town demolished them in the late 1990s, and the site is now part of the village green.

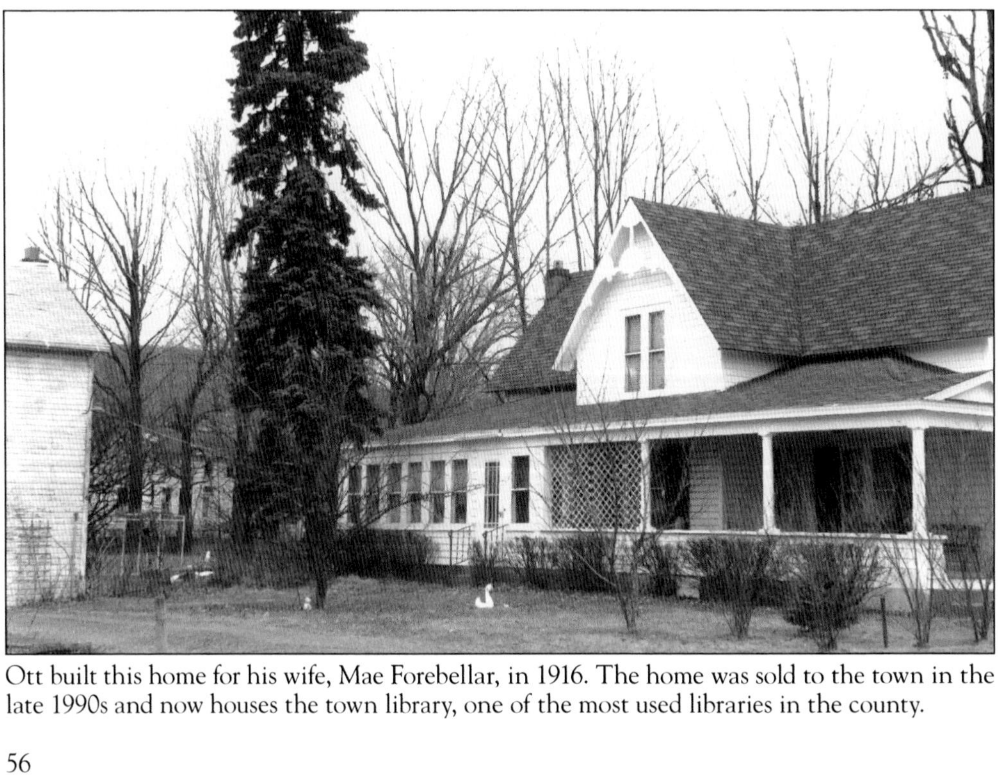

Ott built this home for his wife, Mae Forebellar, in 1916. The home was sold to the town in the late 1990s and now houses the town library, one of the most used libraries in the county.

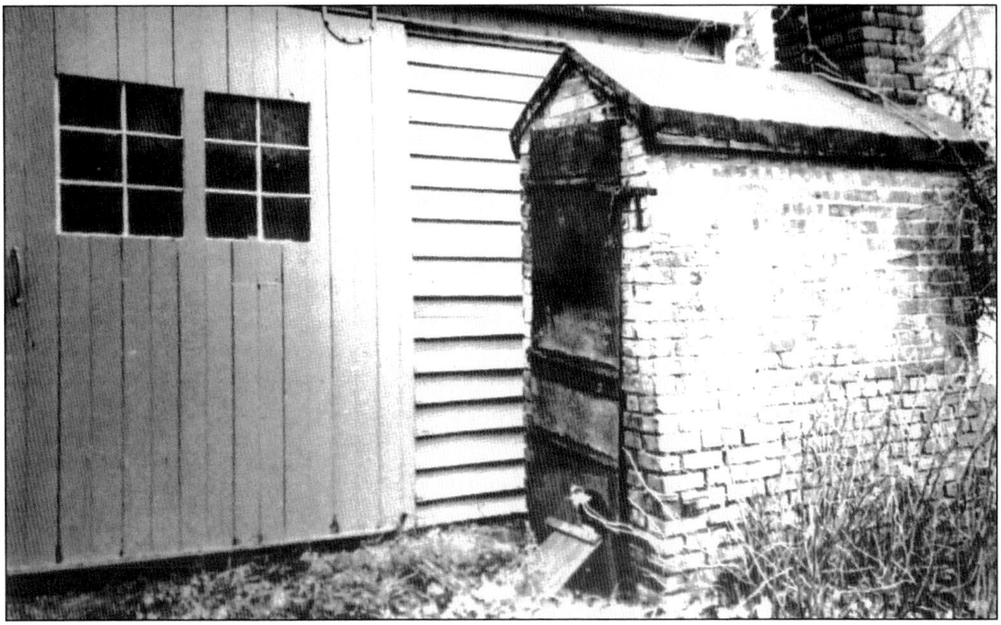

This brick forge was behind the Bosch home on Plank Road. Here is where Peter Bosch heated and then bent iron to fit on wagon wheels.

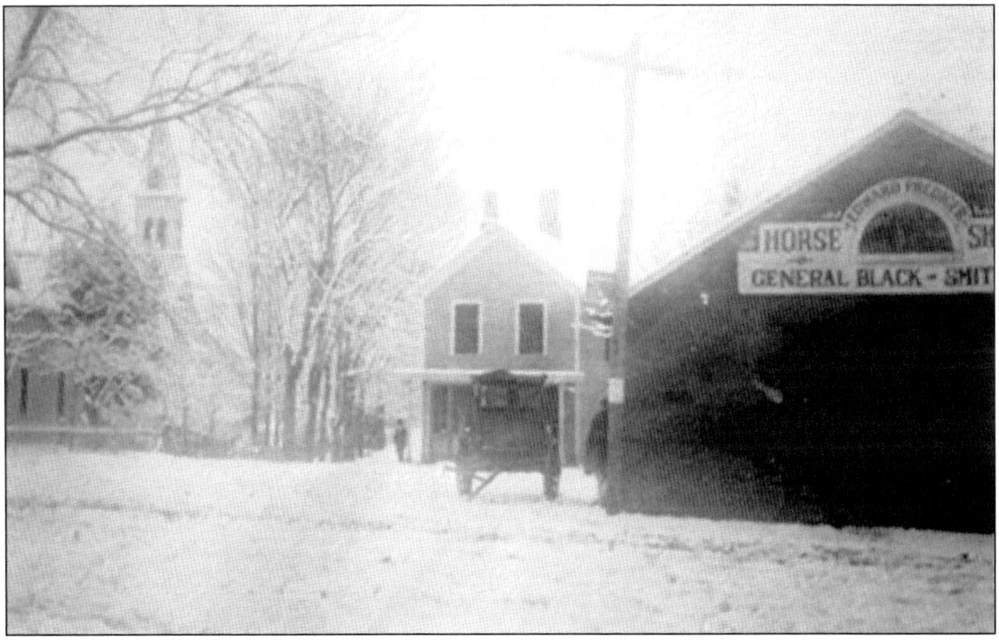


Two blacksmith shops were next to each other on Main Street. The brick one was owned and operated by a Mr. Clark. Just west of it was a wooden structure operated by Edward Prediger. To the left of the blacksmith shop was the home of Earl Wilker and his family. At one time, there was a bakery in the building.

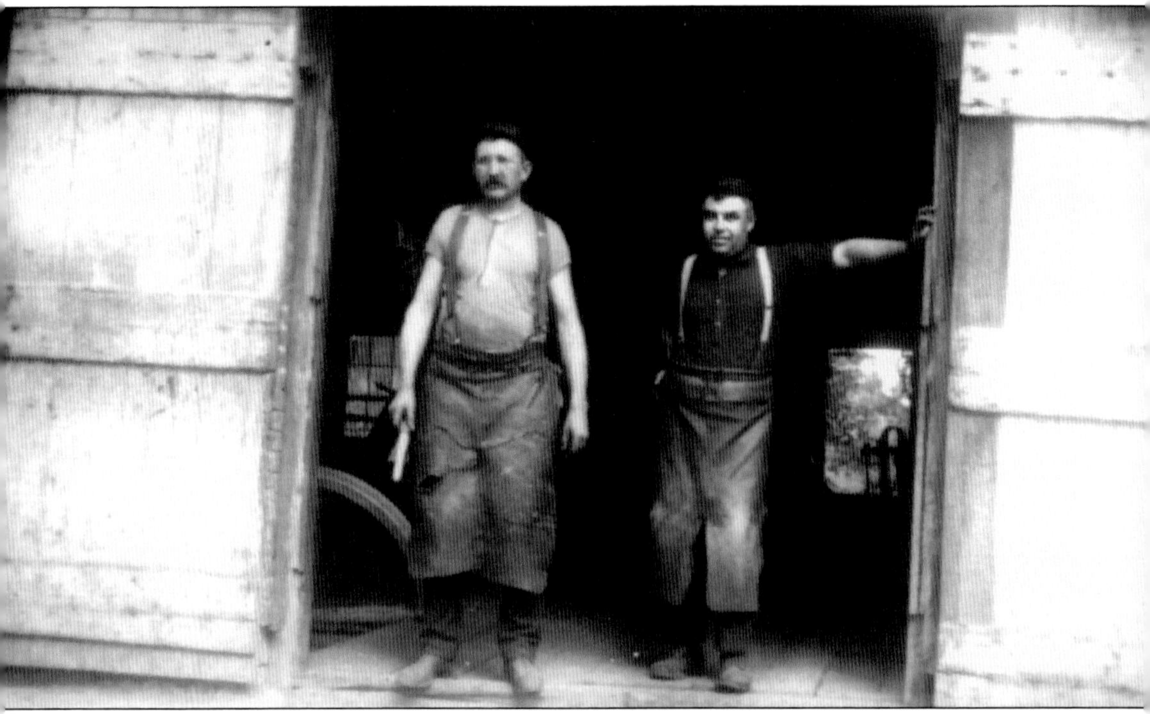

Edward Prediger and William Weinbrecht stand in the doorway of the old wood blacksmith shop, located next to the other blacksmith shop in the village. The building was later demolished to make way for highway construction.

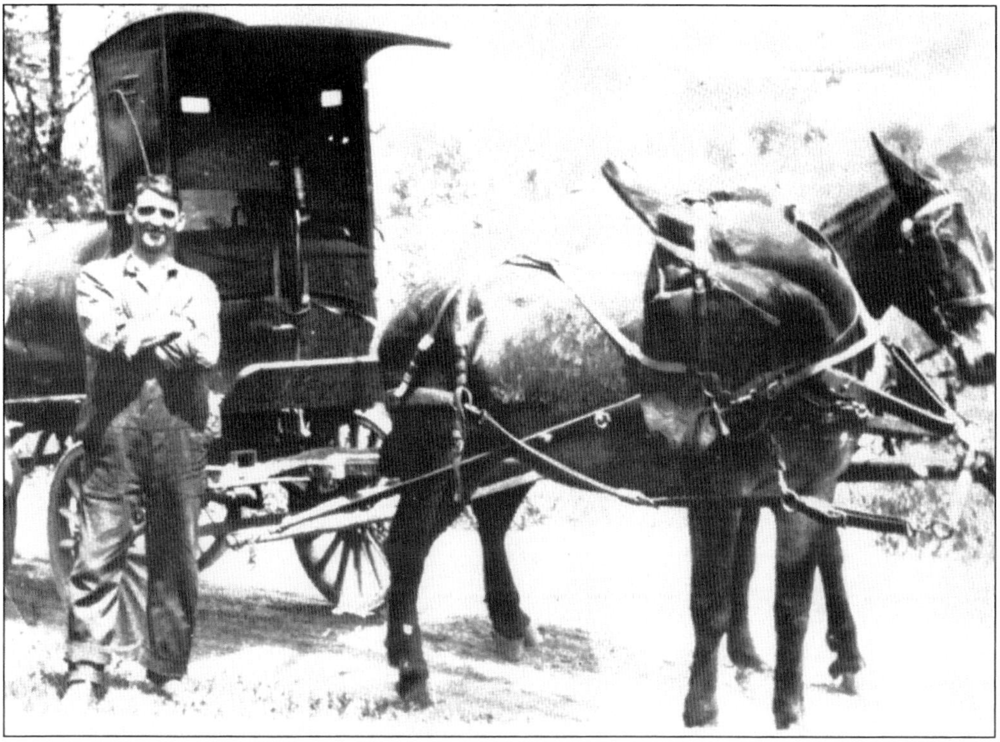

Nicholas Legenbauer (Mindy) poses in 1916 after delivering fuel oil to local residents with his team of mules and wagon. He, along with several Legenbauer family members, ran an oil business that continues to operate today.

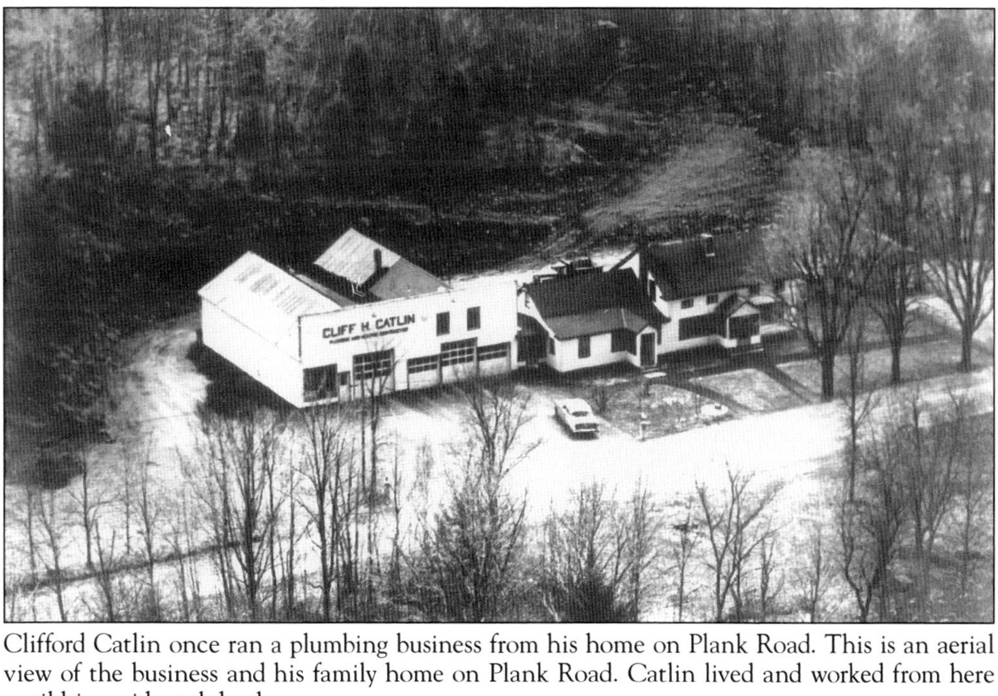


Clifford Catlin once ran a plumbing business from his home on Plank Road. This is an aerial view of the business and his family home on Plank Road. Catlin lived and worked from here until his accidental death.

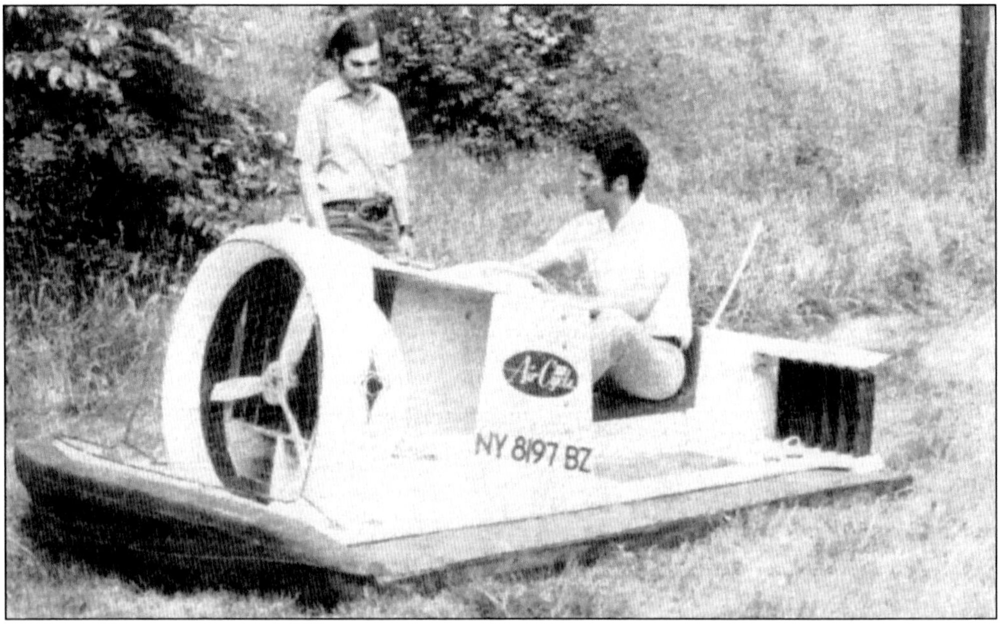


In 1962, Hugo Ferguson constructed Duffer's Associates, where he worked on his Air Cycle, the first economical hovercraft-type vehicle. The company, now called Dynamic Systems Inc., is where the Gleeble is manufactured.

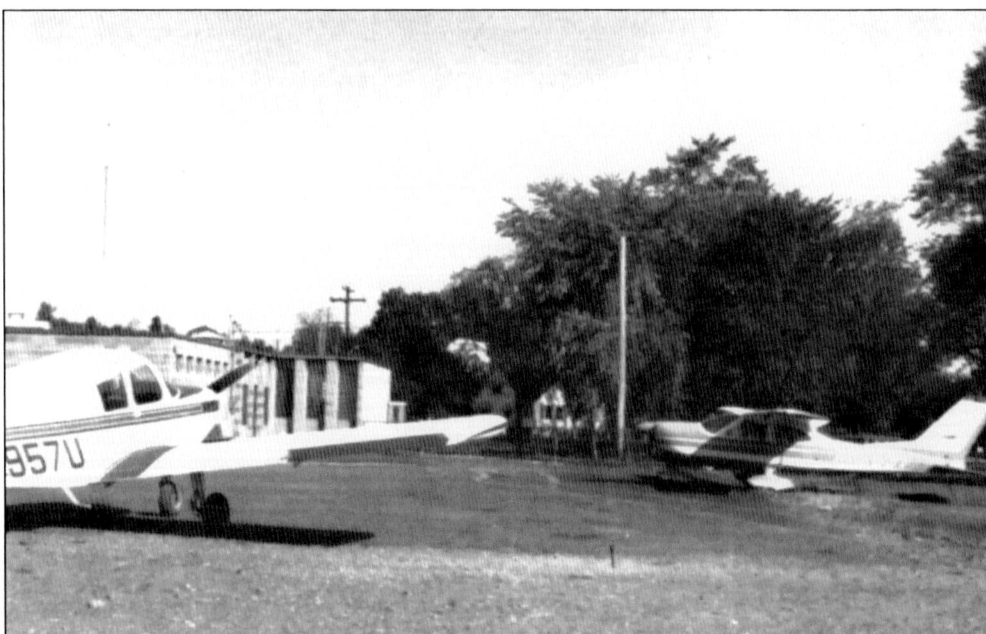


Poestenkill Airport was built where small planes could land. Several people leave their private planes there at the field.

*Four*

# School Days

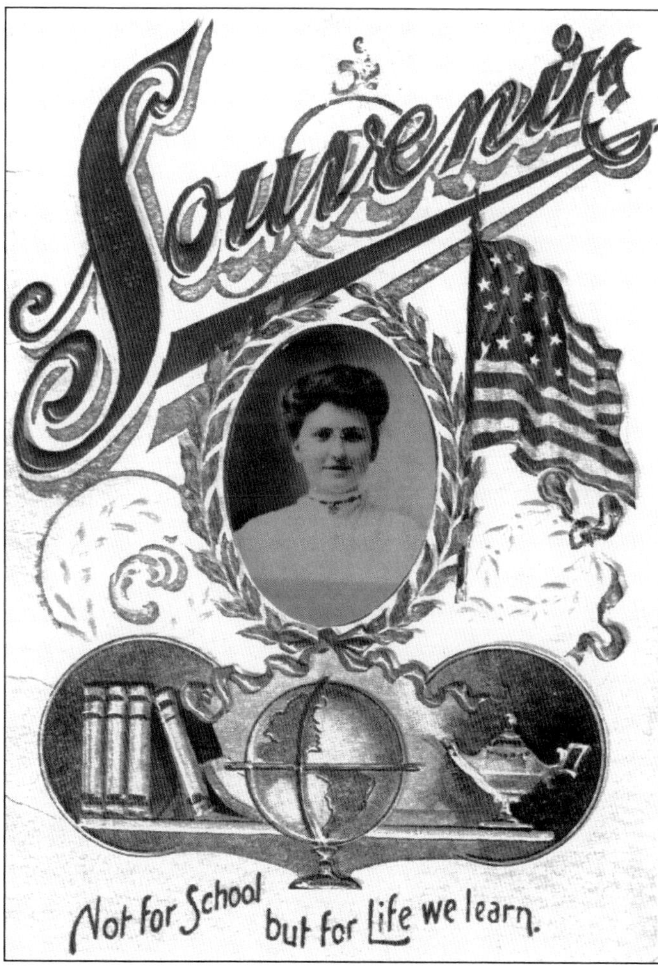


At the close of the school year, teachers gave their students a souvenir booklet containing the names of teachers, students, and school board members. This 1908 booklet is from the District No. 3 school; the teacher is Carrie Radz.

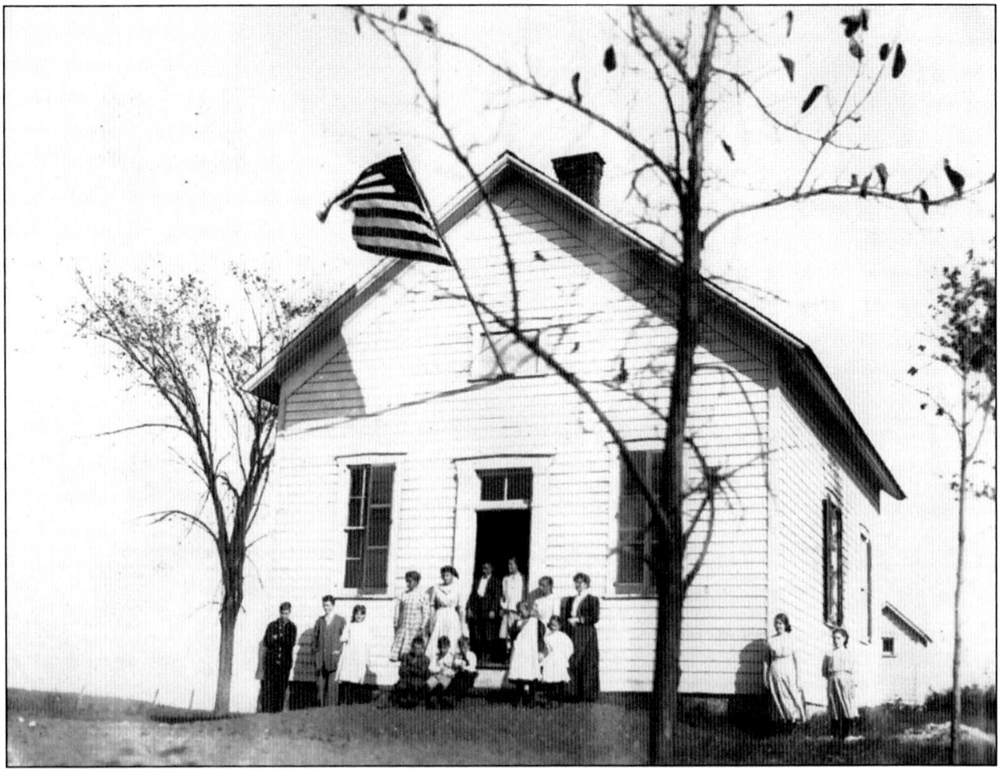

District No. 1 was known as Round Top School, because the original building had a dome-shaped roof or round top. This original school was located near Liberty Lane. The second Round Top School building (above) was at the intersection of Route 66 and Round Top Road. The class is seen below about 1898 with its teacher Edward Bower, who later received a doctorate in education and became superintendent of schools in Lindenhurst, Long Island.

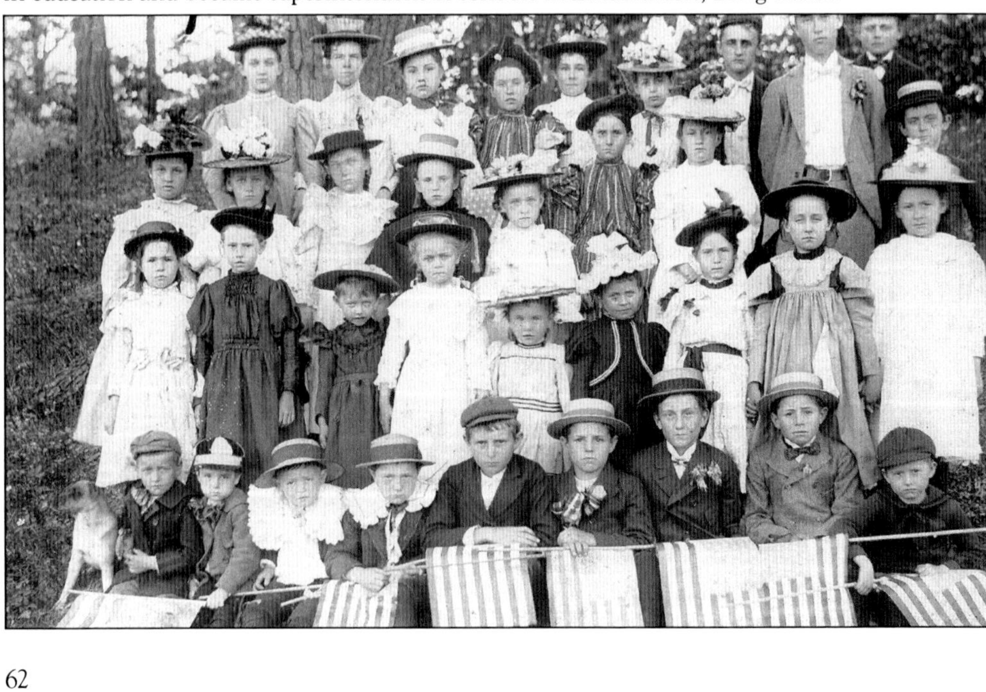

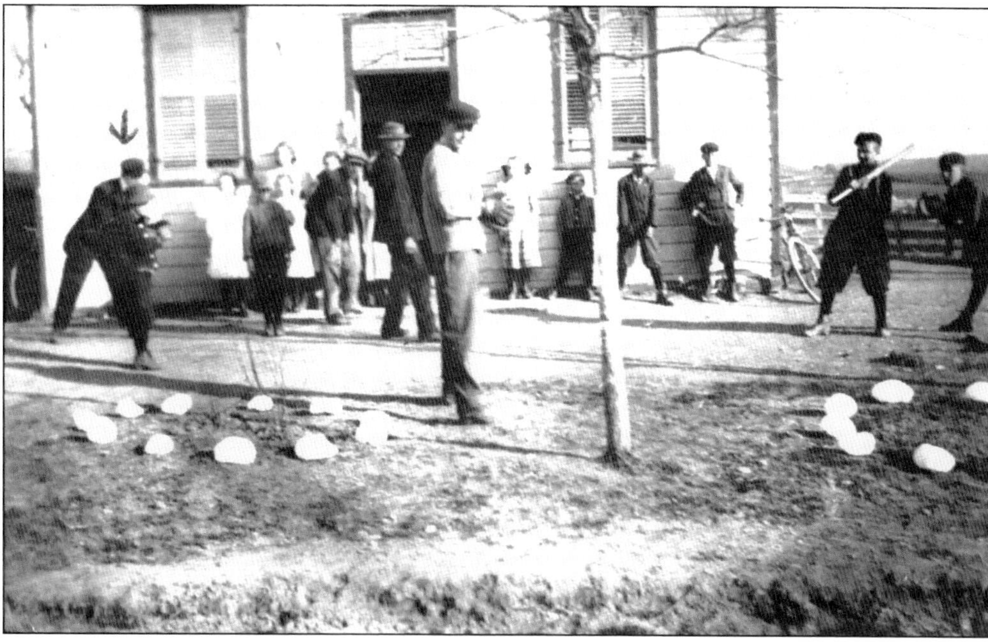

District No. 2 was the Weatherwax School, named for the several Weatherwax families living in the vicinity. Above are students at recess time in front of the school. This was the only one-room school in Poestenkill (below) to have two entrances, one for boys and one for girls. Some of the children attending this school were from the families of Abbott, Brod, Heaver, Ryan, Carner, Stristman, and Weatherwax.

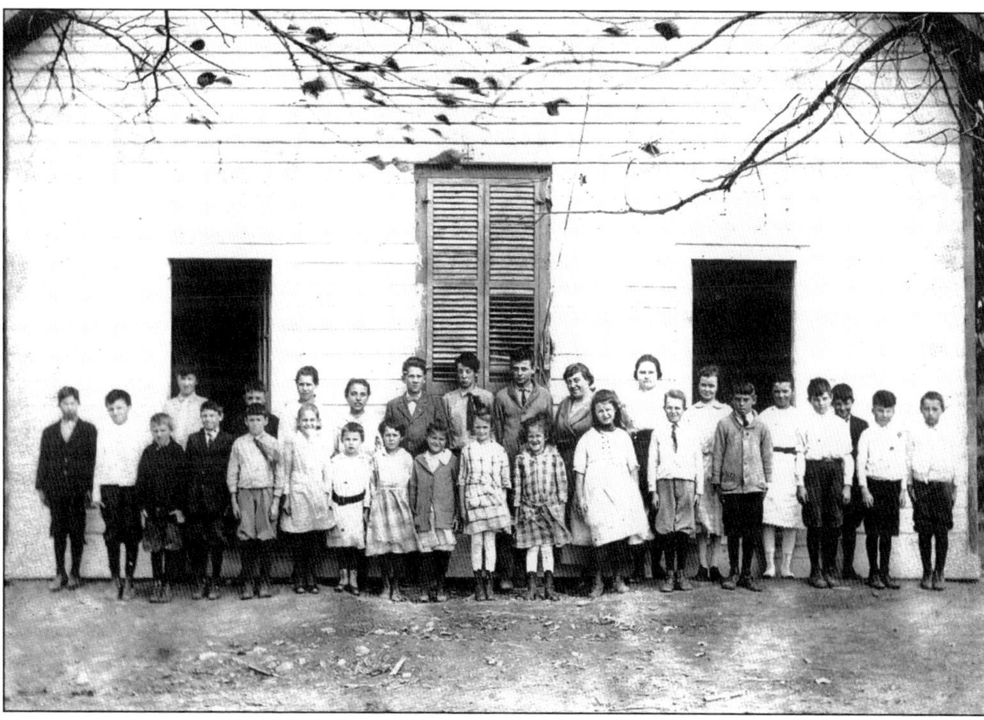

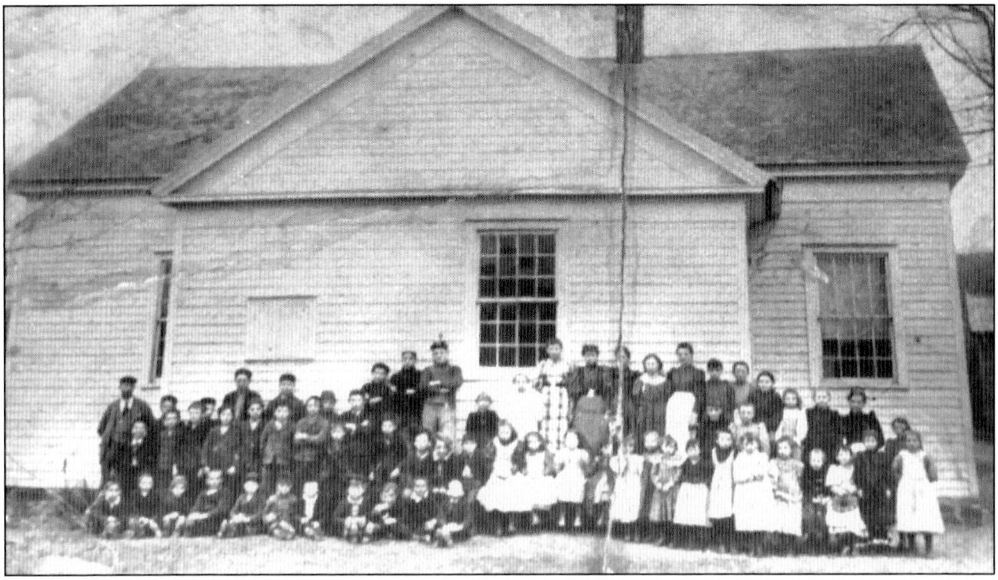

The District No. 3 school was called the Village School (above). This was the only two-room school in Poestenkill. The children are pictured below in the backyard of the school. The teachers are Bertha Clickner on the left and a Mr. Bauer on the right.

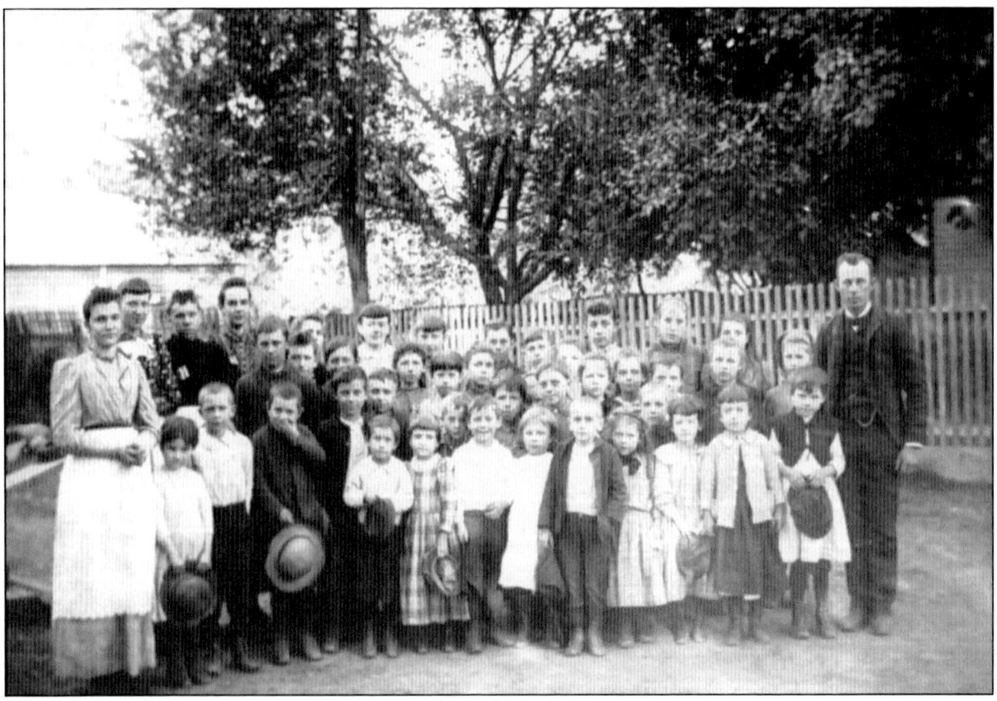

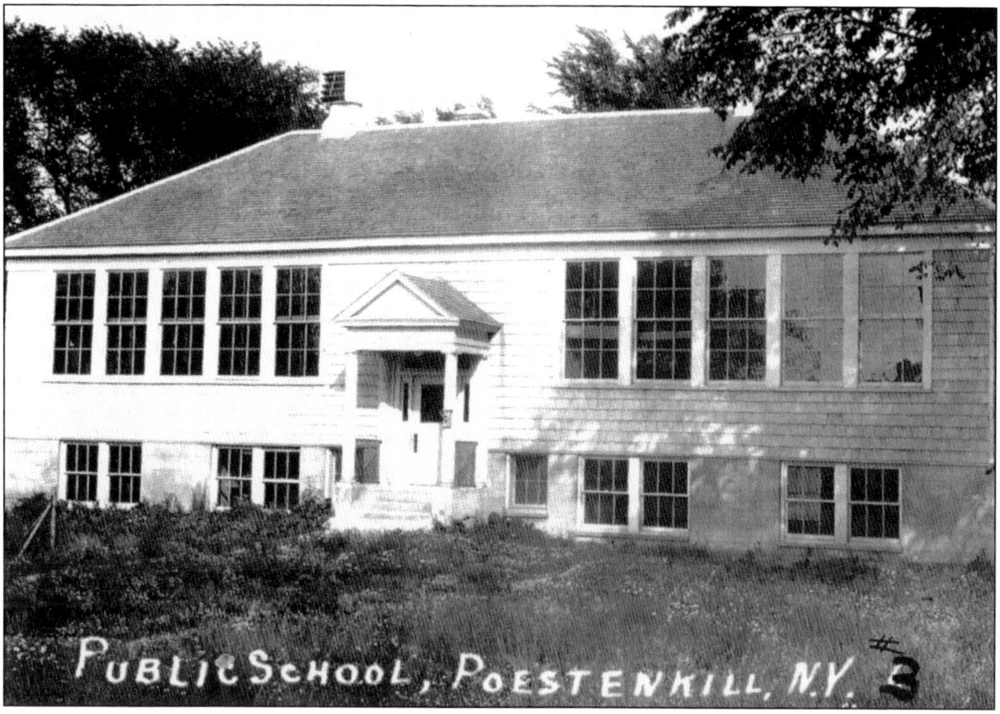


The Village School was replaced with a four-room school in late 1928. Above is a photograph of the front of the building, while below is the back of the building with playground. This building closed in 1951 due to crowded conditions, and students moved into the new Poestenkill Elementary School.

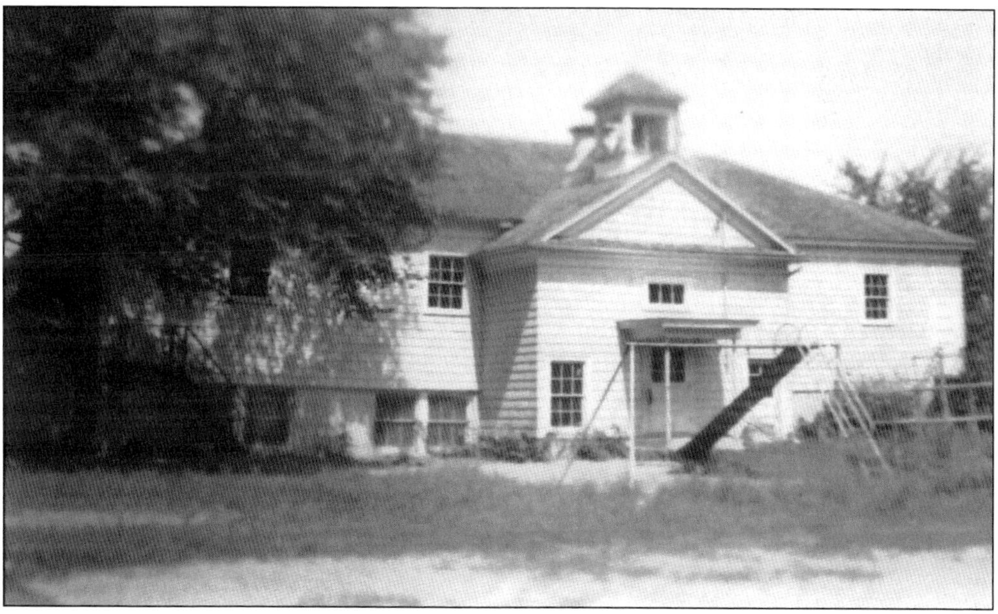

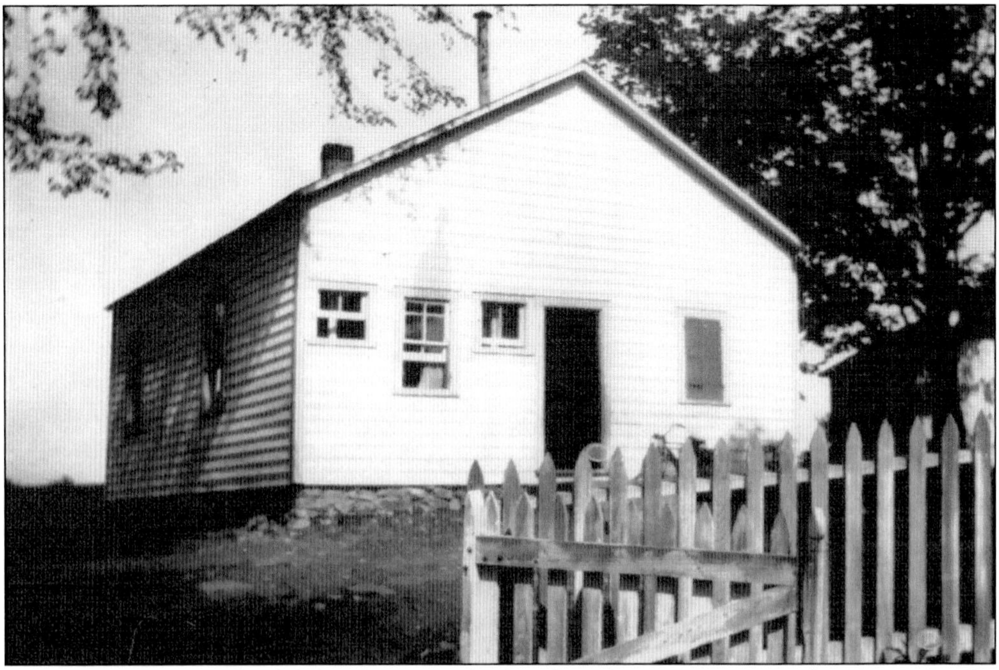

The District No. 4 school (above) was in the hamlet of Ives Corners on the Henry Searles farm. This school originally had two cloakrooms, one for boys and one for girls. Below is a class photograph from 1896.

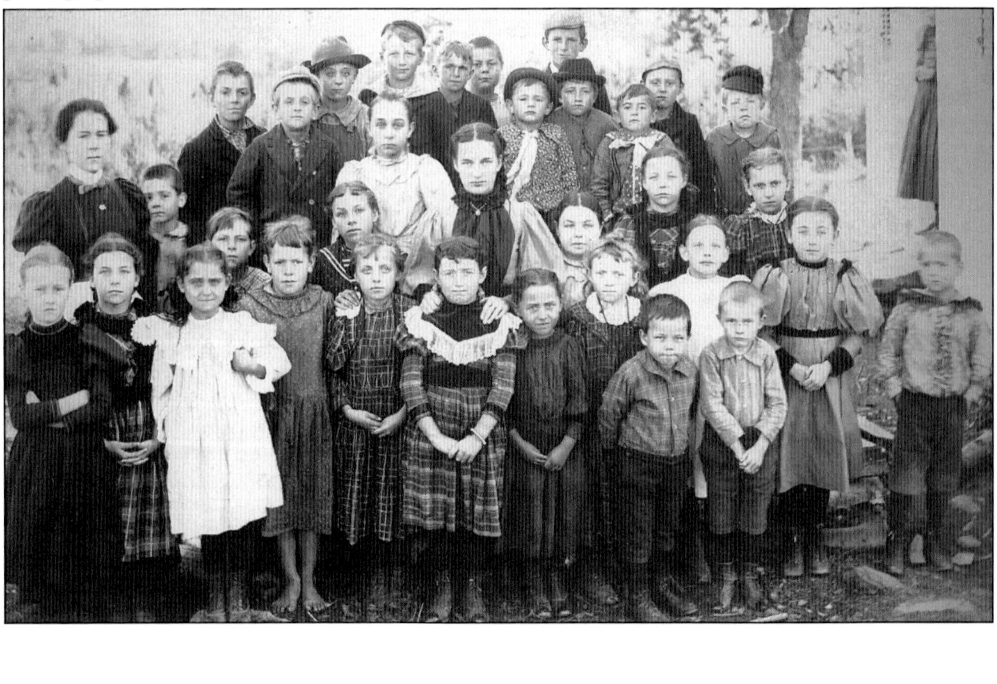

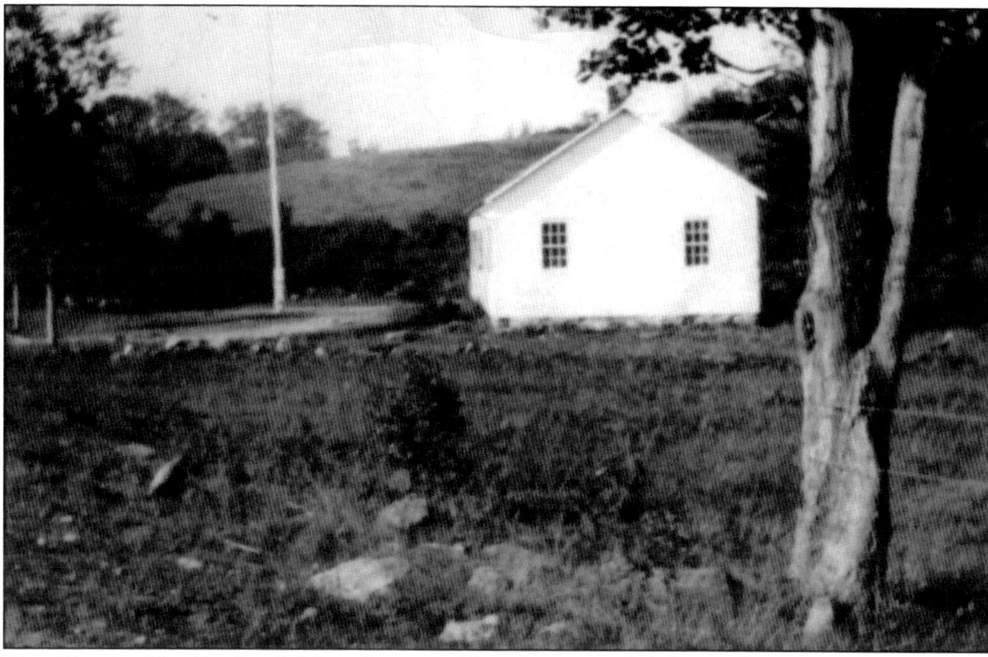

The District No. 5 school (above) was in East Poestenkill. This is the only school in town known to have its own school song. Below is a class photograph taken in 1924, showing Norma Teal, Eva Flint, Irene Flint, Mildred Catlin, William Kaiser, Violet Kaiser, Edna Kaiser, Helen Teal, Etola Teal, Mildred Teal, Marion Flint, Evelyn Catlin, Laura Catlin, Alice Kaiser, Sanford Catlin, Theodore Catlin, Walter Schroeder, Wilson Miller, Elwin Flint, Maurice Bly, and Merritt Cropsey.

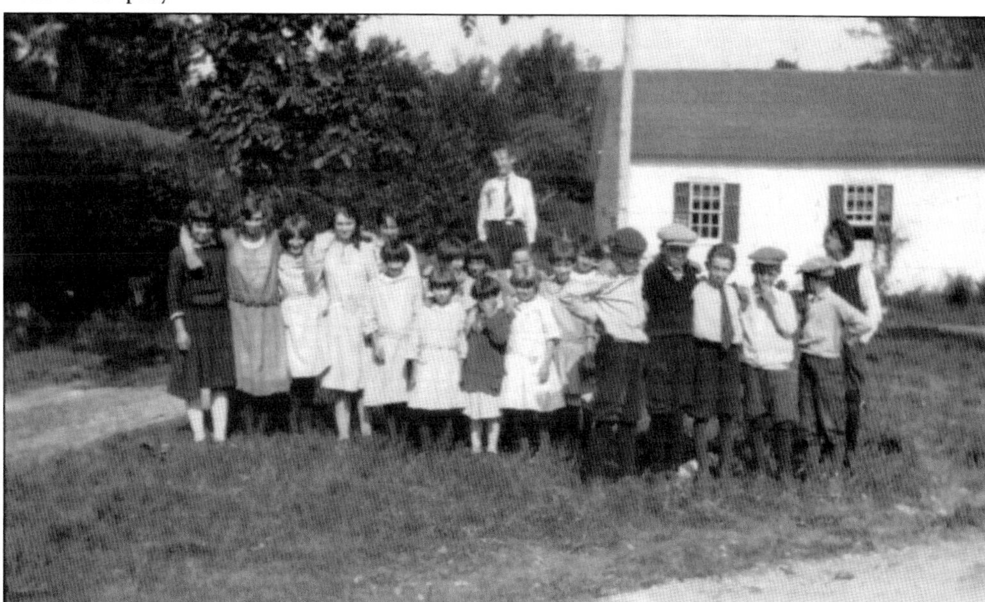

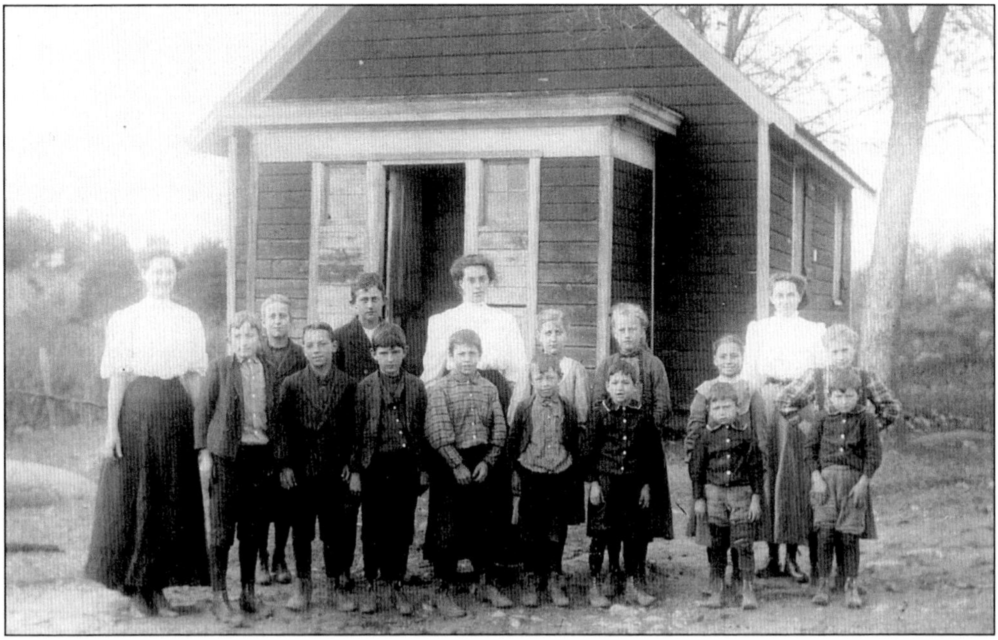

The District No. 6 school (above) was near the Poestenkill-Berlin town line and was known as the King School around the early 1900s. In the early days, it served as school and meetinghouse for that tiny hamlet. In later years, Verner Cropsey and his son Merritt purchased the building and moved it to their property to convert it to a garage. Below is Louise Wiegner's teacher's contract, dated August 19, 1909.

## TEACHER'S CONTRACT

SECTIONS 562 TO 567 INCLUSIVE OF THE EDUCATION LAW OF 1909

I [illegible] of [illegible] county of [illegible] a duly qualified teacher, hereby contract with the board of trustees of district no. 6 town of [illegible] county of [illegible] to teach the public school of said district for the term of 32 consecutive weeks, except as hereafter provided, commencing [illegible] 1909 at a weekly compensation of 9 dollars and — cents payable at the end of each thirty days during the term of such employment.

And the board of trustees of said district hereby contract to employ said teacher for said period at the said rate of compensation, payable at the times herein stated.

Said board of trustees reserve the right to provide for a vacation or vacations of not more than 2 weeks in the aggregate, during said term, which vacation shall not count as a part of the term of service above referred to.

Dated [illegible] 19 1909

[illegible]
Teacher

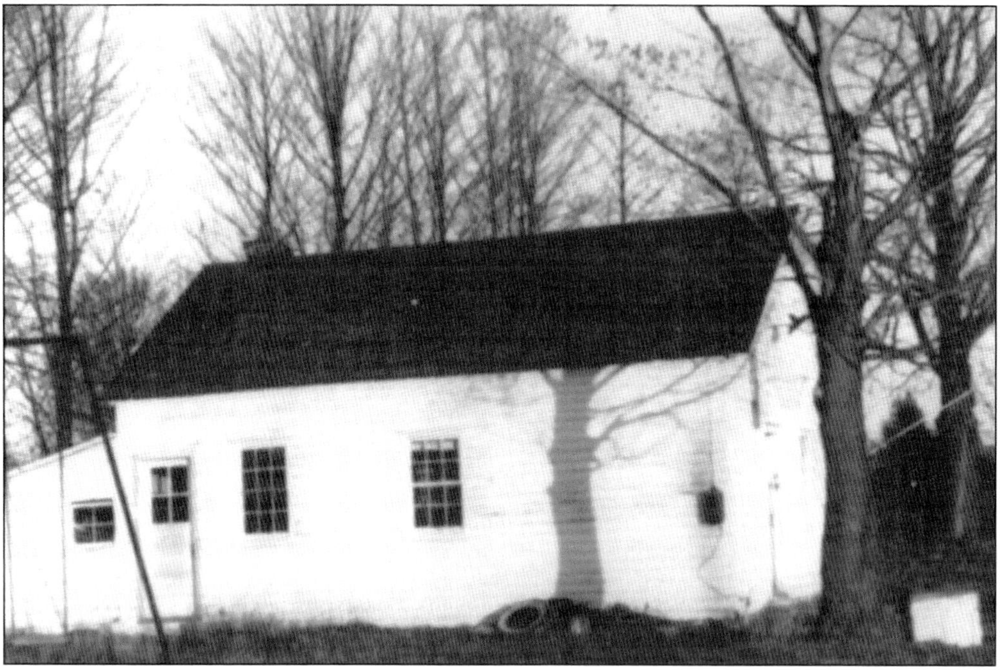

The District No. 7 school (above) was called the North Road School and was located on North Road opposite the former home of Philip Ernst. Below is a *c.* 1902 class picture of children in eight grades in the one-room school of learning.

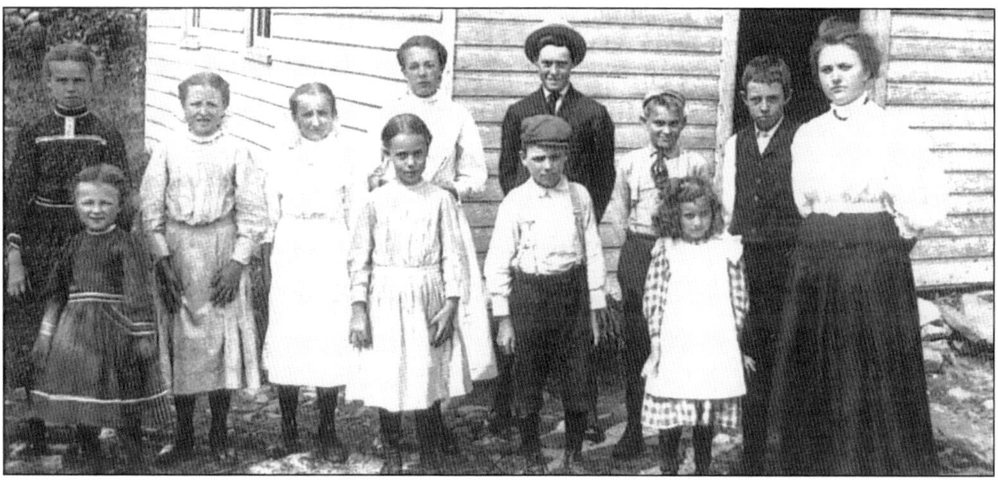

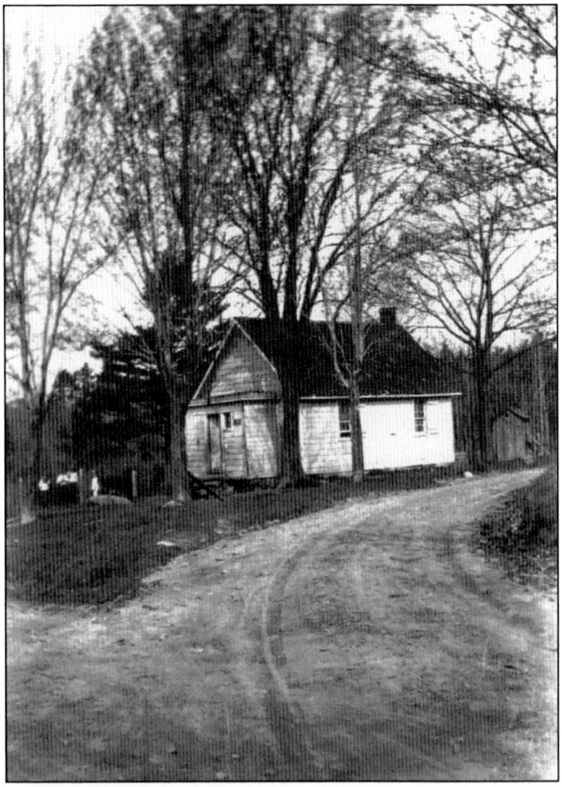

The District No. 8 school was called the Oak Hill School (left). Below is an early group photograph. It must have been a special occasion as some students are wearing corsages.

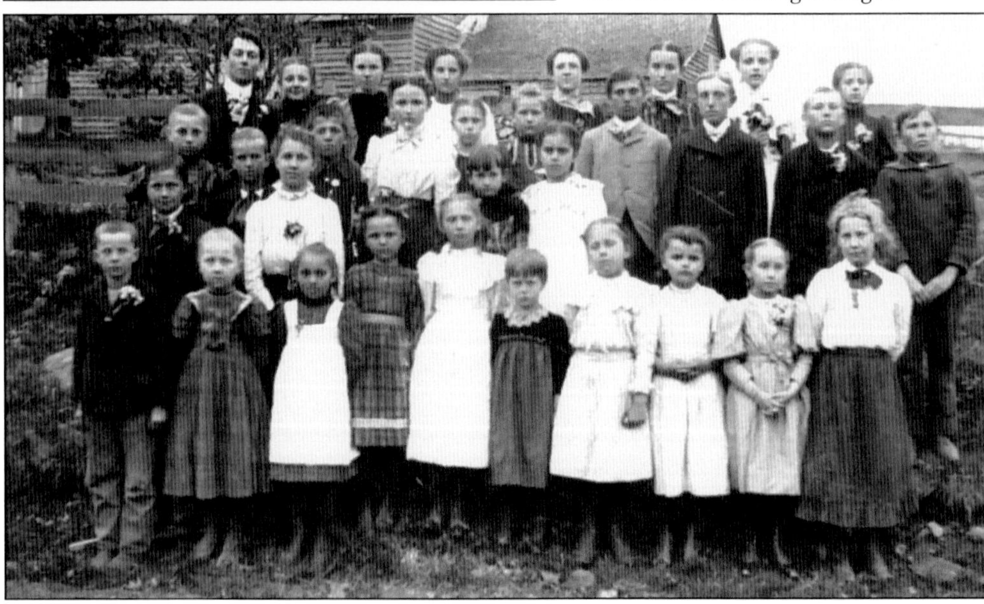

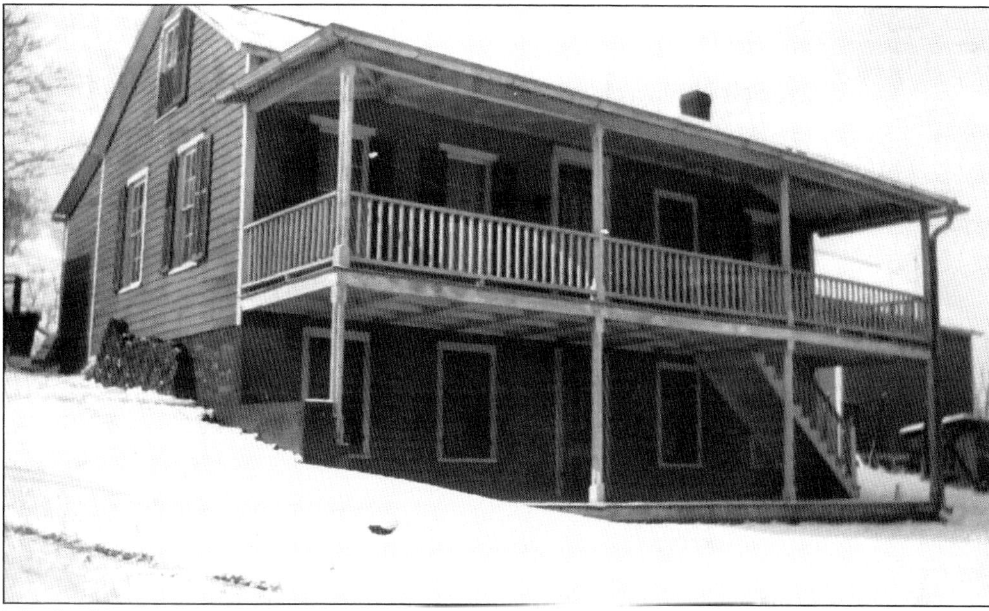

This building, at the bottom of Snake Hill Road, was once a select school, a private, postgraduate school that operated for only a few years in the 1850s.

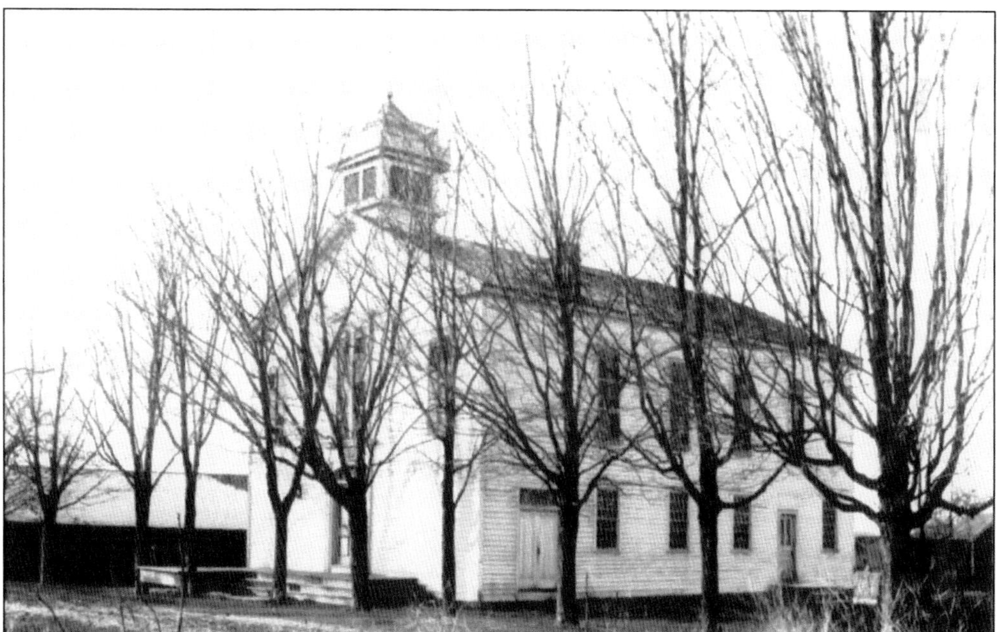

The Poestenkill Academy was located on Snyders Corners Road on the site of the Poestenkill Christian Church (Disciples of Christ) and operated during the 1850s.

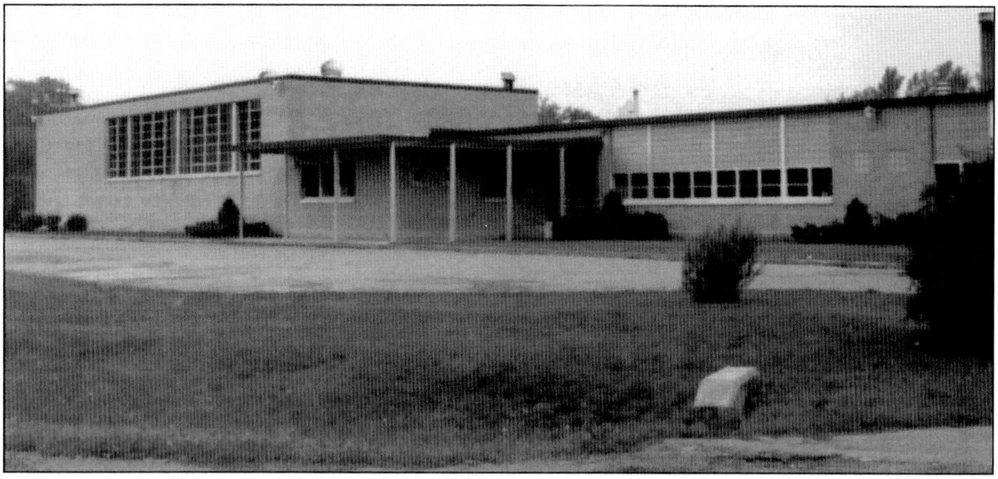

Poestenkill Elementary School was built in 1950–1951 at a cost of $254,637 to consolidate several of the one-room schools. The original Poestenkill schools joined the Central School District, known as Averill Park Central School District between the years 1929 and 1958. Two additions have been attached to this original building.

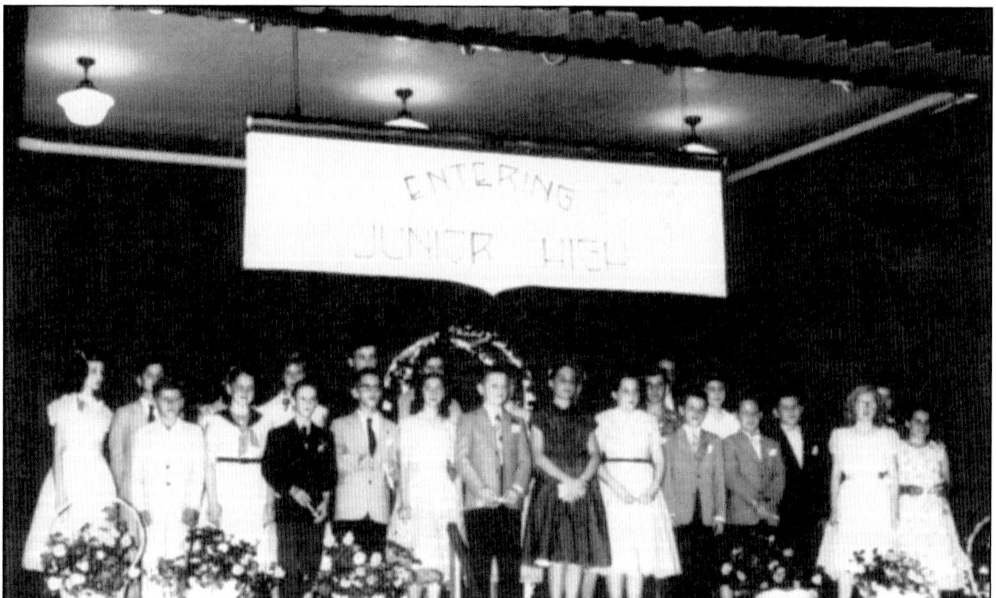

The sixth-grade class of 1955 leaves Poestenkill Elementary School and moves on to Averill Park Junior High School.

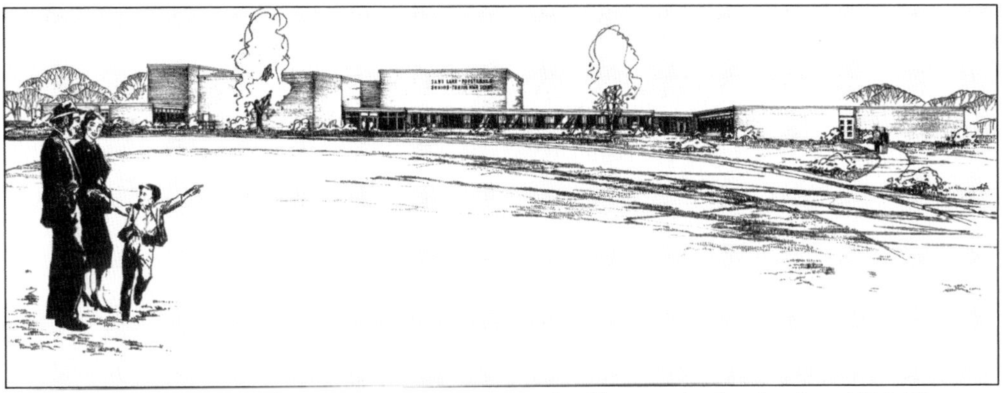

Due to overcrowded conditions, it was necessary to build a new high school in 1956. The new high school is seen here as a sketch presented to voters for their approval in 1955 at a projected total cost of $1,620,000.

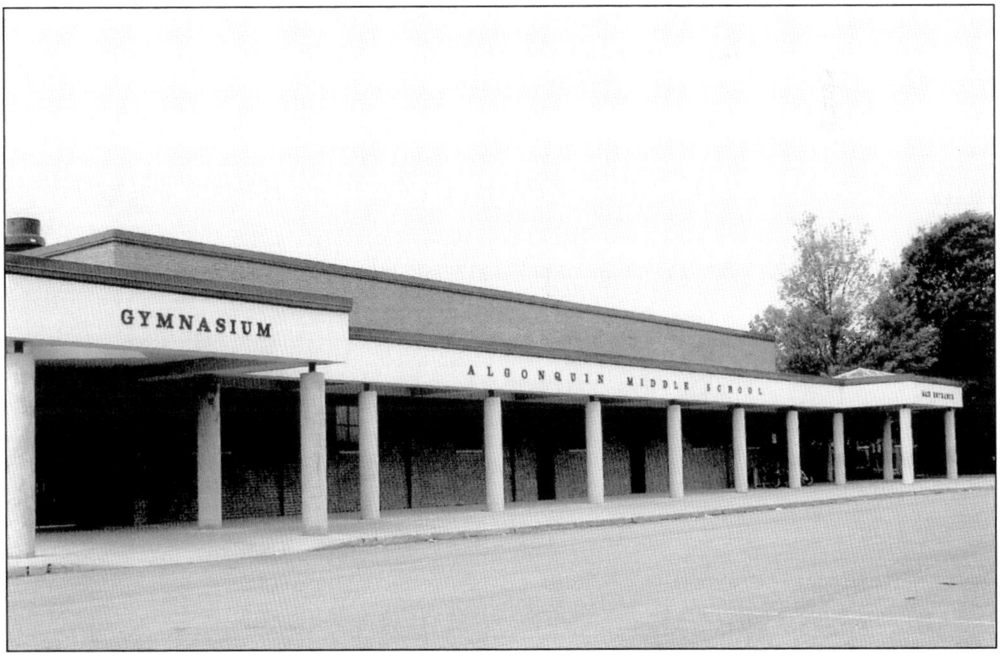


When the high school became too crowded, it was again necessary to build another school. In 1966, grades six through eight moved into the newly constructed Algonquin Middle School.

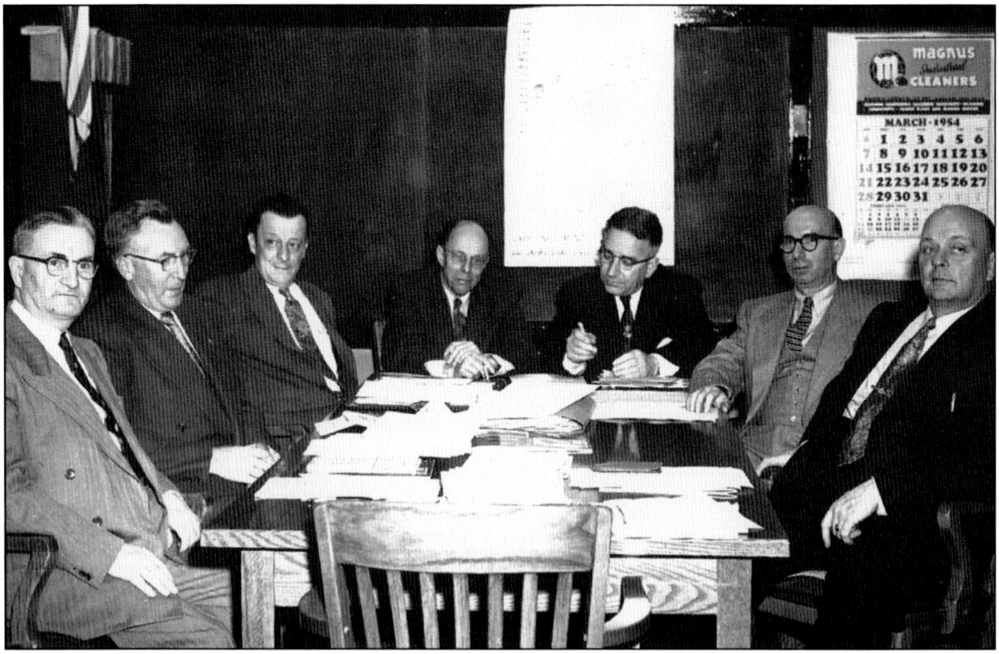


The 1954 board of education of the Averill Park Central School District was made up of, clockwise from bottom left, Lewis Griffin of Stephentown; Carl Beck of Sand Lake; Roland Trathan of Poestenkill; Kimball Sprague of West Sand Lake; Herford Smith, business supervisor; Elmer Stahlman, supervising principal; and Merrill Zweig from Poestenkill.

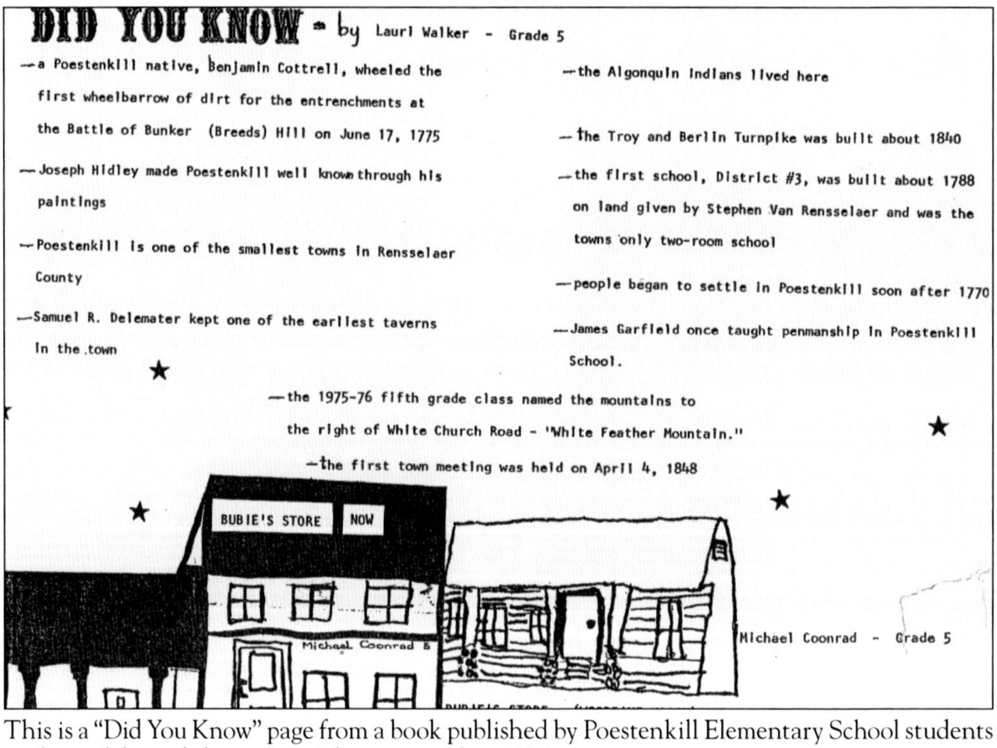

**DID YOU KNOW** - by Laurl Walker - Grade 5

—a Poestenkill native, Benjamin Cottrell, wheeled the first wheelbarrow of dirt for the entrenchments at the Battle of Bunker (Breeds) Hill on June 17, 1775

—Joseph Hidley made Poestenkill well known through his paintings

—Poestenkill is one of the smallest towns in Rensselaer County

—Samuel R. Delemater kept one of the earliest taverns in the town

—the Algonquin Indians lived here

—the Troy and Berlin Turnpike was built about 1840

—the first school, District #3, was built about 1788 on land given by Stephen Van Rensselaer and was the towns only two-room school

—people began to settle in Poestenkill soon after 1770

—James Garfield once taught penmanship in Poestenkill School.

—the 1975-76 fifth grade class named the mountains to the right of White Church Road - "White Feather Mountain."

—the first town meeting was held on April 4, 1848



Michael Coonrad - Grade 5

This is a "Did You Know" page from a book published by Poestenkill Elementary School students as they celebrated the country's bicentennial in 1976.

# *Five*

# CHURCHES

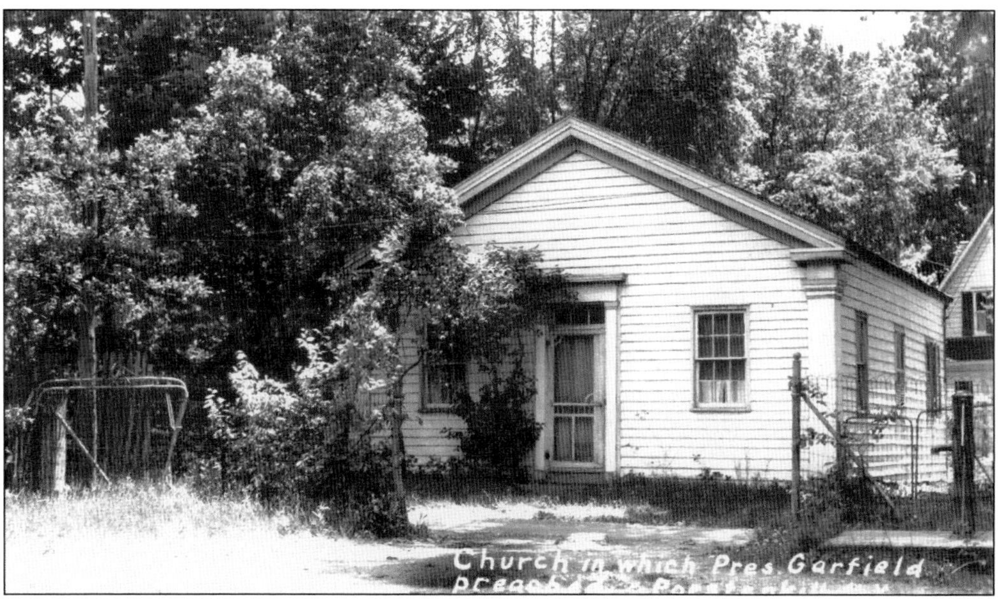


Here is the original meetinghouse of the Church of Christ around 1959. In this building, James A. Garfield, the martyred president, preached his first sermon while a student at Williams College in 1854. The building was used as a church from 1850 to 1864. It was then converted into a dwelling.

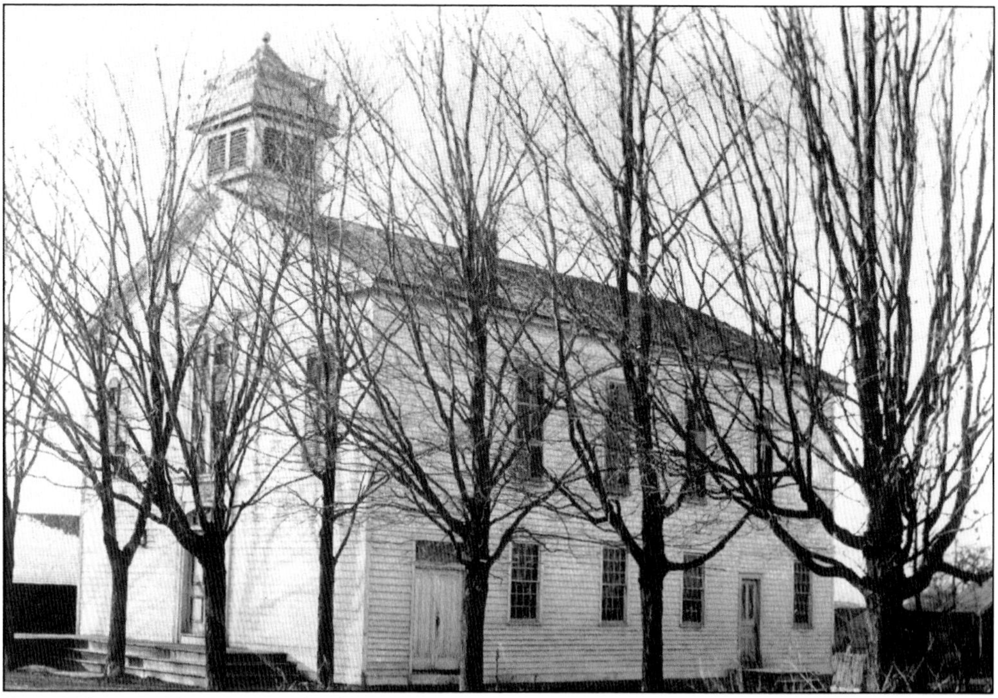

From February 23, 1864, until February 17, 1901, the Poestenkill Academy (above) stood on the present site and was used as the Christian Church (Church of Christ Disciples) until the current building (below) was erected.

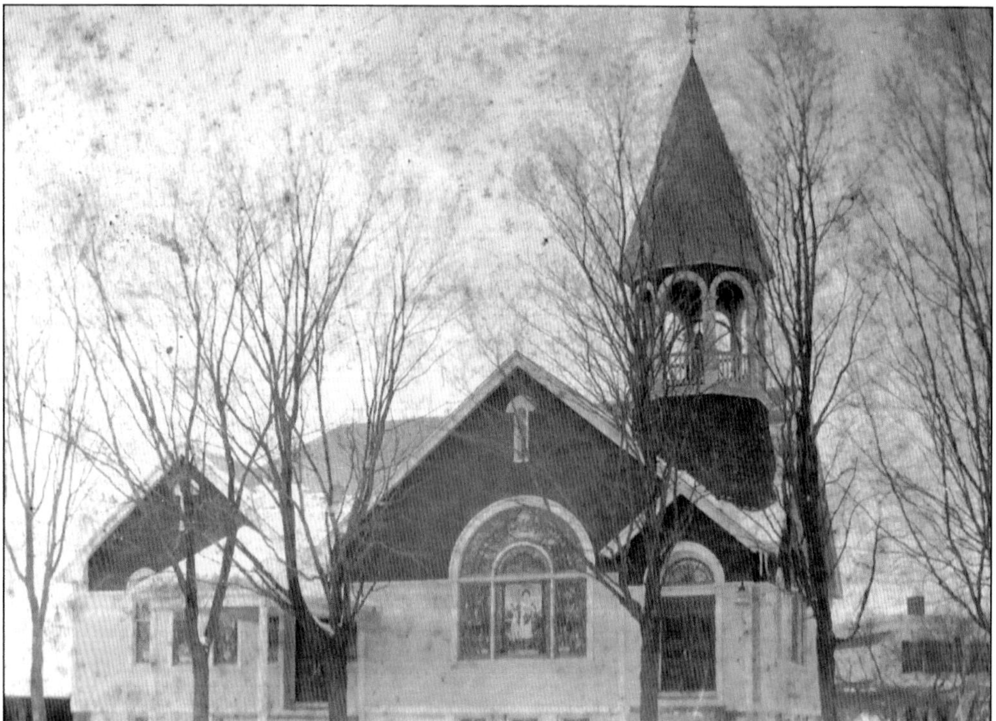

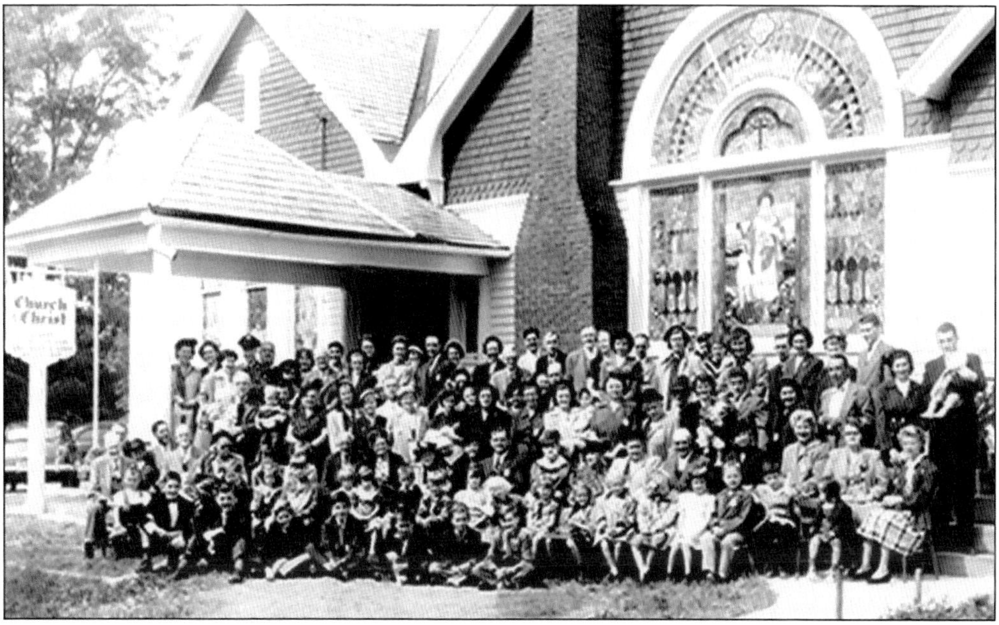


This picture shows the congregation of the Church of Christ in 1950. The members are celebrating their centennial anniversary and are posed in front of the unusual stained-glass window.

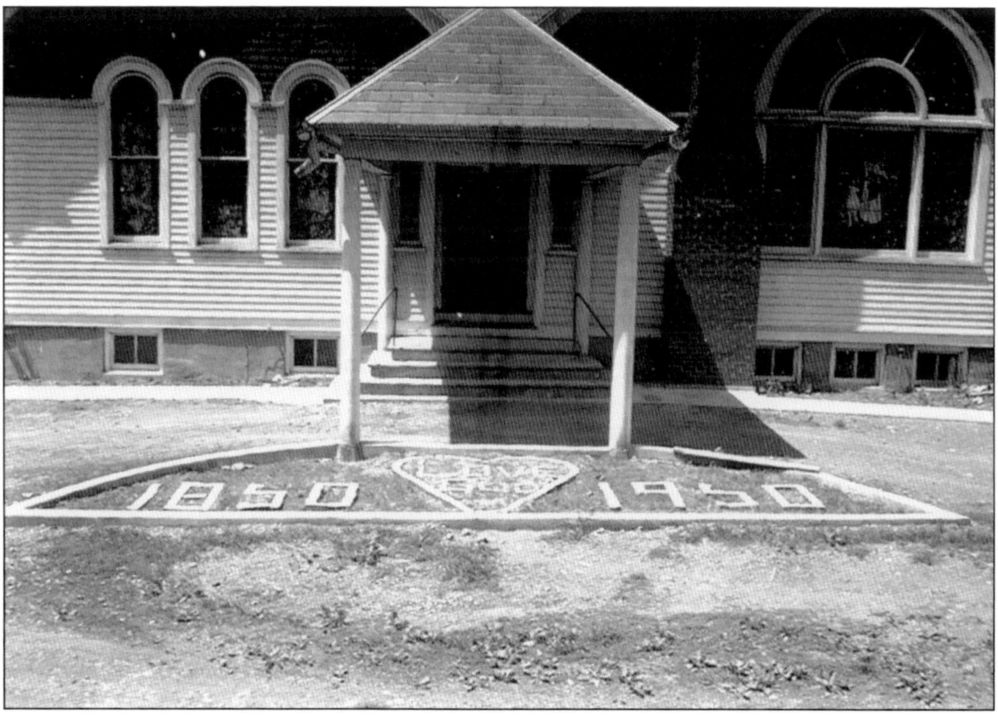


This shows the front of the Church of Christ at its centennial anniversary around 1950. A special sculpture was made in front of the church, designating the dates of the anniversary, 1850 to 1950.

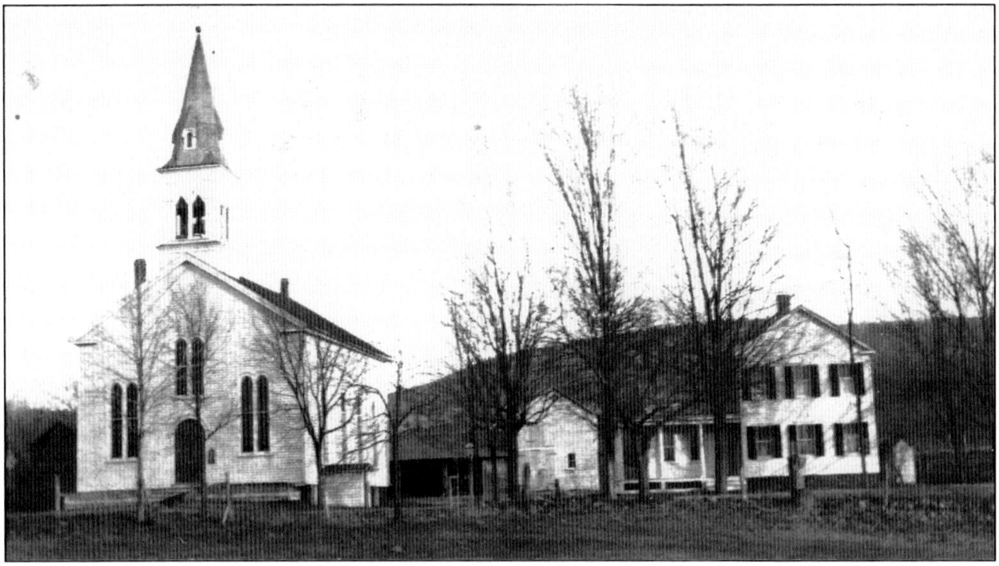

This is the exterior view of the Evangelical Lutheran Church and parsonage complex showing the barn and horse sheds behind the church that were used each Sunday while services were being held.

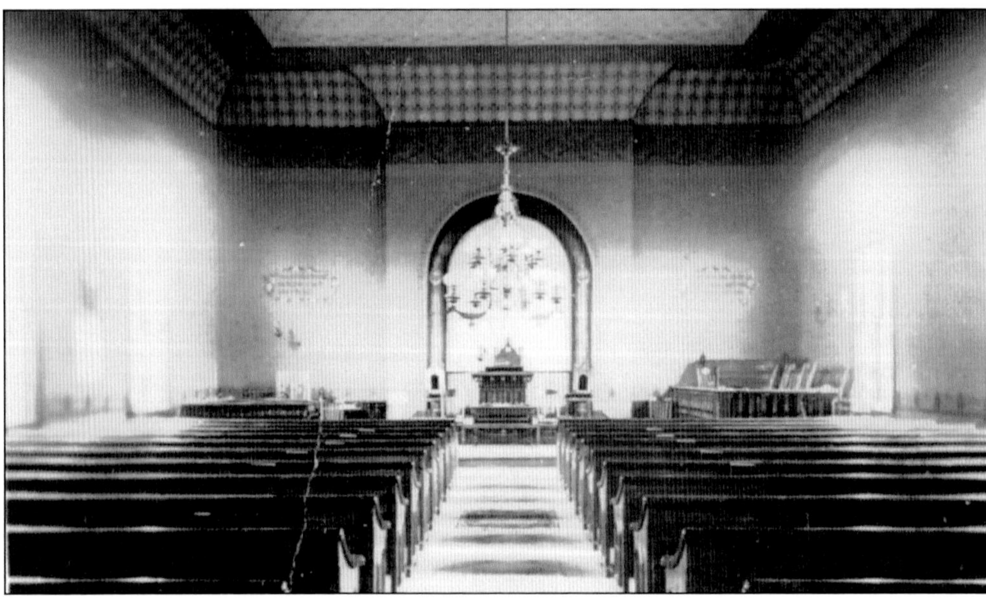

An interior view of the Evangelical Lutheran Church before extensive renovations took place in 1958 is shown here. The altar, pulpit, lectern, and choir chairs were all made of oak. The benches are still in use today.

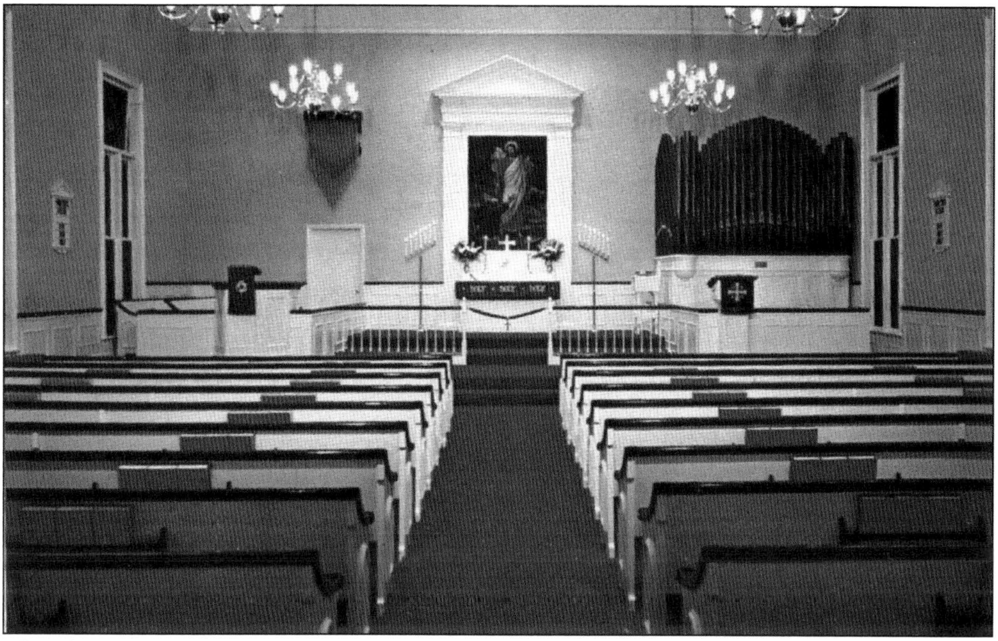

This shows the newly renovated sanctuary of the Evangelical Lutheran Church around 1958. The pipe organ, not seen in the previous photograph, was restored to its original glory. The lighter color, along with red carpeting, enhances the beauty of this old church.

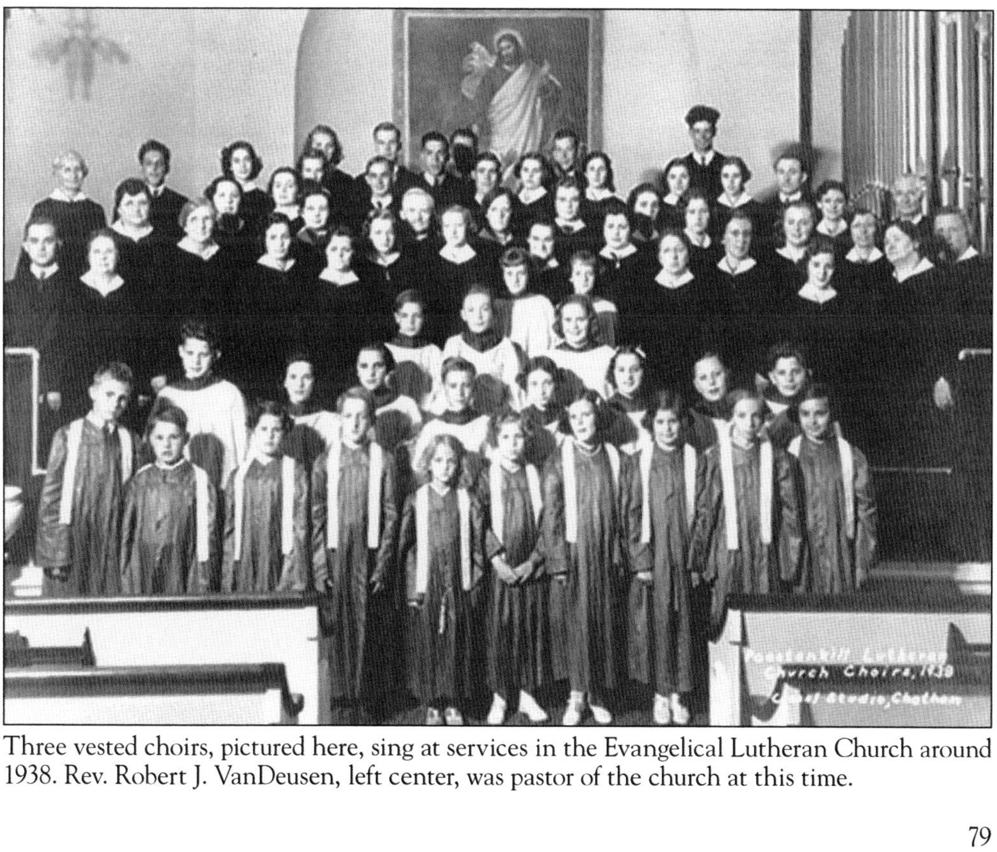


Three vested choirs, pictured here, sing at services in the Evangelical Lutheran Church around 1938. Rev. Robert J. VanDeusen, left center, was pastor of the church at this time.

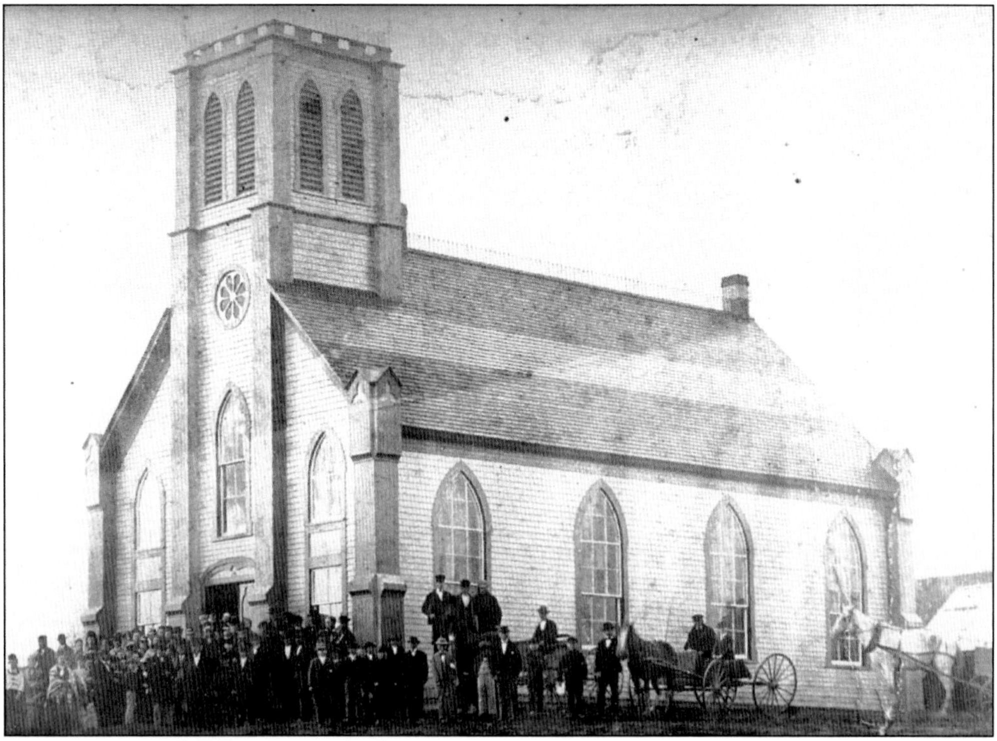

The Union Gospel Church in East Poestenkill was originally part of the Methodist Episcopal Conference. The church dates from 1872. It is seen here in 1920. The edifice cost $6,500 with an additional $350 for the bell that was placed in the tower of the church.

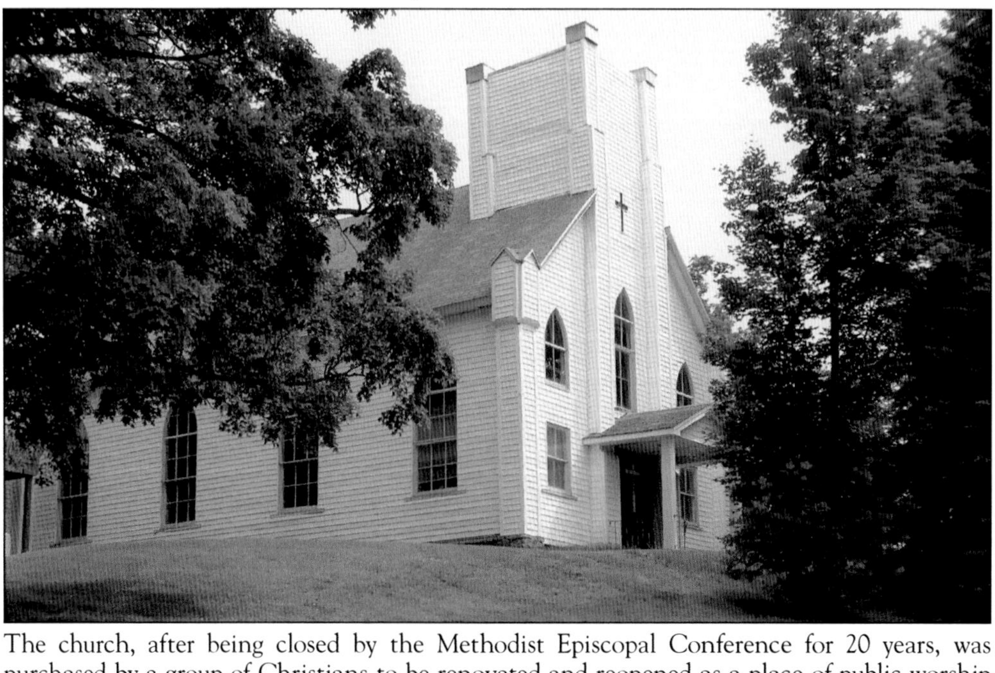

The church, after being closed by the Methodist Episcopal Conference for 20 years, was purchased by a group of Christians to be renovated and reopened as a place of public worship and was renamed the Union Gospel Church when it reopened on July 6, 1941.

This poster advertises a strawberry festival held at the Union Gospel Church on June 11, 1879. Festivals like this were very popular in the early days. Strawberries were grown locally and shipped to the city for sale.

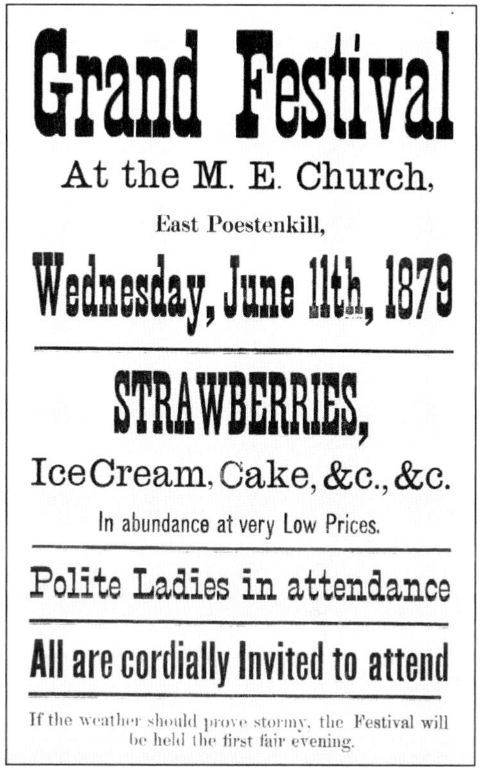


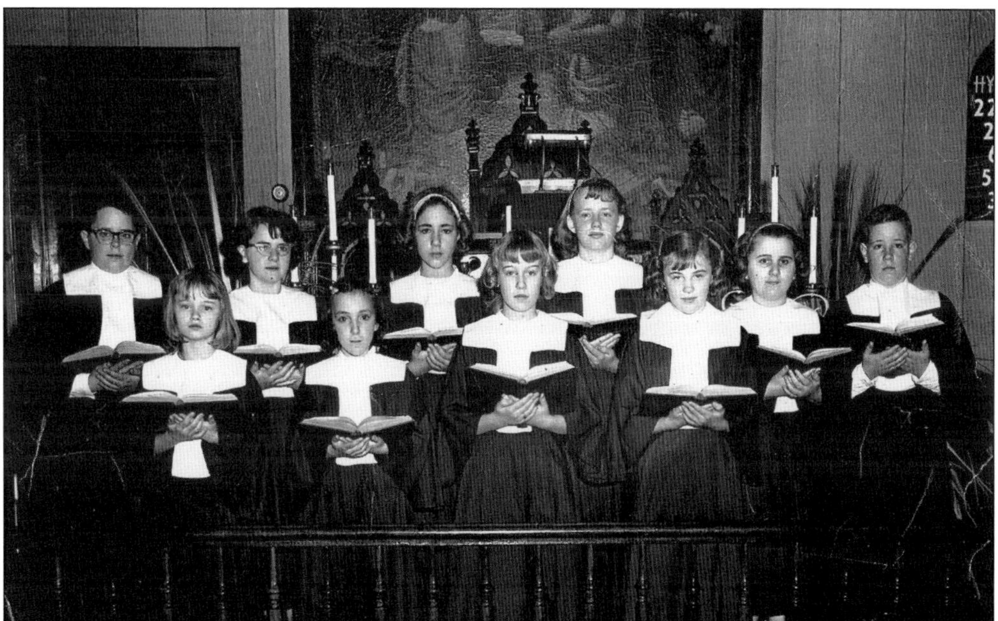

The youth choir of the Union Gospel Church stand in front of the altar ready to present its hymns for the service. Seen are, from left to right, (first row) Lisa Smith, Martha Naylor, Alice Grunge, and Sonya Wagar; (second row) James Flint, Cheryl Whitney, Karen Gooley, Shirley Wagar, Colleen Whitney, and Daryl Gooley.

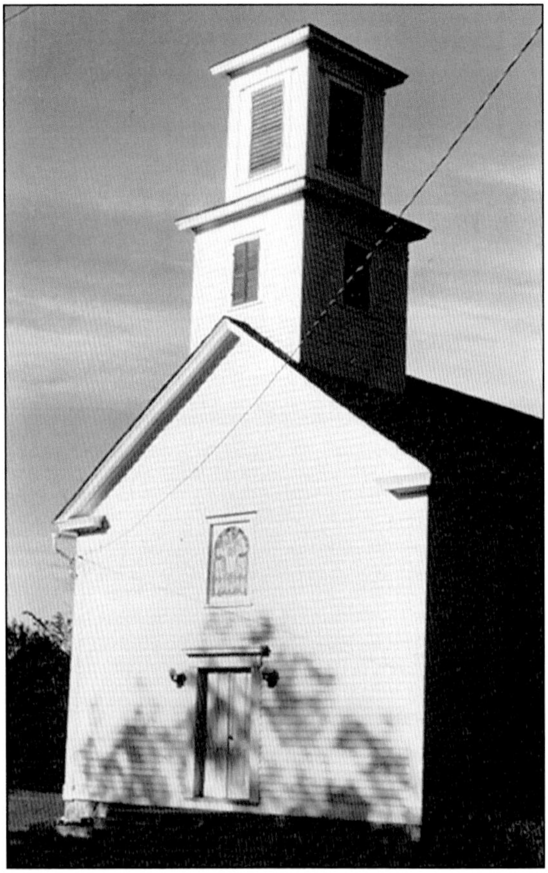

The edifice of the Baptist church on Legenbauer Road in East Poestenkill has remained basically unchanged since it was built in 1856. It still serves the community.

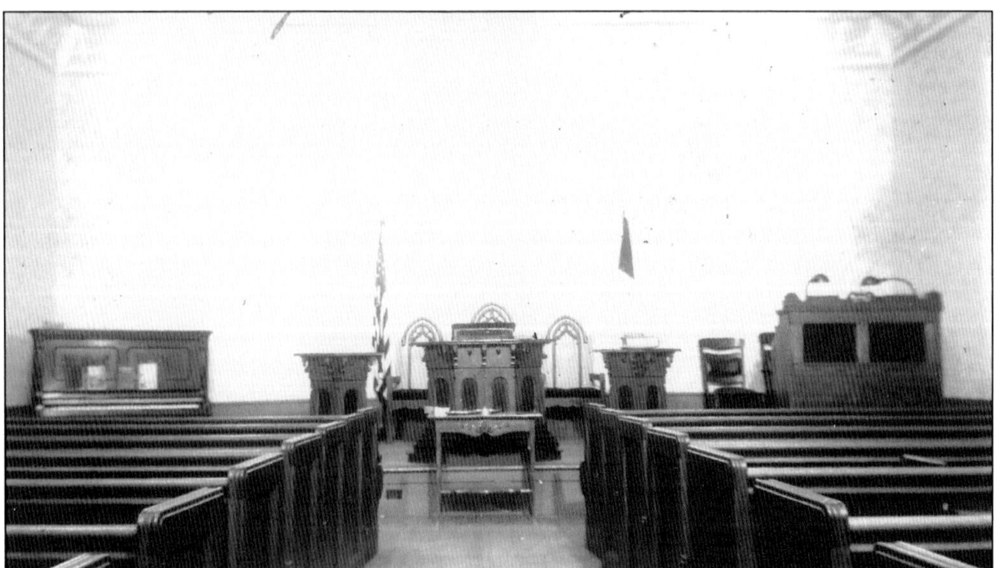

This photograph shows the sanctuary of the Baptist church. The founding of the church was in 1814. Stained-glass windows were installed in 1906 at a cost of $17 each and are engraved with the name of the family who donated the window.

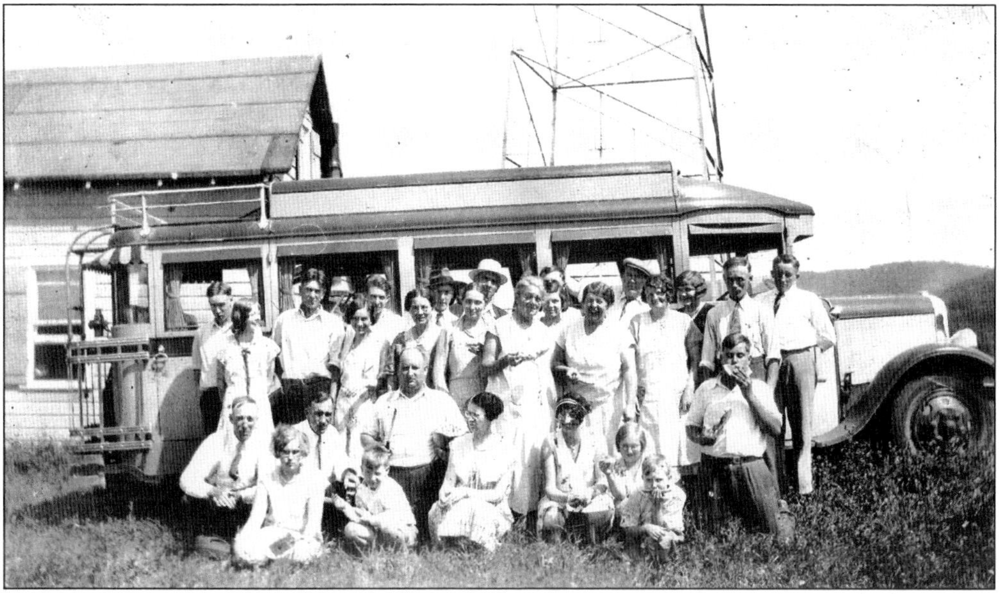

Here members of the Baptist church gather to board Otto Miller's bus as they ready themselves to travel to Lake Champlain for a summer picnic.

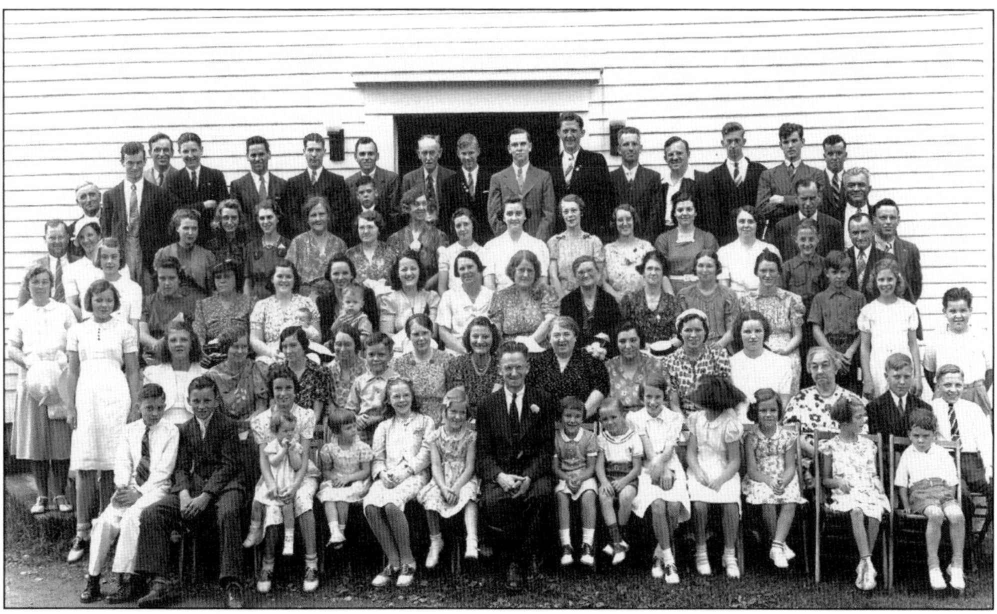

This photograph shows the Baptist church congregation in 1940.

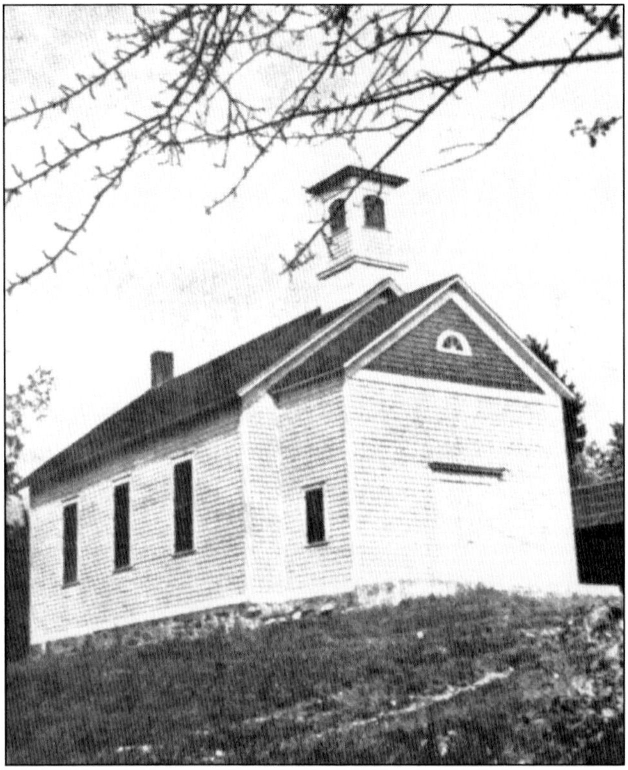

East Poestenkill's Zion Lutheran Church is also known as the German Church, the 56 Church, and the North Road Church, as it was built by German families at the intersection of 56 Road and North Road.

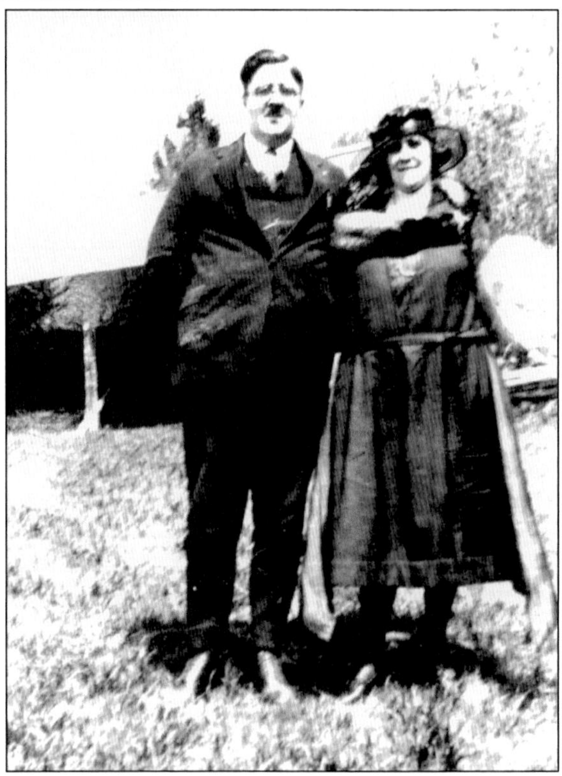

Rev. Oscar Egli and his wife, Anna Egli, are standing in front of the carriage shed. Reverend Egli served the church from 1919 to 1947.

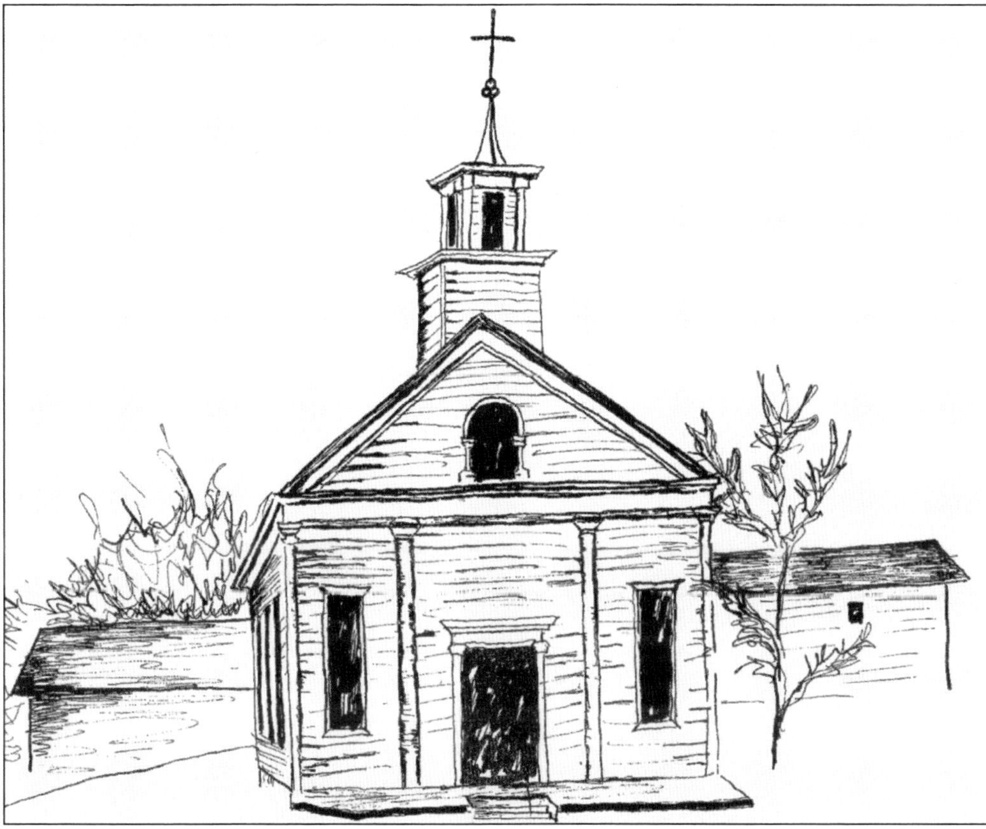

This is a sketch of the Free Will Baptist Church, located on Plank Road at the corner of Powers Road and organized in 1843.

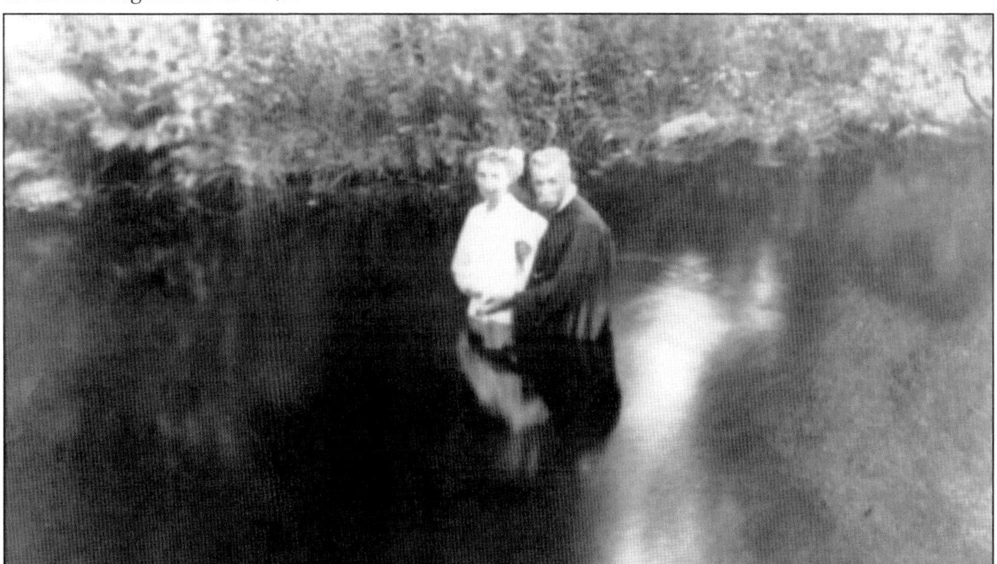

The minister of the Free Will Baptist Church baptizes Grace B. Mulson in the Poestenkill Creek in 1908.

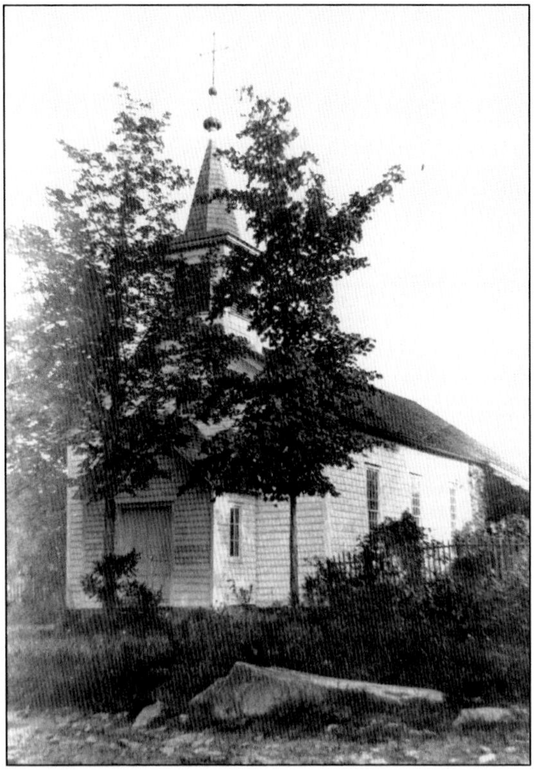

Seen here is the exterior of St. Mary's of the Woods, which was built by German immigrants in 1860 on a parcel of land given by William Weigand.

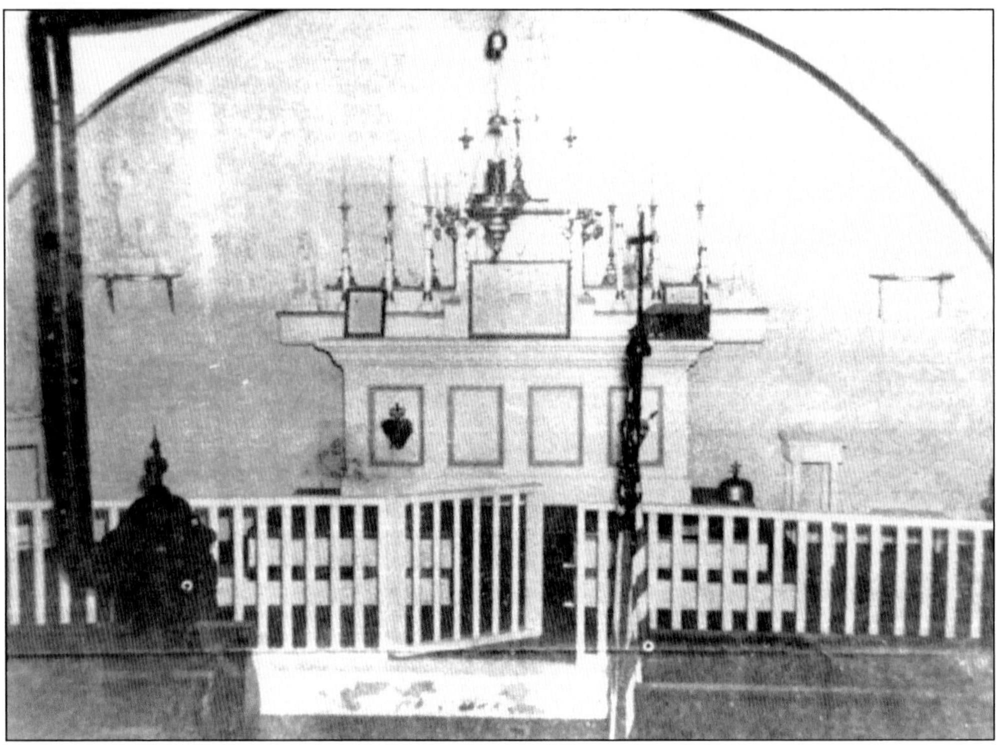

The interior of St. Mary's of the Woods shows the stove used to heat the church.

*Six*

# Getting Around Town

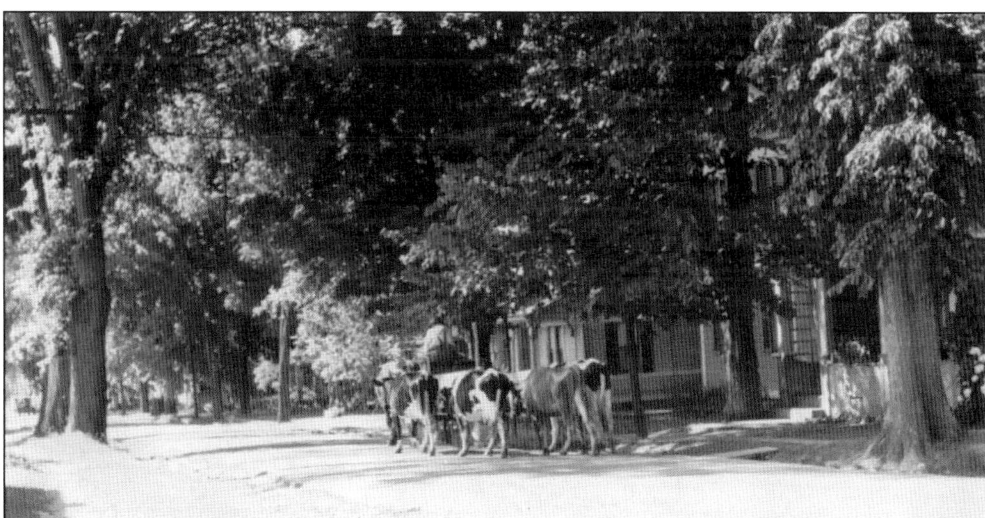

This is Main Street in the village of Poestenkill, showing Edward Miller returning home with his cows.

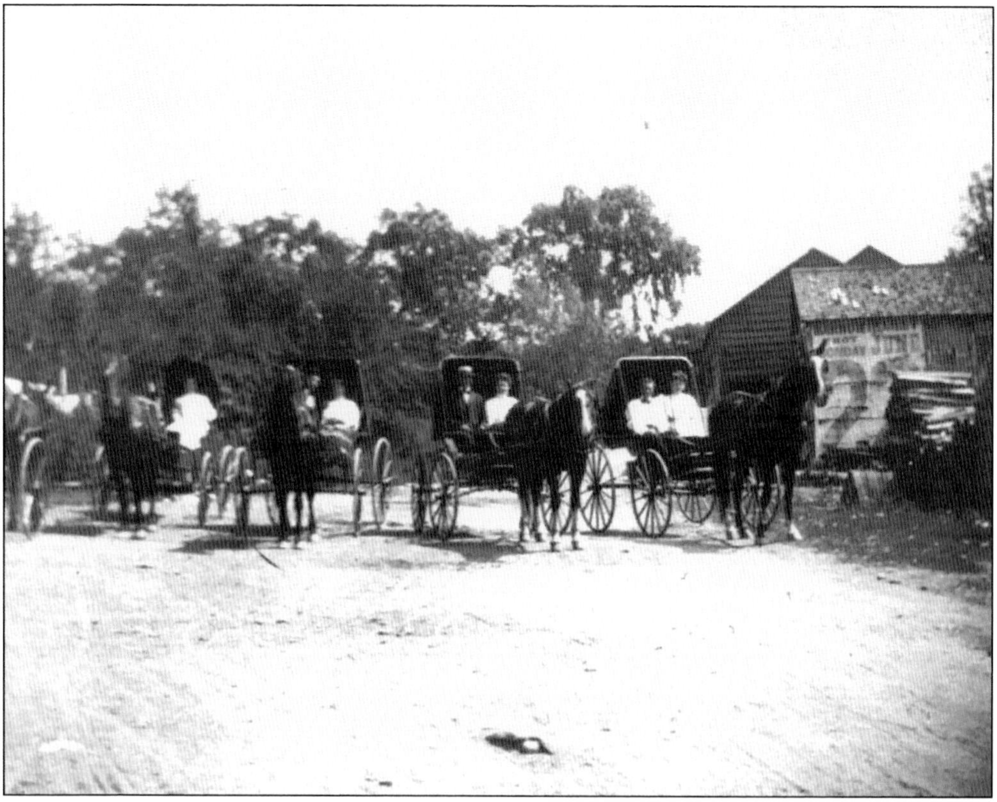

Seen here are people in their finery going to church on a nice Sunday morning around the late 1800s.

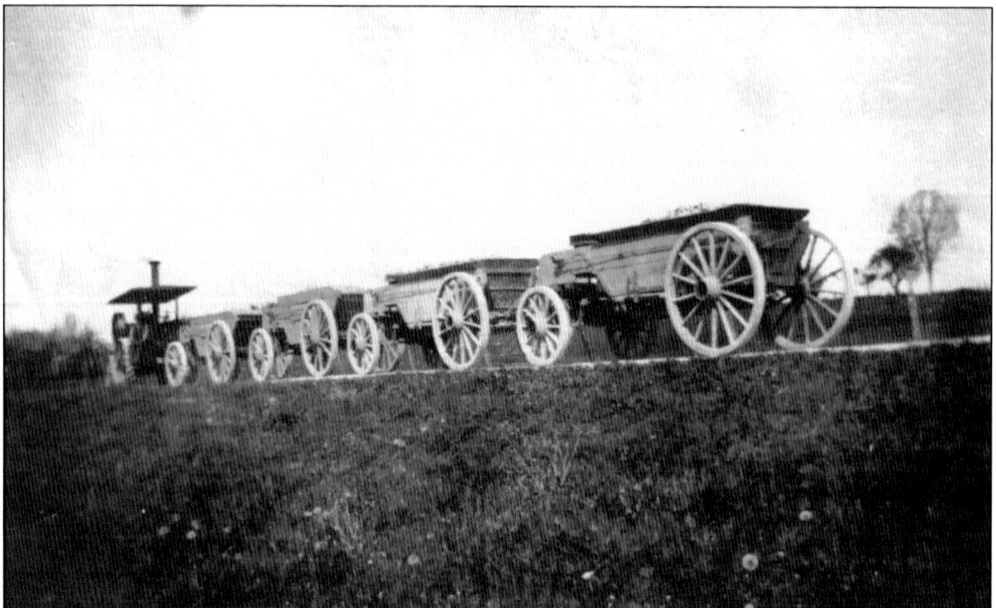

Here cars are taking crushed stone on the town's only railway down to the village so the macadam road could be built in 1906.

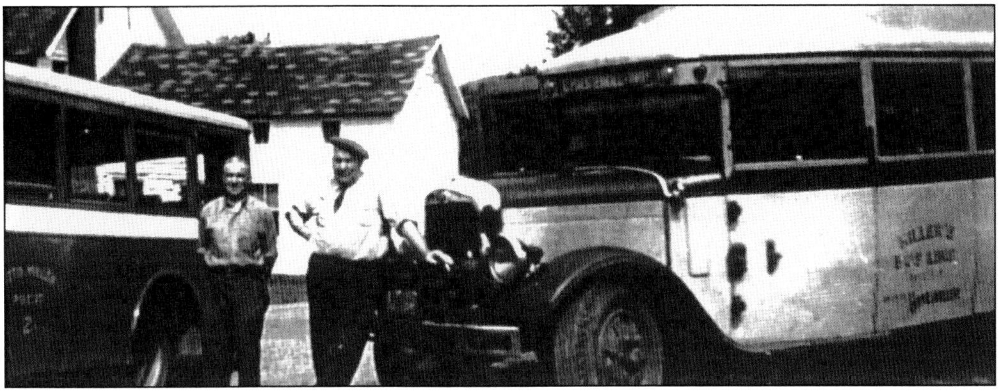

Seen here in 1948, Otto Miller and his brother Lewis ran a bus service from Barberville to Troy every morning and back in the evening for community members working in the city or for those who were just shopping.

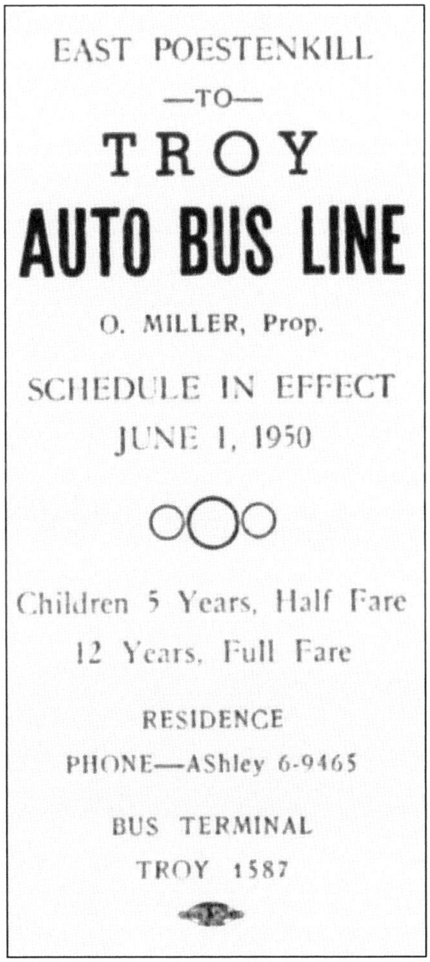

EAST POESTENKILL

—TO—

TROY

AUTO BUS LINE

O. MILLER, Prop.

SCHEDULE IN EFFECT

JUNE 1, 1950

Children 5 Years, Half Fare

12 Years, Full Fare

RESIDENCE

PHONE—AShley 6-9465

BUS TERMINAL

TROY 1587

Schedules of the East Poestenkill-to-Troy bus line were given out to those who rode the bus. This schedule is from 1950.

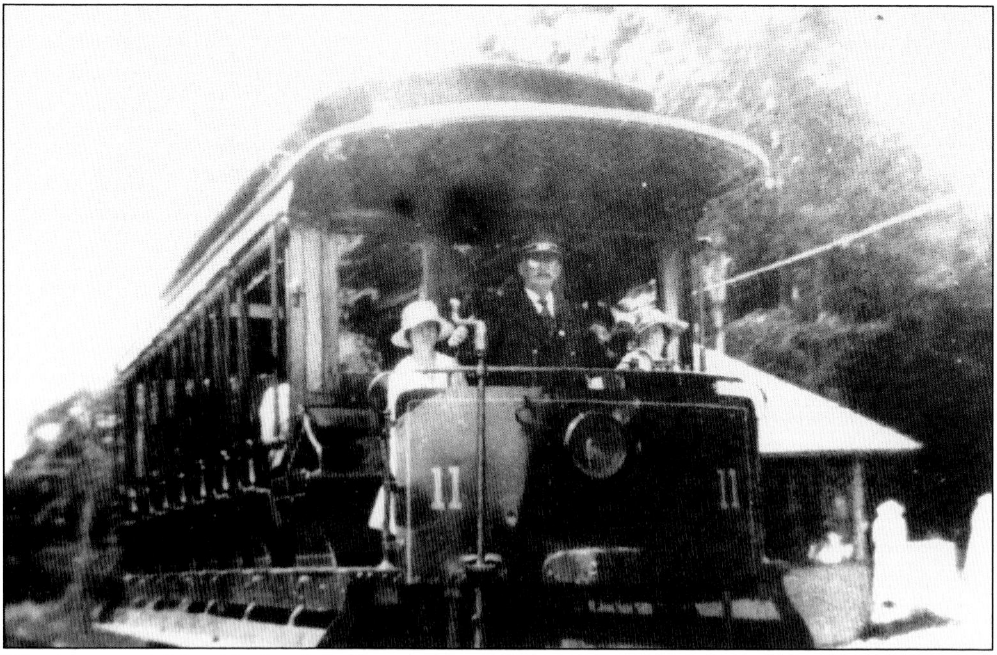
The Troy and New England trolley open-car No. 11 ran through the southwest corner of Poestenkill, stop 13, during the summer months.

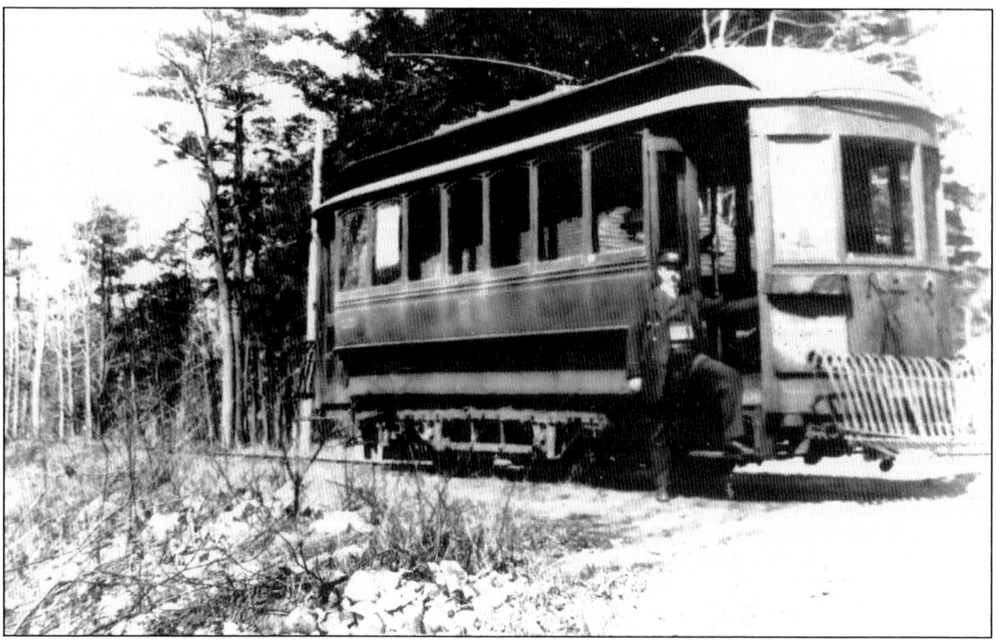
The Troy and New England closed-car trolley No. 6 is on its last run on March 31, 1925.

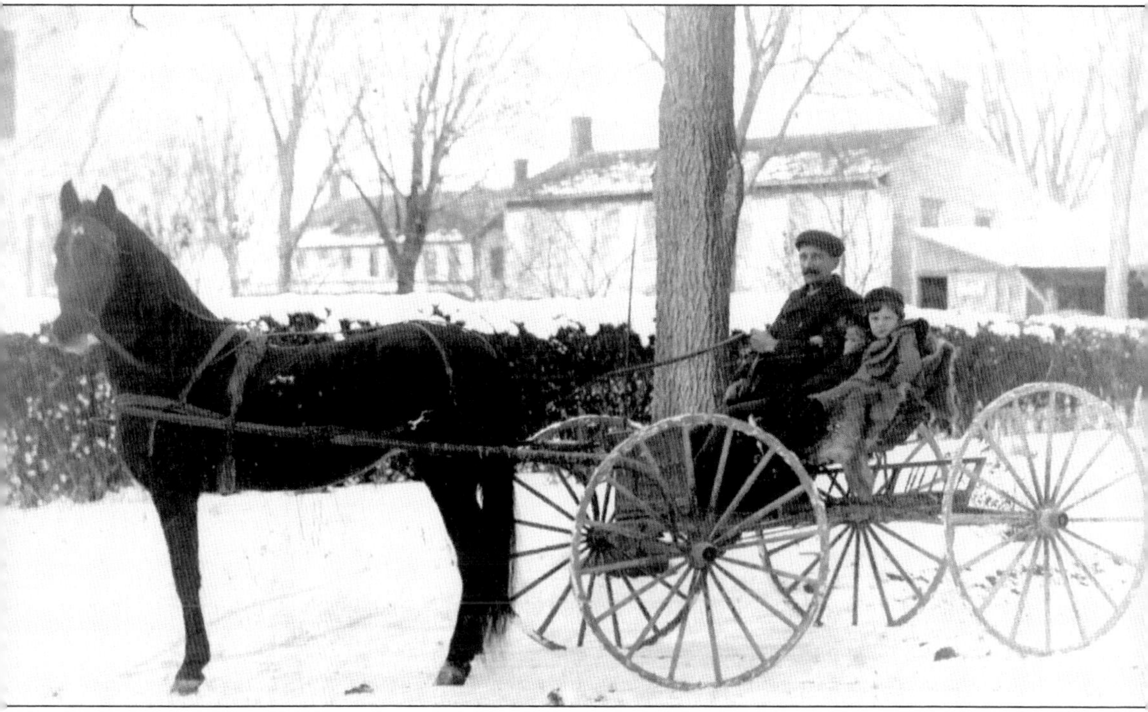

Charlie Hilton and Howard Cole are bundled up ready to go. In the background, the Woodbine Hotel, later Bubie's General Store, can be seen. To the right is Union Hall.

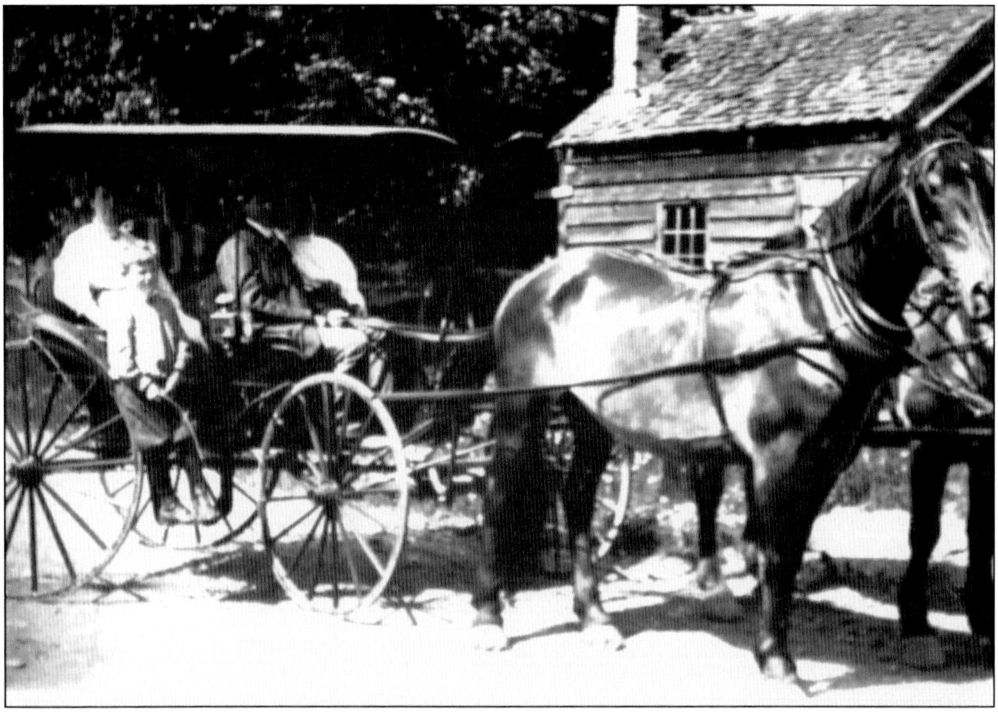

The Clickner family is off to church in its Sunday wagon. Seen here in front are Ward and Clara Clickner and in the back are Sophia Ebbing and Rev. Frank Jones's son Milton. The photograph was taken in front of their farm on Snake Hill Road.

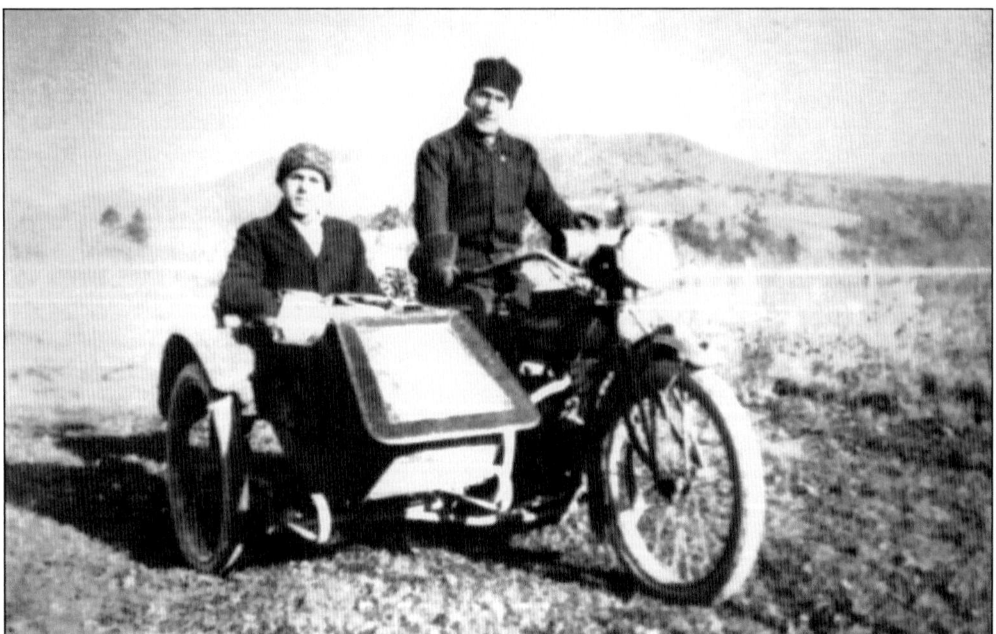

Lester (left) and Walter Forebellar take a spin on their motorcycle as Snake Hill looms in the background. Snake Hill Road was a small dirt road, at this time with very few motorists on the road.

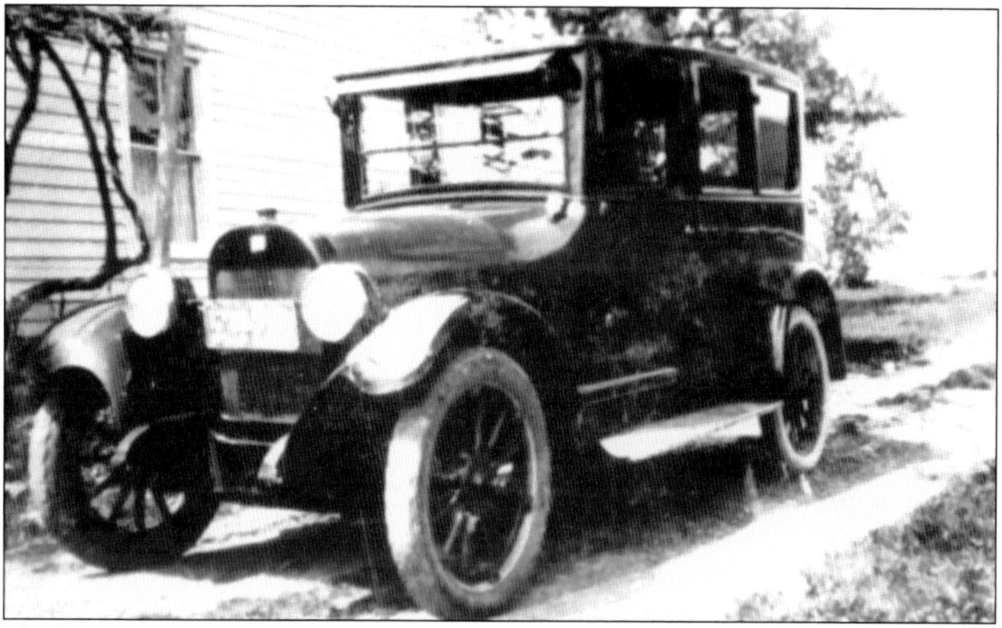

Charles L. Ballard's uncle Edward Ott owned this 1923 Buick sedan, which sits in the driveway of John Forebellar's home on Snake Hill Road.

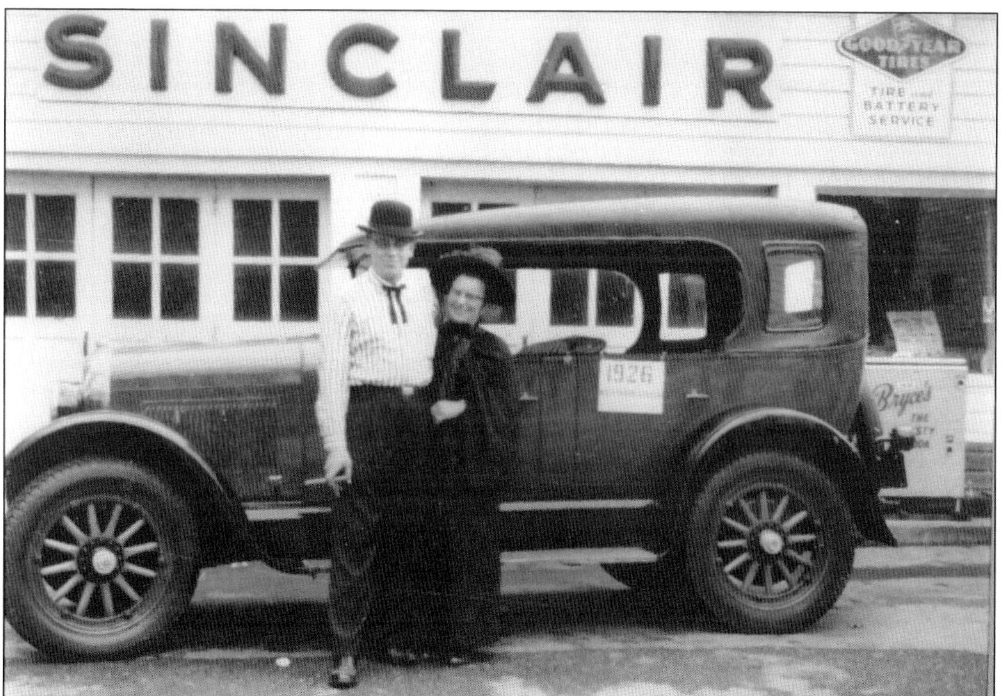


Clifford Catlin and his wife, Elizabeth Bubie Catlin, pose in front of their 1926 car parked in front of Raymond Bubie's garage on Main Street before participating in one of Poestenkill's many parades.

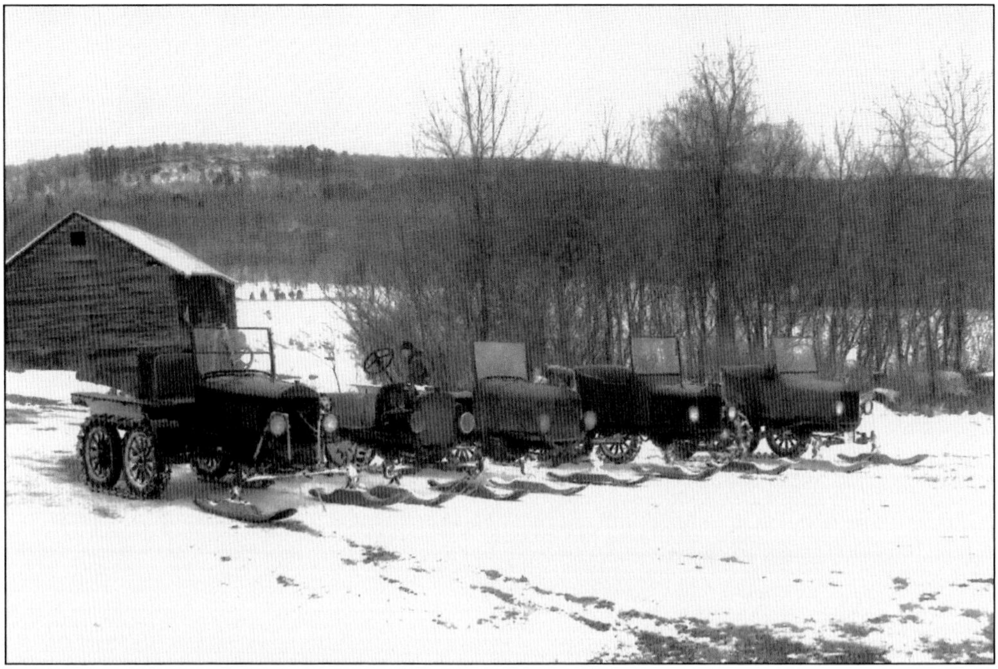

Charles M. Ballard shows off his fleet of restored Model T snowmobiles in front of the barn once owned by his great-grandfather John Forebellar.

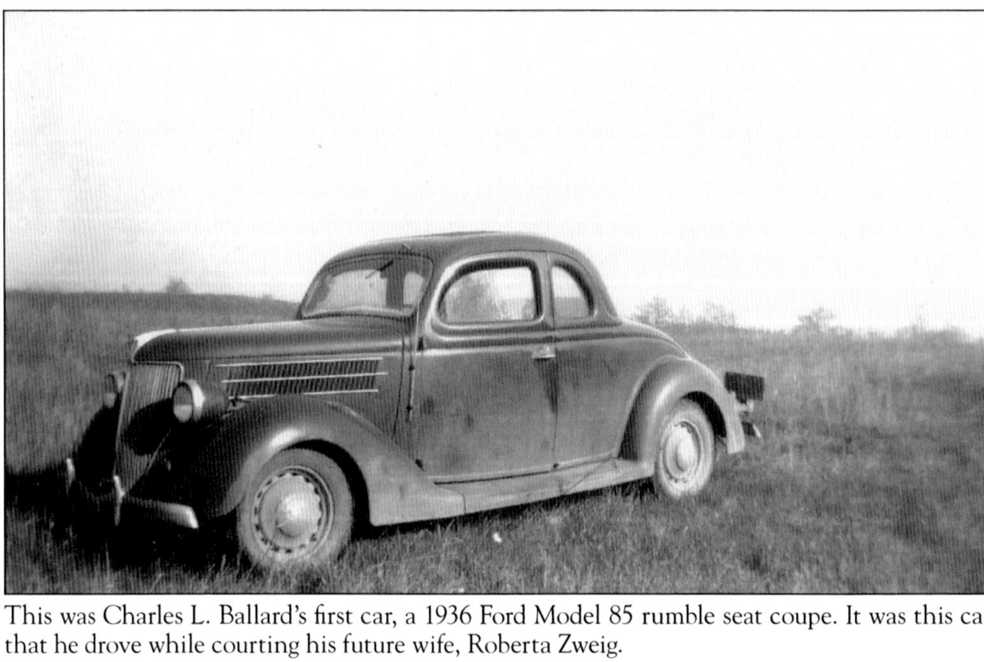

This was Charles L. Ballard's first car, a 1936 Ford Model 85 rumble seat coupe. It was this car that he drove while courting his future wife, Roberta Zweig.

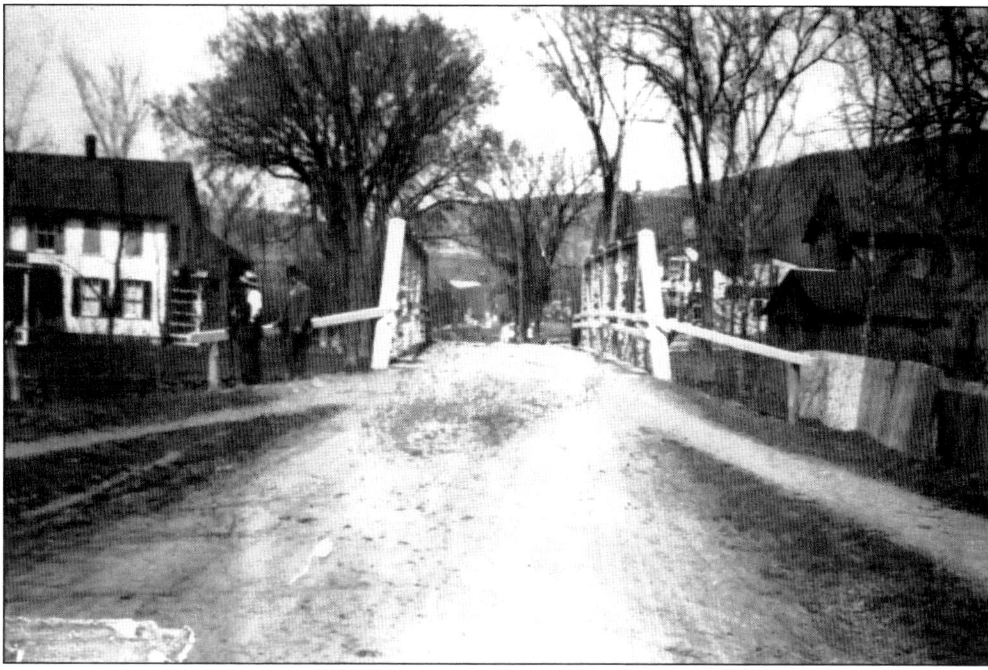

The 1908 bridge crossing the Poesten Kill on Farm-to-Market Road was an iron bridge with dirt roads fore and aft. The small building on the right was the cobbler shop known as the "10-footer."

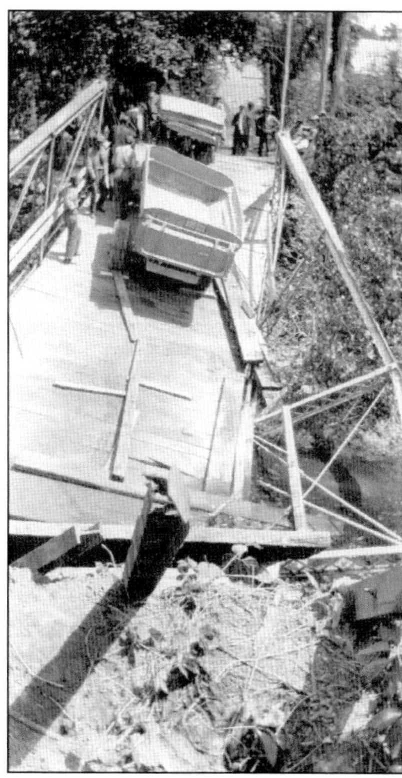

Following the collapse of the 1908 bridge in June 1922, a truck is rescued as bystanders watch the retrieval progress.

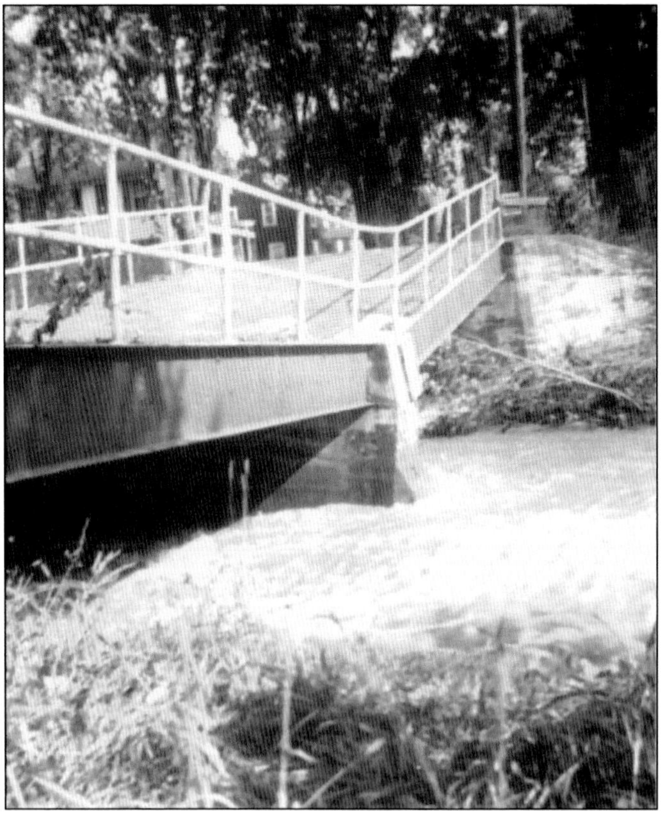

The collapse of the new 1922 bridge was caused by the 1938 flood of the Poesten Kill. The rushing waters caused the steel girders to collapse.

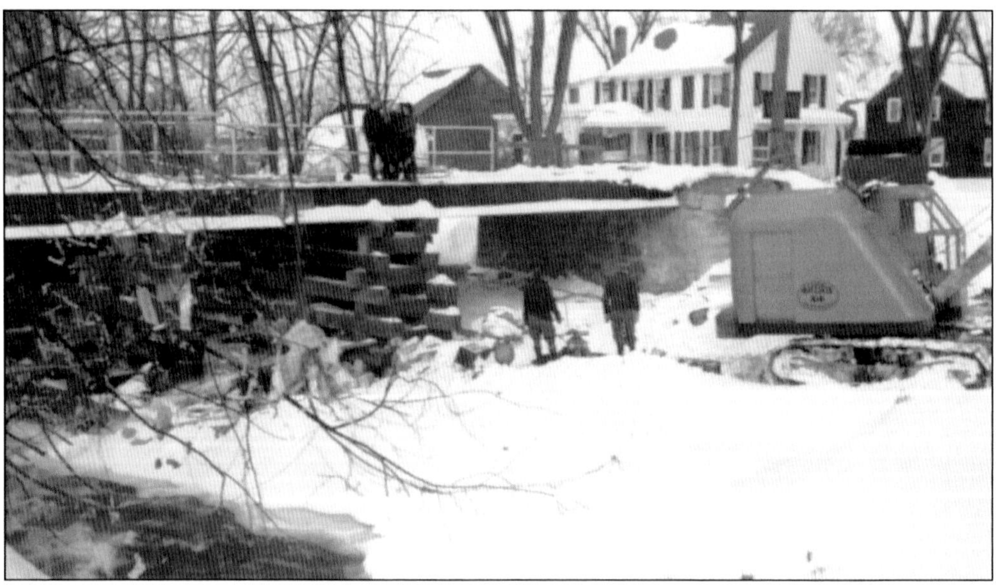

Rebuilding the bridge occurred during the winter of 1938–1939, while the ground was frozen and the creek was low.

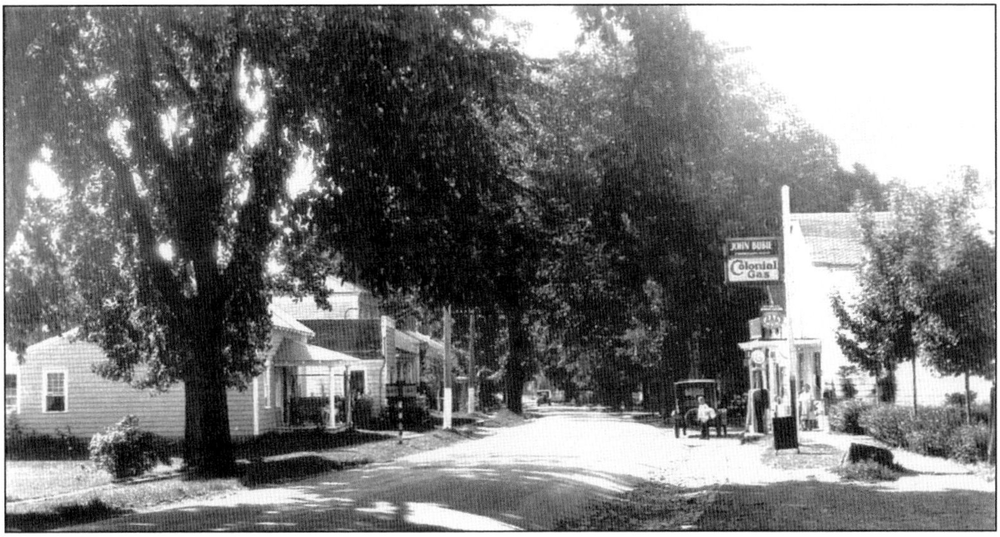

This is an early 1900s scene of Main Street in Poestenkill looking west. John Bubie's gas station is on the right. Note the dirt road. The gas station is now the auto parts store run by Bubie's grandsons.

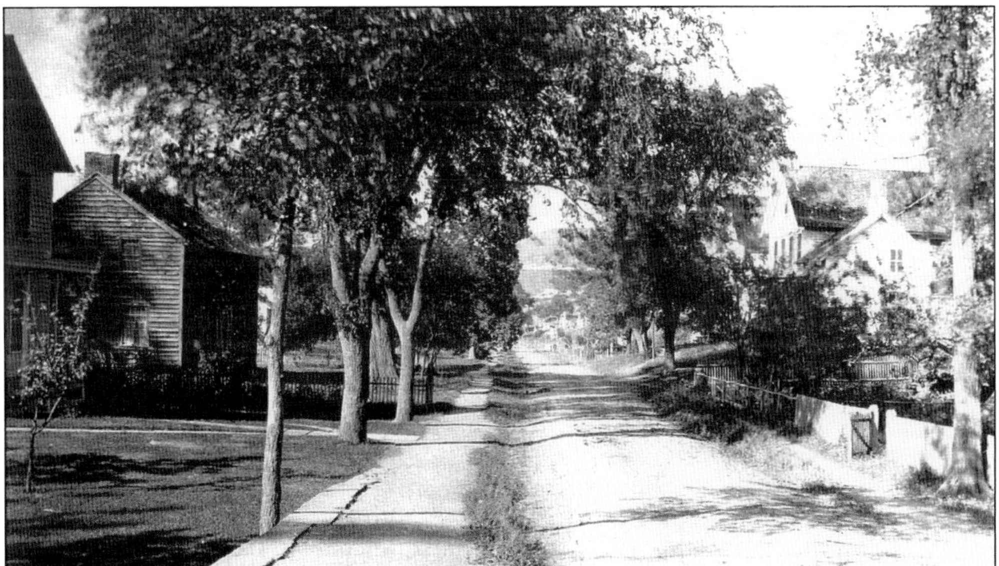
This is Farm-to-Market Road looking north after crossing the previously shown bridge. The second house on the left is the oldest remaining home in Poestenkill, built by Archelaus Lynd.

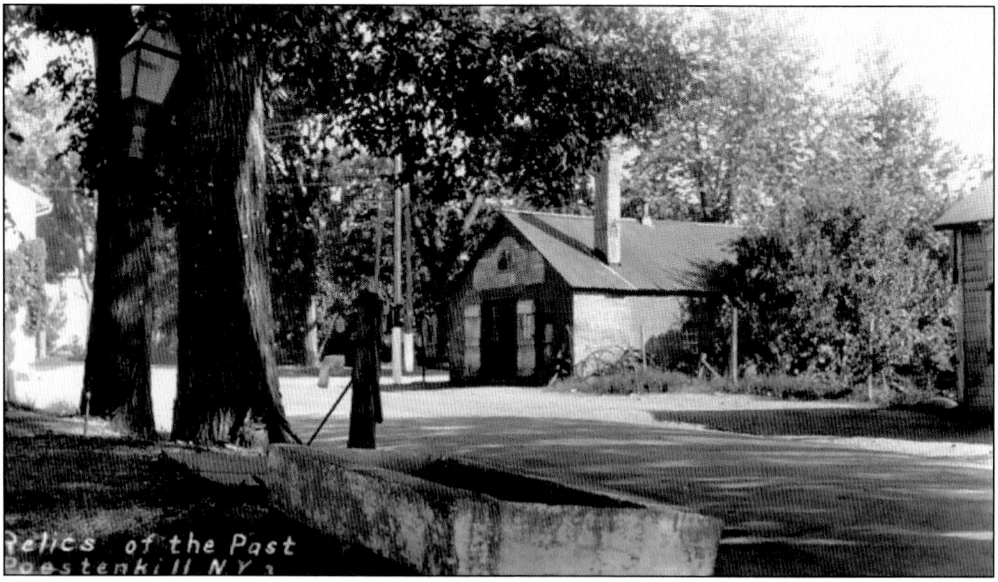


This view is of the village of Poestenkill's main intersection, showing the old brick blacksmith shop and a corner of the wooden blacksmith shop on the far right. On the left is the front of the Woodbine Hotel with the gaslight, hand pump, and watering troth.

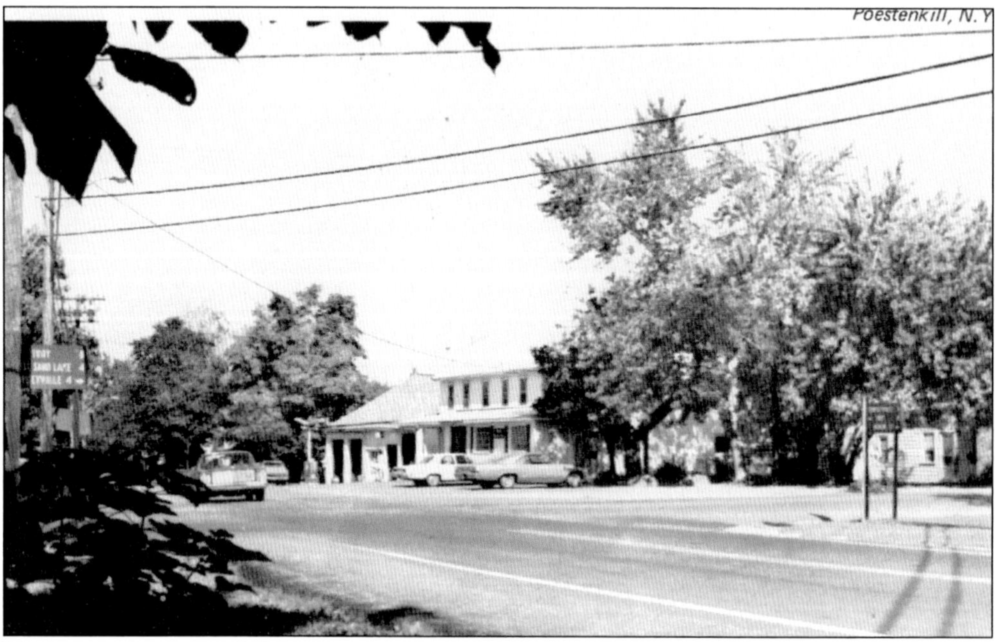


This is a 1950s view of the main intersection showing Bubie's General Store and Gas Station to its left.

*Seven*

# COMMUNITY SERVICES

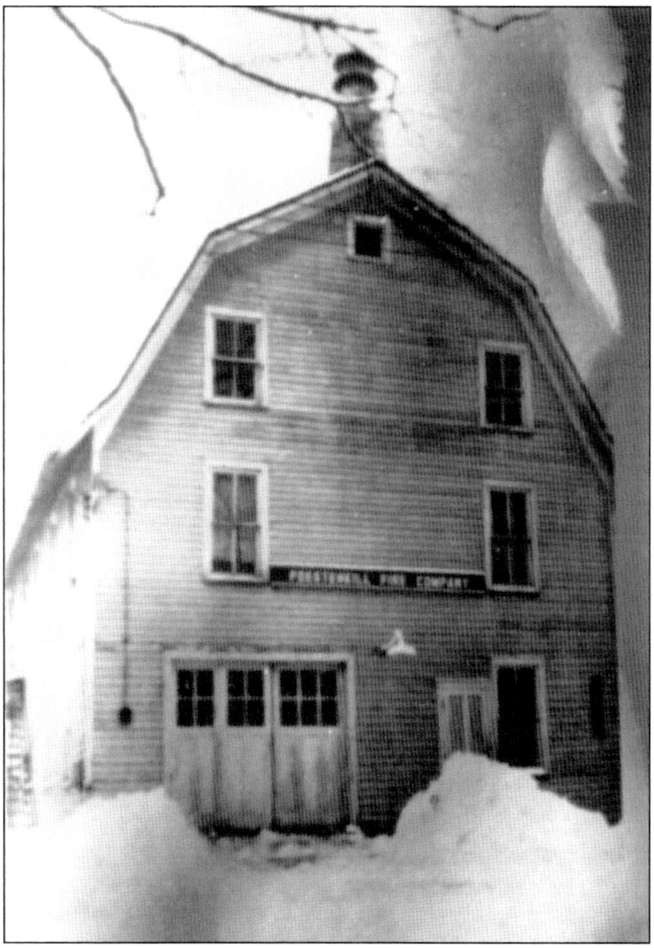

The first firehouse was built in 1920, when a small group of civic-minded men worked to organize and equip a community fire department. The organization grew rapidly, as did the need for more firefighting equipment, and an addition was constructed on each side of the building allowing for more equipment to be housed. The Poestenkill Fire Company is one of the few in Rensselaer County owned by the membership. The town contracts with the fire company on a yearly basis for fire protection.

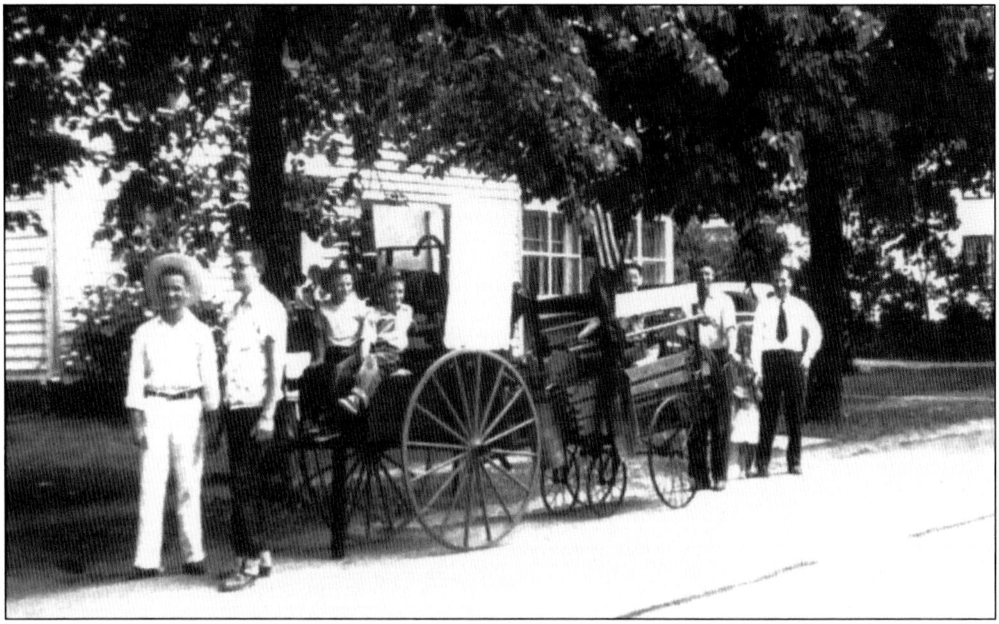

Hand pumper No. 2 was made by Lucien Wager in 1910. This little pumper once saved a house and 200 chickens. It has been used in several parades, and in this image with the pumper are, from left to right, Jack Petropol, Charles Bubie, Robert Bubie, Earl Campbell, June Butler, and Tod Butler.

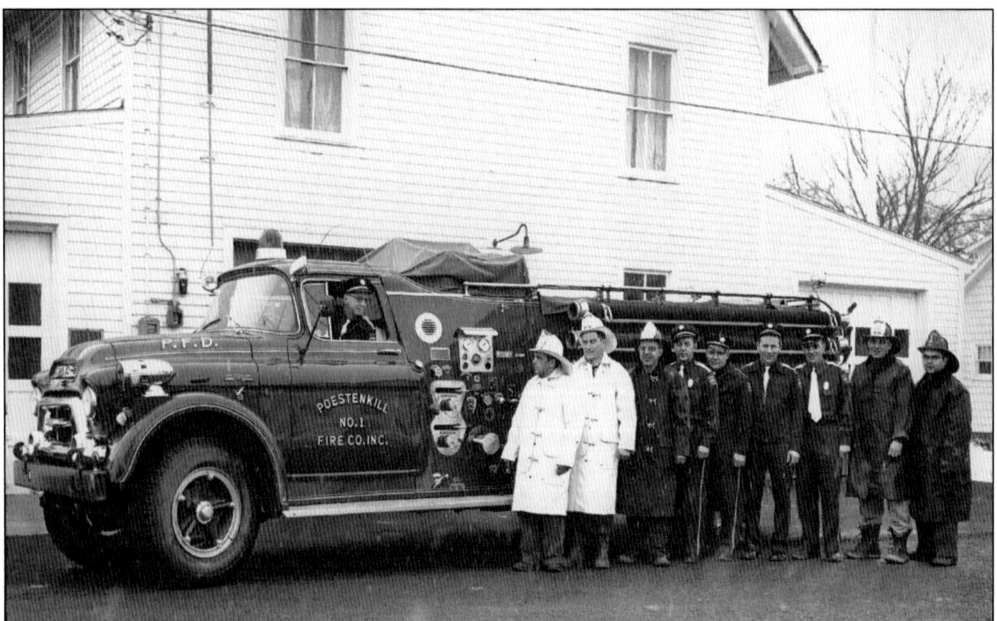


This is the first new pumper, purchased on September 6, 1957, and delivered in February 1958. Company volunteers are, from left to right, John Finley, Chief Raymond Bubie, Assistant Chief William Ackner, Lt. Edward Hughs, Capt. Thomas Slavin, chief of fire police Gene Miner, Samuel Dzembo, company president Harry Taylor, Edward Walsh, and secretary Robert Bubie.

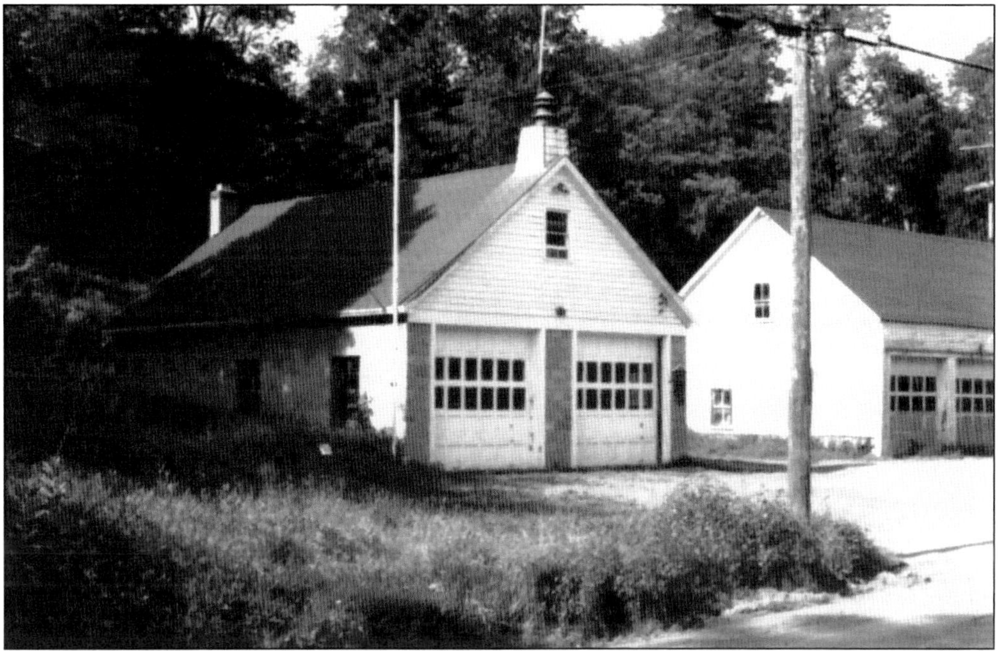

The Poestenkill Fire Company continued its expansion program when it placed fire apparatus in East Poestenkill. Early in 1951, a new building was erected in East Poestenkill, and shortly thereafter, Fire District No. 2 received a tank truck.

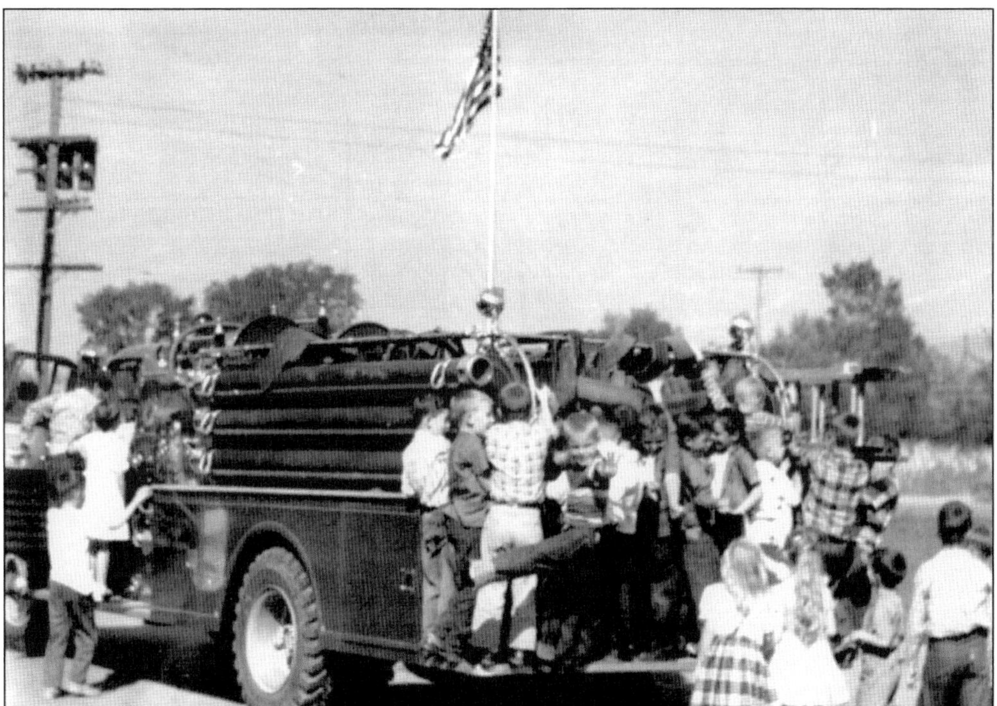

Fire Prevention Week is an important week at Poestenkill Elementary School. Here members of the fire company demonstrate, drill, and lecture students in 1957.

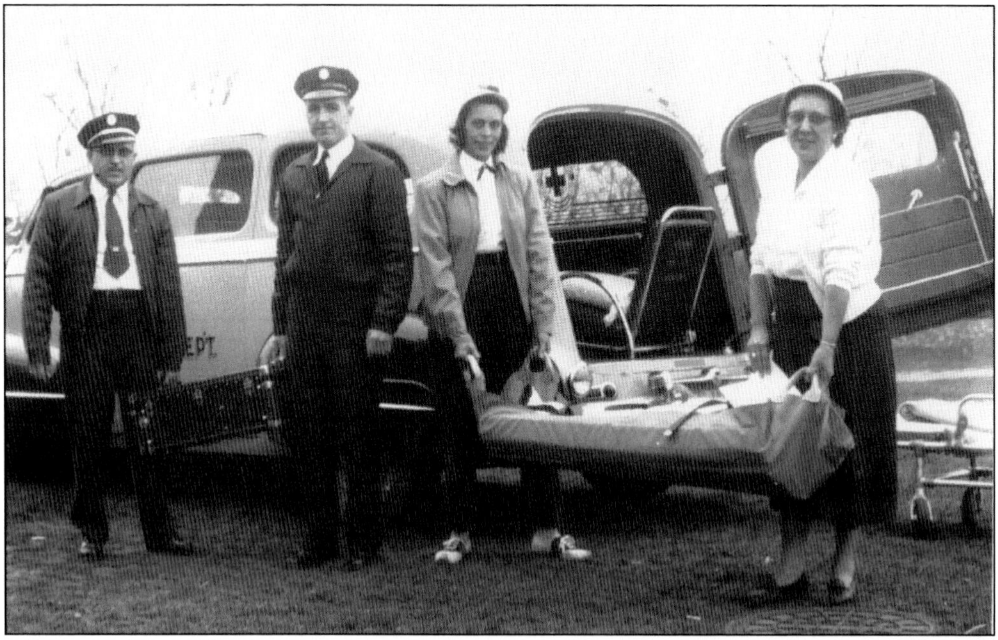

The town's first ambulance, a 1942 gray Buick, was used for several years. When the next vehicle was purchased, this one was given to the Town of Grafton. Squad members seen here are, from left to right, Walter Bubie, Frank Wittman, Alice Prediger, and Florence Miller Hill.

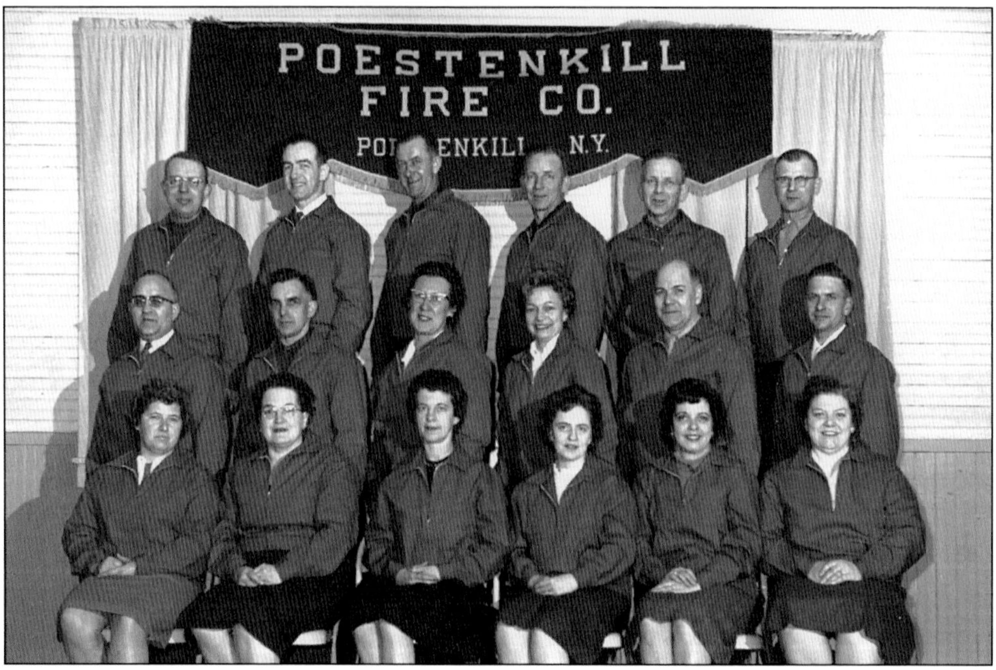


This is the ambulance squad, from around the late 1950s. Members are, from left to right, (first row) Grace Bubie, Margaret Walsh Brod, Helen Bentner, Shirley Hughs, Patsy Roach Fisher, and Ellen Legenbauer Dzembo; (second row) Walter Bubie, Raymond Bubie, Florence Miller Hill, Mildred Miller Fleming, Gene Miner, and Fred Reichard; (third row) Edward Hughs, Frank Wittman, Steve Synintski, Sam Dzembo, Joseph Fleming, and Henry King.

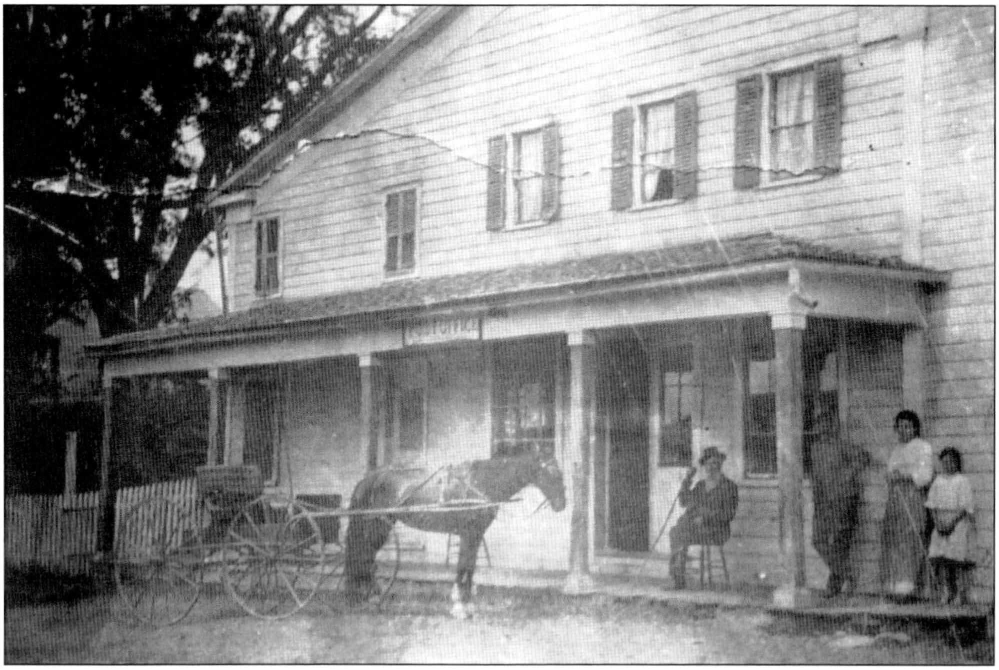

George Barber's store also housed the East Poestenkill Post Office. Seen here in 1910, the building was later destroyed by a fire caused by lightning. The East Poestenkill Fire District No. 2 was built on this site.

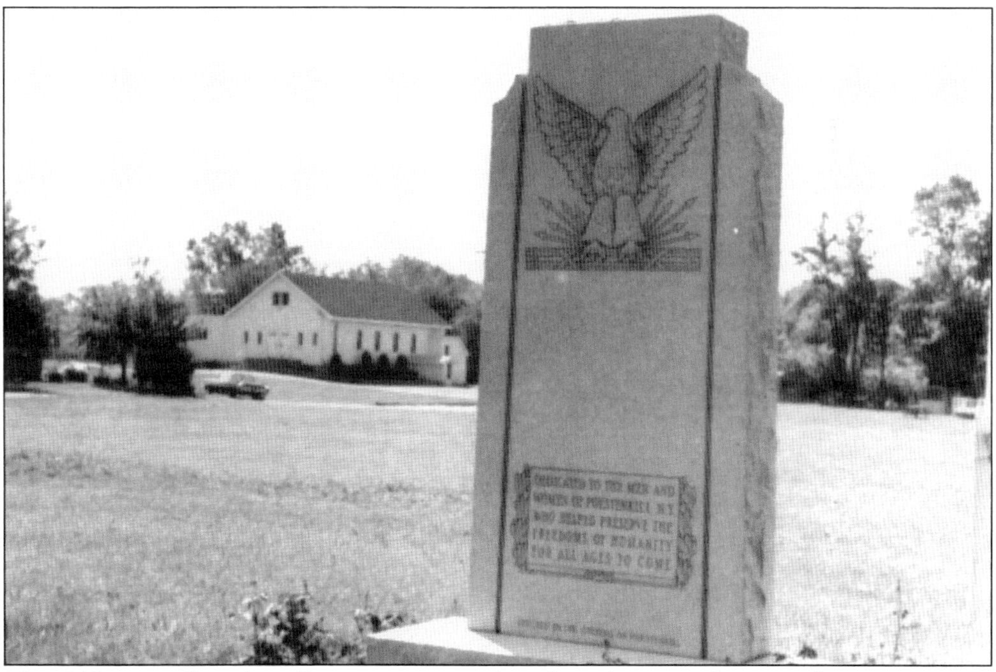

The old honor roll in the village center was taken down because of new road construction. A new granite marker was erected in the Poestenkill Chapter of the Veterans of Foreign Wars field adjoining the Sullivan Jones Post No. 7466.

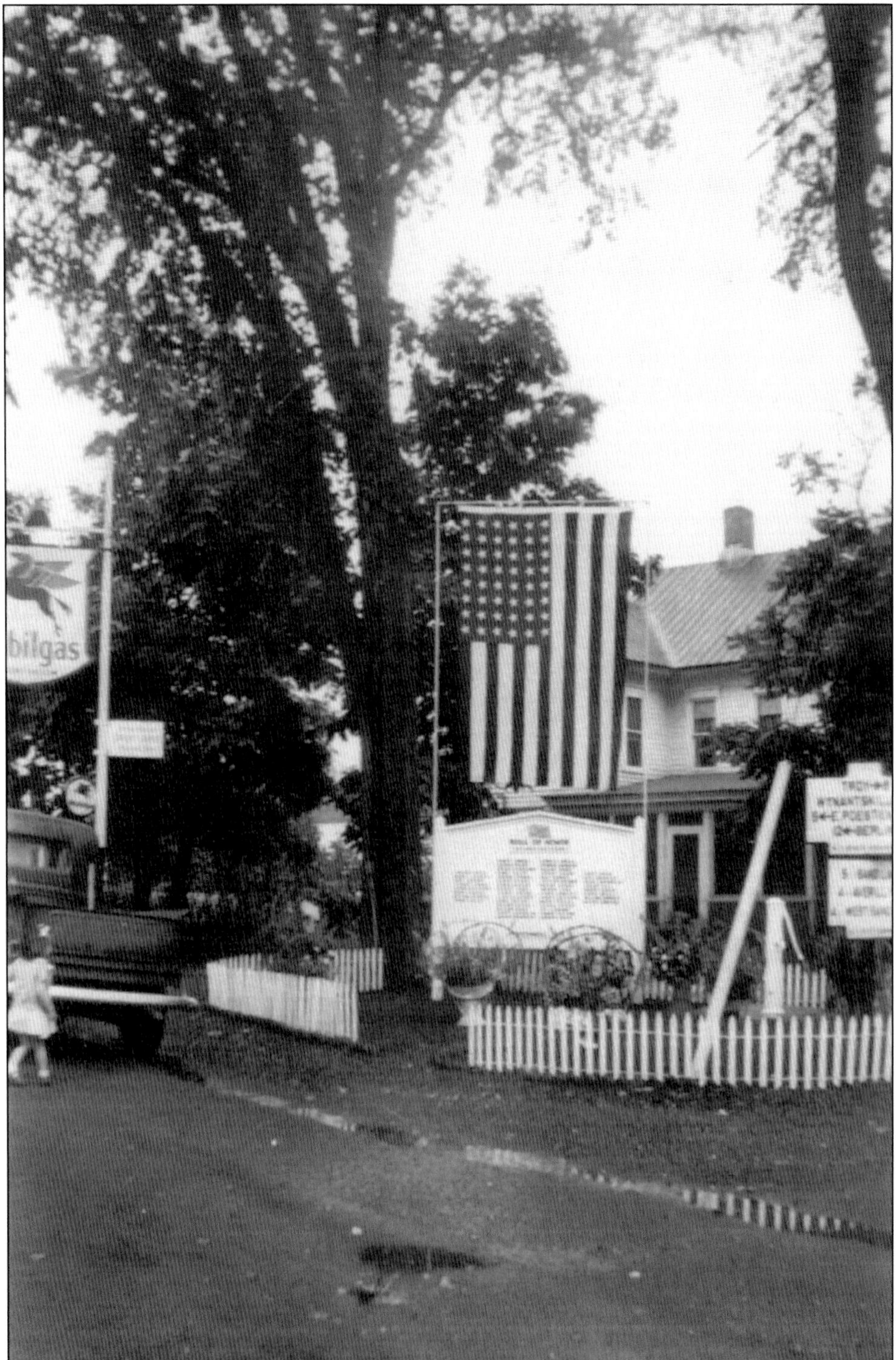

Seen here is the original honor roll, located in the center of the village, listing those who served their country. This photograph was taken on June 3, 1942, the day of the honor roll's dedication. Later it was necessary to add a panel to each side of the board.

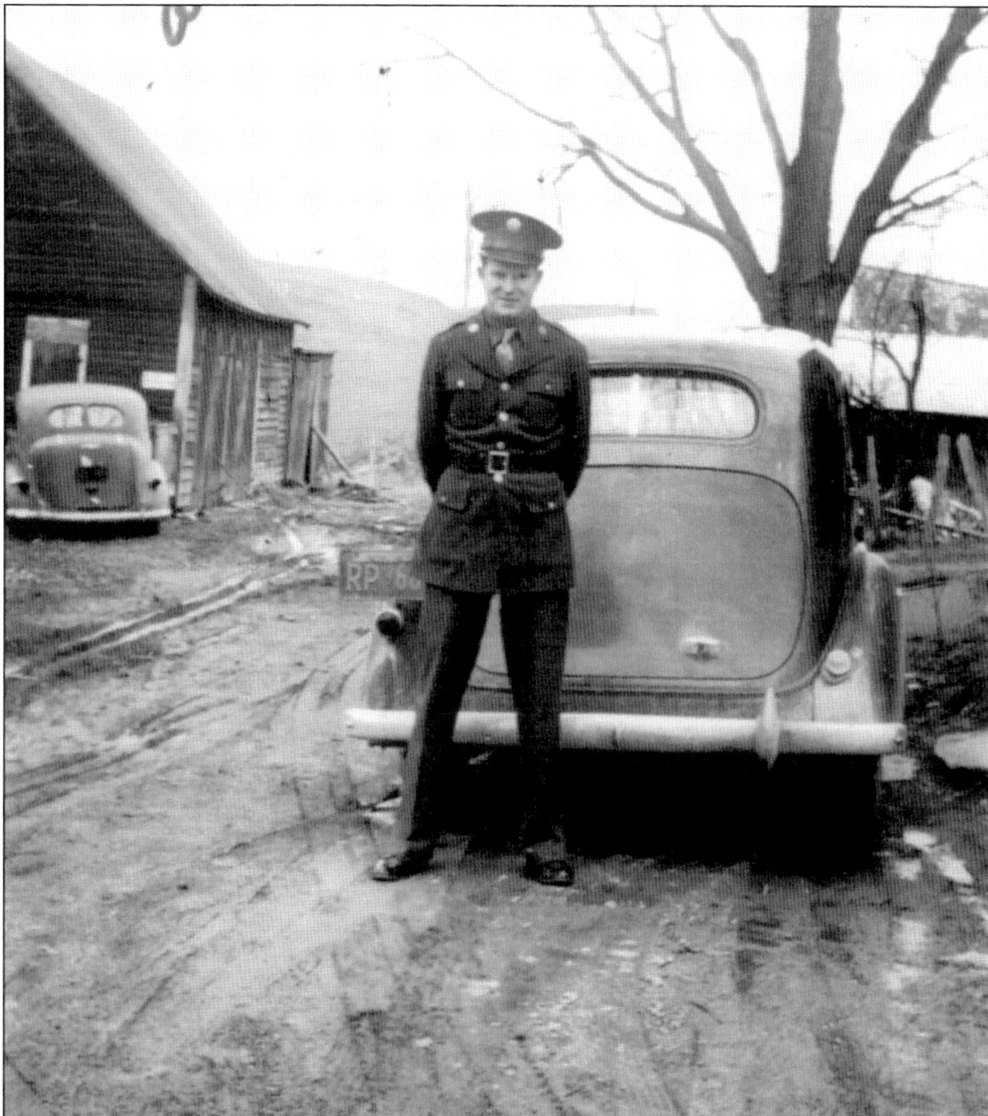

Donald Dunham is home on leave during World War II. The Dunham farm was on Snyders Corners Road. Dunham later came home and settled in the village of Poestenkill.

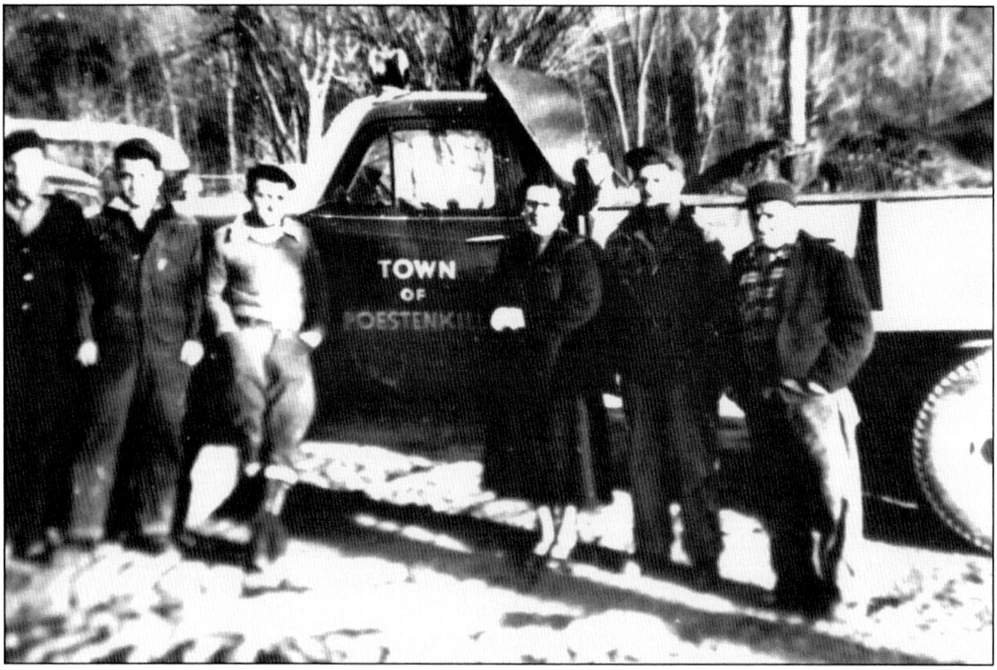


Florence Miller Hill was appointed as acting highway superintendent from October 1952 to January 1953, completing her husband Kenneth's term following his death. Hill was the only female to hold that position.

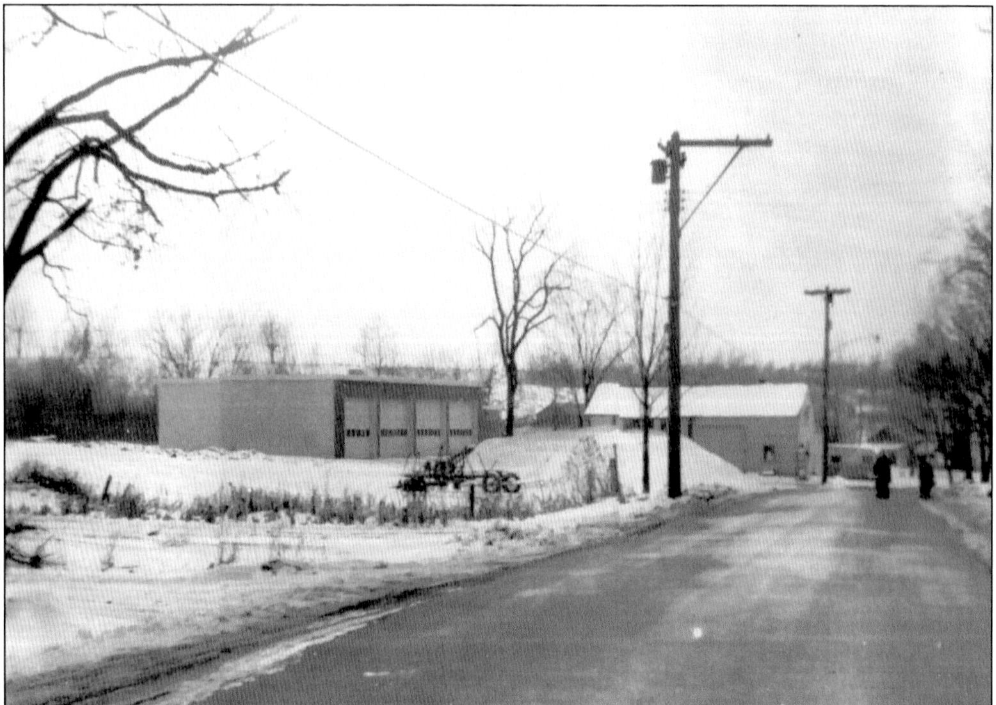

Plank Road is the site of the old (right) town highway department and the new (left) highway department.

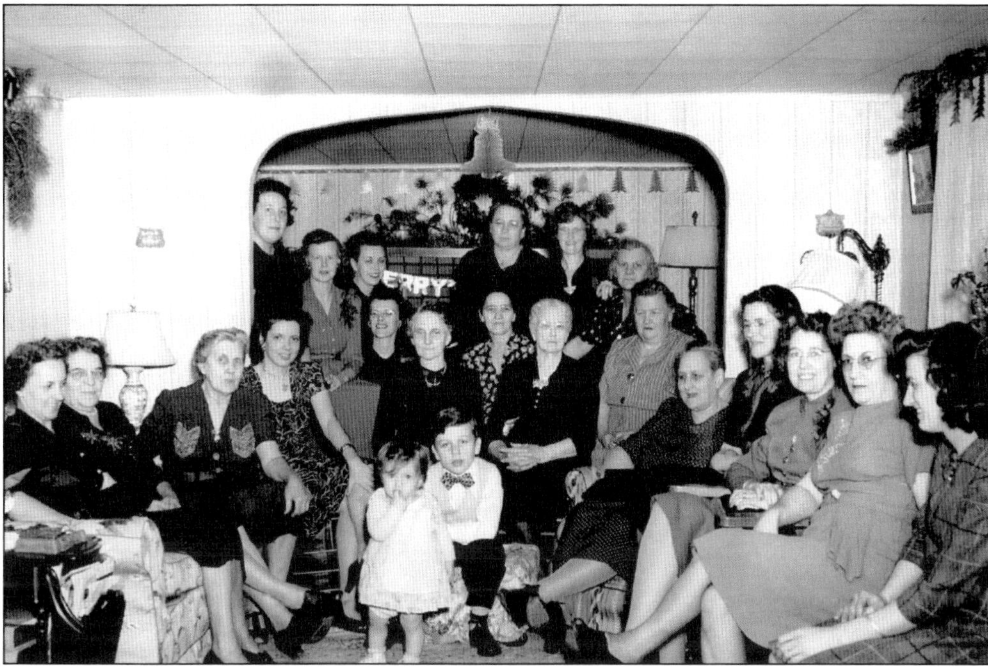

This image shows a Poestenkill Hills Home Bureau meeting at the home of Althea Buehler, around 1947. Standing in the back row, from left to right, are Martha Ripple, Janet Pinney, Alice Prediger, Ruth Moody, Hattie Hayner, and Althea Buehler. Others pictured are a Mrs. Jones, Foneta Prediger, Patsy Fisher, a Mrs. Reichard, Irma Fisher, Beatrice Haines, and Marguerite Fisher. The little boy is Paul Fisher. This group has been active for more then 50 years.

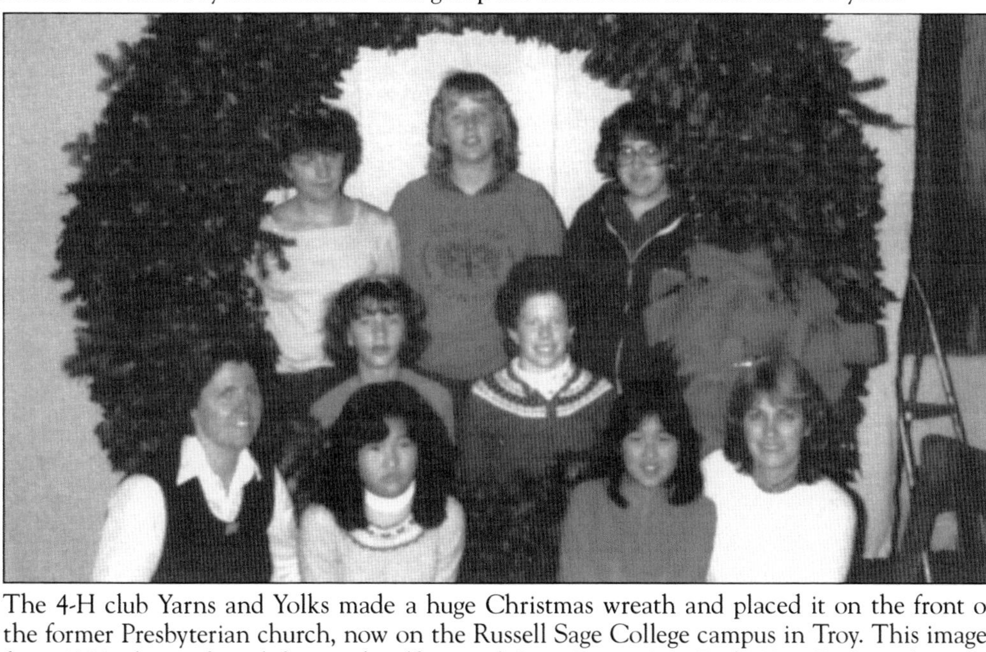

The 4-H club Yarns and Yolks made a huge Christmas wreath and placed it on the front of the former Presbyterian church, now on the Russell Sage College campus in Troy. This image, from 1982, shows, from left to right, (first row) Joan Zweig, Lisa Fink, Kim Fink, and Nancy Fink; (second row) Jessica Zweig and Katie Bashford; (third row) Janine Zweig, Jennifer Zweig, and Christine Geise.

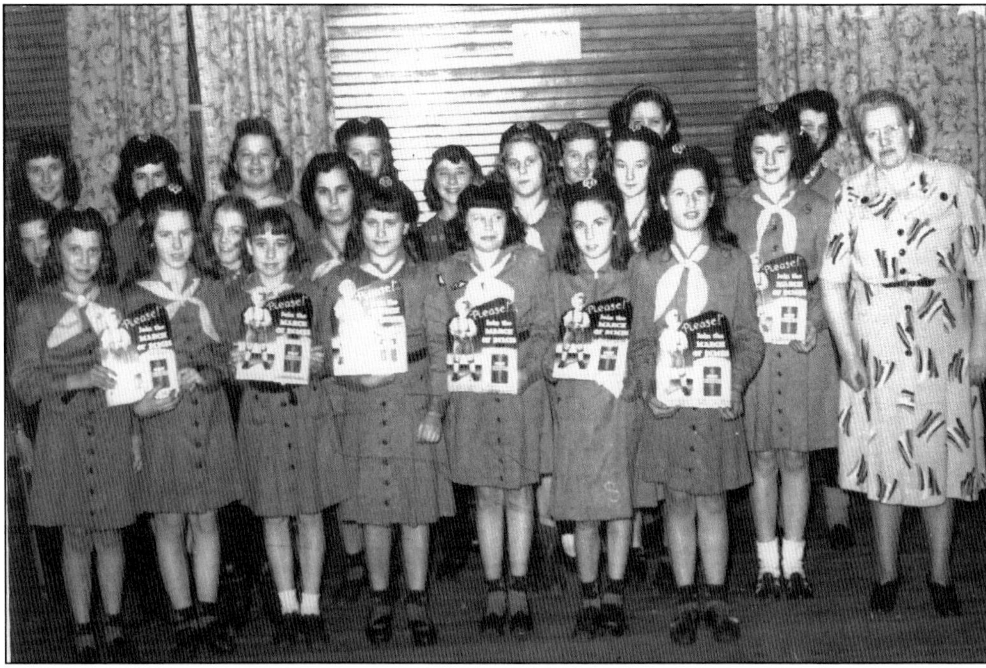

Poestenkill Girl Scouts are involved in collecting money for the March of Dimes around 1950. Among the girls shown here with March of Dimes chairperson Ann Lebentritt are Pat Hogan, Wilma Miller, Susie Walsh, Karen Bauer, Mary Lou Wilkins, Kathleen Walsh, Ann Petropol, Betty Arnold, Margie Hogan, Shirley Collins, Kay Jorgenson, Cindy Bayley, Janet Hoffay, Janet Shaw, Lois Ryan, and Arlene Miller.

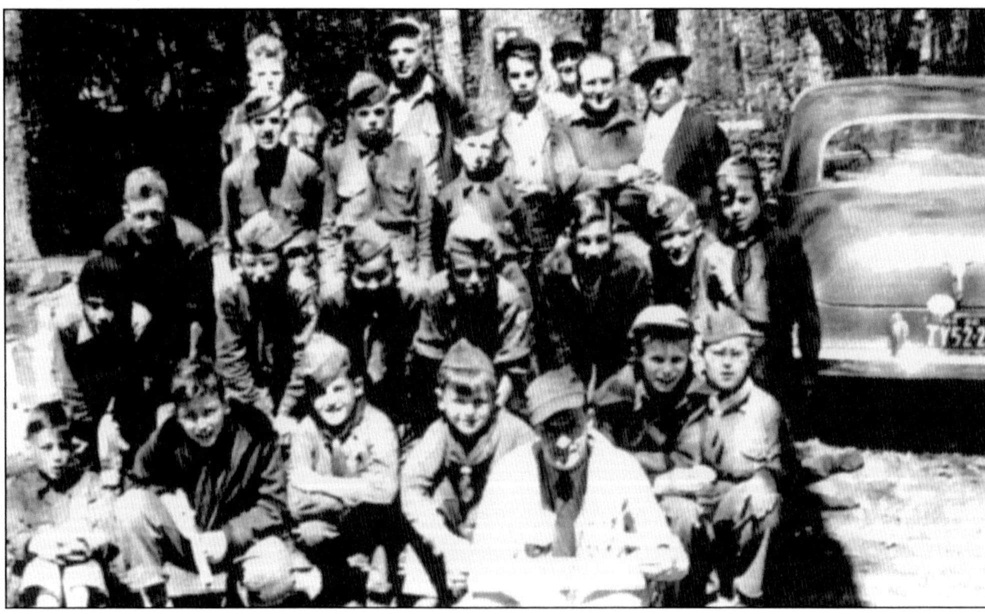

Boy Scout Troop 28 (now Troop 528) has a long history of achievement and enthusiasm. Included in this camporee photograph, from around 1950, are leaders Ken Davis, Jack Mahaffey, and Roland Trathen, and Scouts Hans Bauer, Stanley Arnold, Robert Bubie, Peter Rosenberg, George Brod, Robert Young, Roger Mitchell, Richard Myott, and George Jorgenson.

# *Eight*

# Celebrations and Fun Times

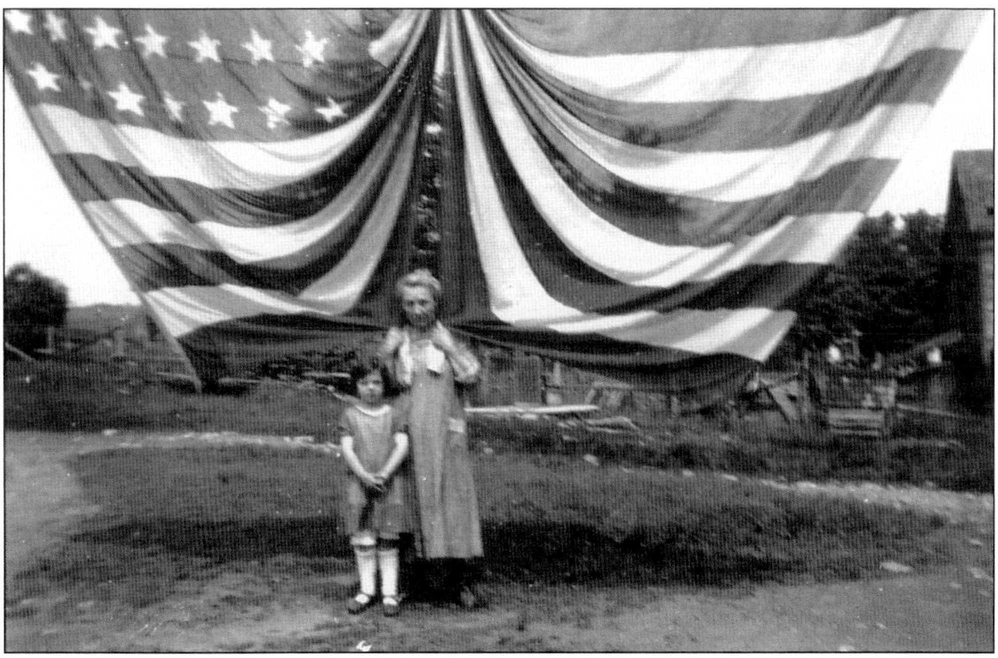

This 12-by-20-foot flag was made during the Civil War by Chloe Ives from East Poestenkill. Ives stitched, by hand, these bright stripes and white stars. A count shows only 35 stars, representing the 35 states. This great flag was flown every Fourth of July at the Ives Corners Hotel. The photograph was taken on July 4, 1922, as Ellen Legenbauer Dzembo and her grandmother Chloe Ives stand below.

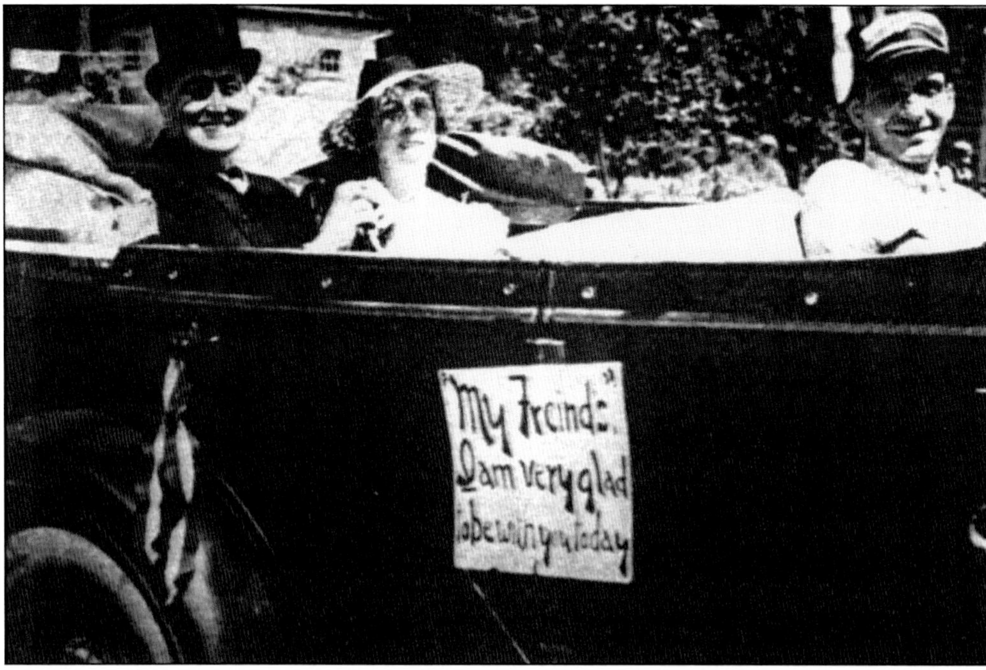


In an image titled "My Friends," Franklin and Eleanor Roosevelt are portrayed by Erma Fisher and Madeline Wood in 1939. Fisher was the founder of the Poestenkill parades, organizing and directing them since the beginning of the 1920s. No child who wanted to be in the parade was ever left out. Fisher herself participated for many years.

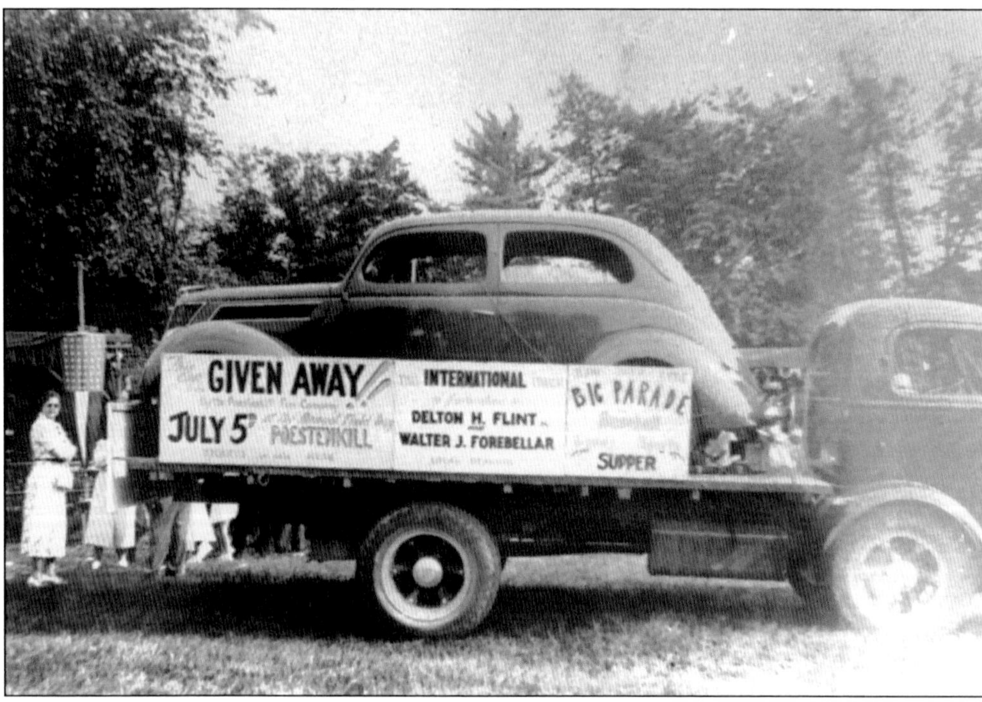


A 1937 Ford was given away at the July 5, 1937, Poestenkill Field Day and parade. E. Marilla Forebellar stands at the left of the float.

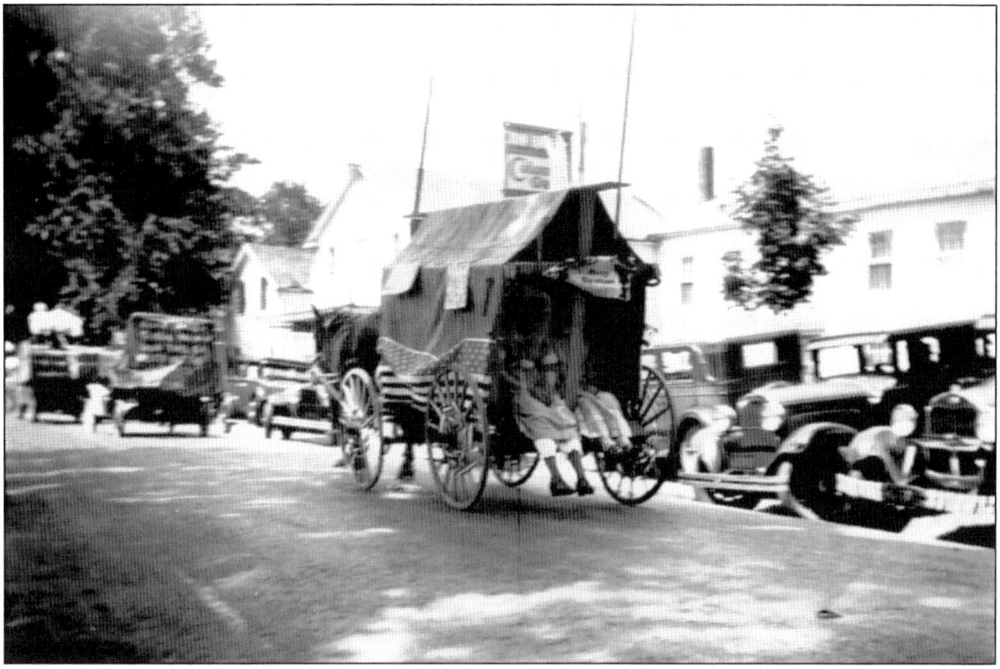

Seen here is a float in the July 4, 1930, parade as it passes Bubie's General Store in the village of Poestenkill.

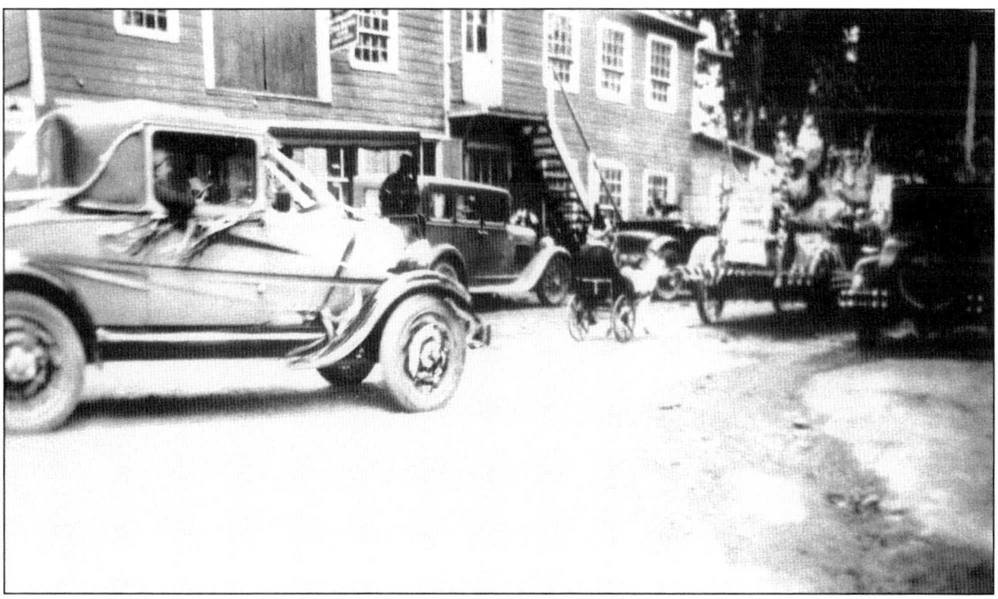

This image shows various old cars in the July 4, 1928, parade. The building in the background is the old wagon maker's shop, later a garage run by Walter Forebellar.

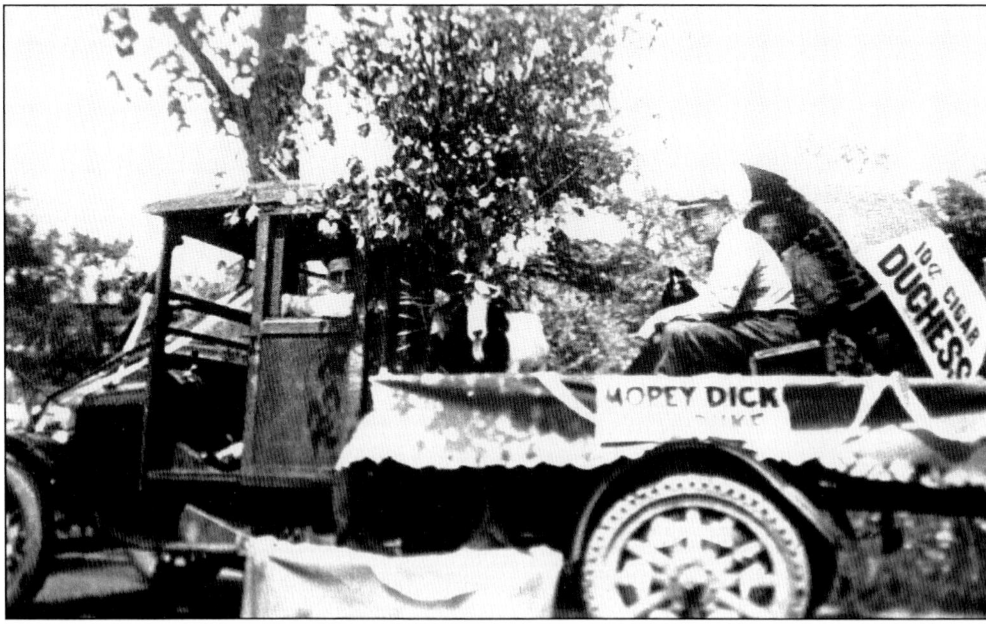


Donald Swankey drives his Ford Model T truck in the Fourth of July parade. Behind the cab of the truck is a nanny goat with Samuel Mill (left) and Charles Farnum sitting in the back. This image is from around the early 1950s.

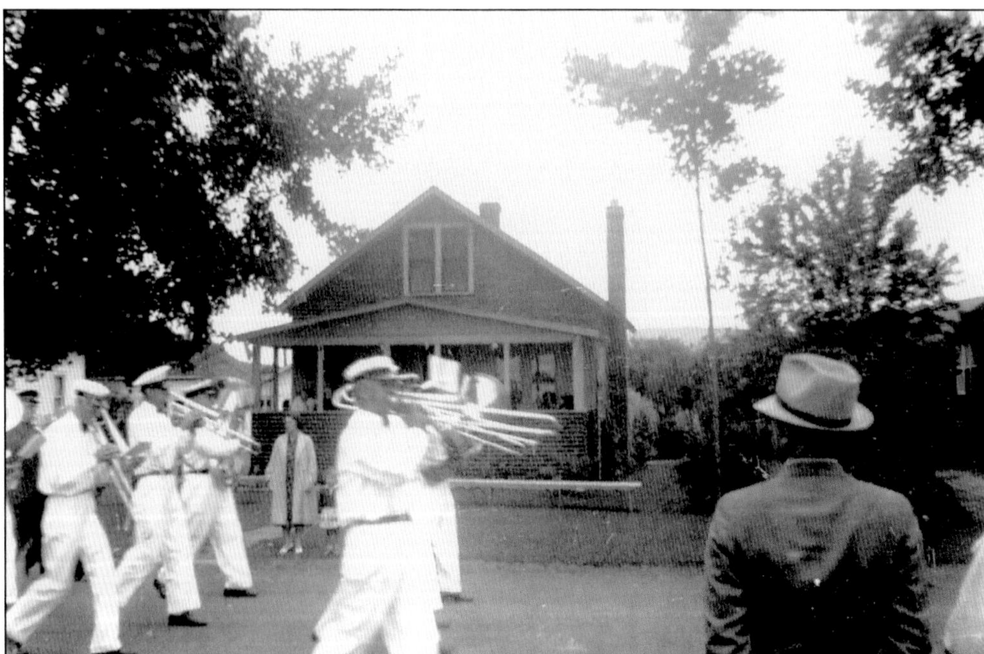

The firemen's band marches in the July 4, 1938, parade. Each year, the Poestenkill Fire Company sponsored a Fourth of July parade and for many years raffled off an automobile. After World War II, the veterans took over the Fourth of July parade organization.

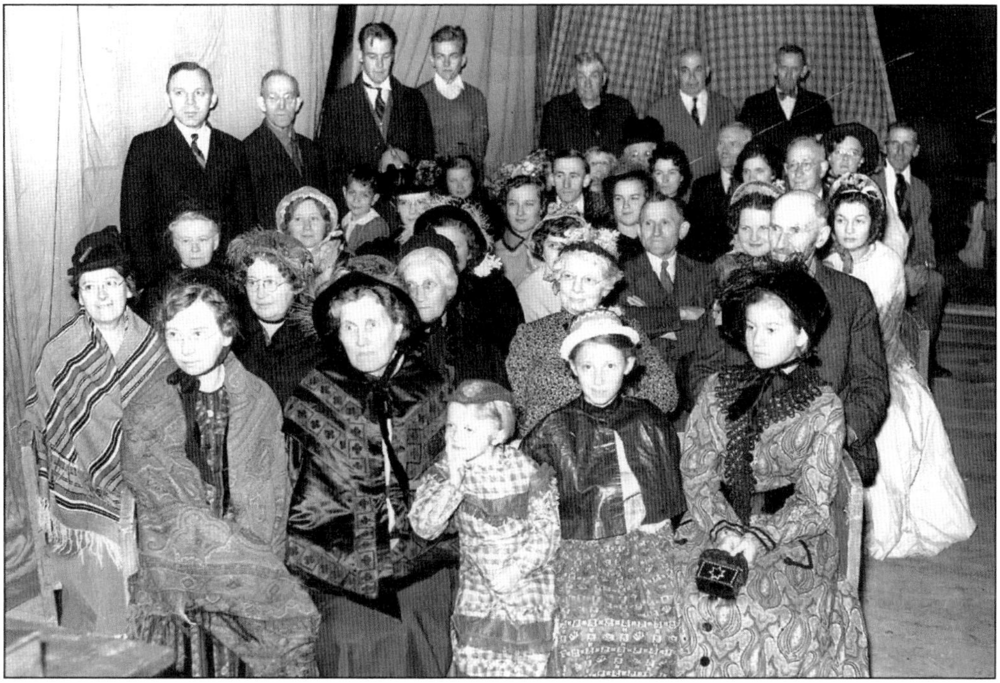

Players pose as they ready themselves for presenting the "Great Garfield Pageant" in 1936. Dr. Henry Garfield, son of the president and then president emeritus of Williams College, attended the festivities.

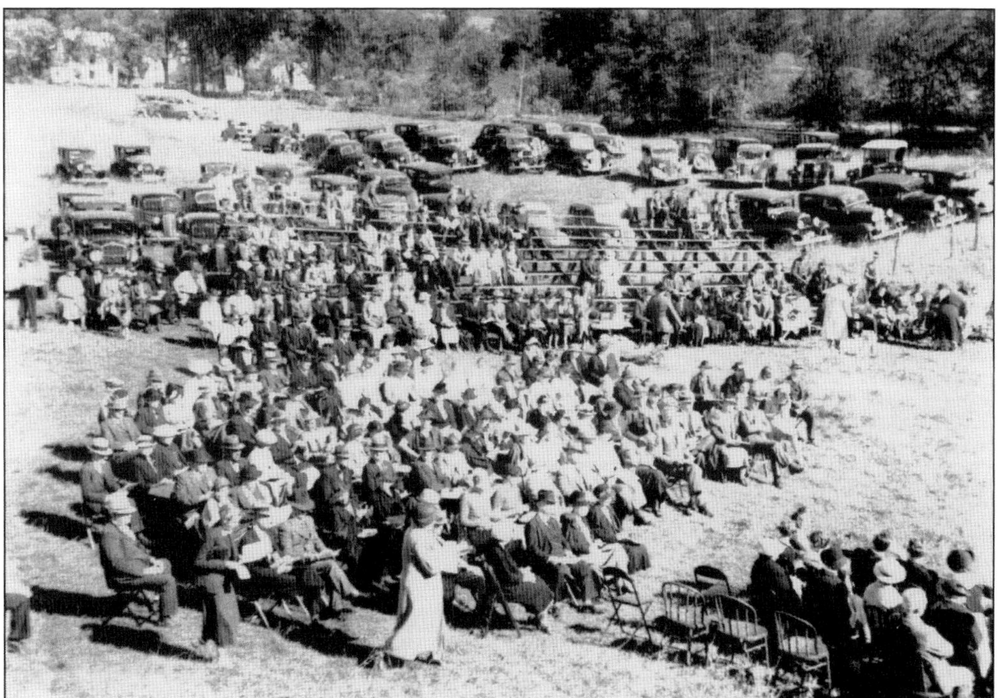

Townsmen watch as the reenactment of the play about Pres. James A. Garfield is presented to the community on September 20, 1936.

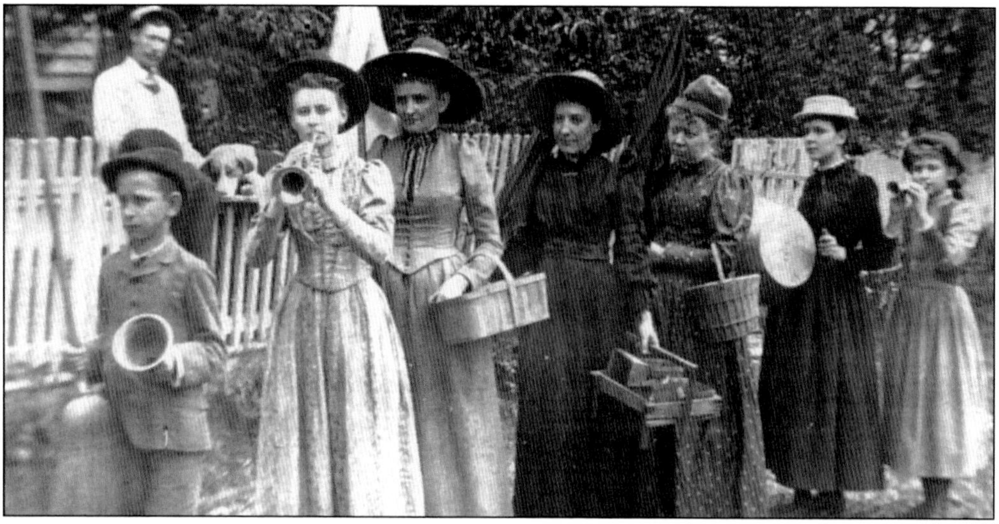

This impromptu marching band shows Fred Obemaier (behind fence), William Morrell, Dell Hayner Obemaier, Mrs. Morrell, Aunt Katie, Mrs. Hayner, and the Morrell girls.

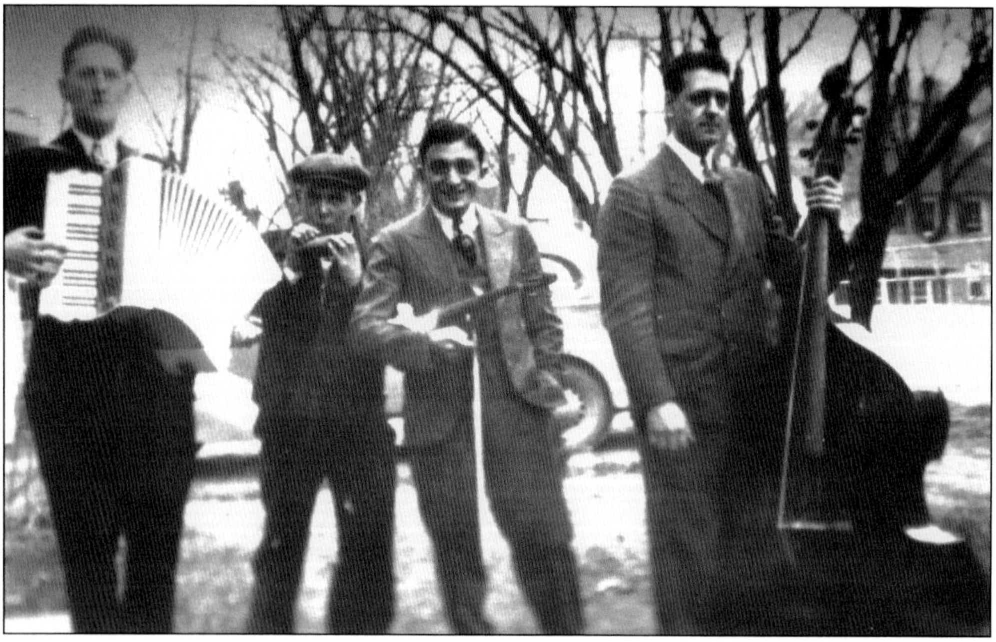

The Snake Hill Sod Busters played for various dances in town. Seen here in 1930, these men, from left to right, Bruce Fisher, Walter Hoffman, Willie Verillo, and Paul Fisher, once tried out on Major Bowes Amateur Hour radio program featuring Fred Allen in New York City.

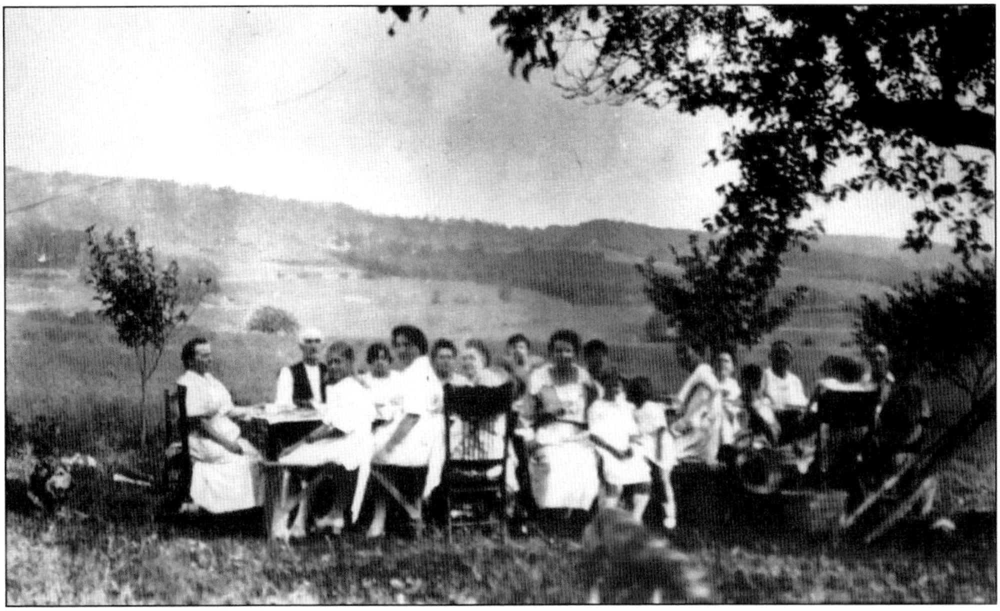

This is the Ballard family clam steam in the early 1920s. Friends and family gather from downstate and Poestenkill for their annual clamsteam at the Hull farm on Snake Hill Road. Snake Hill looms in the background.

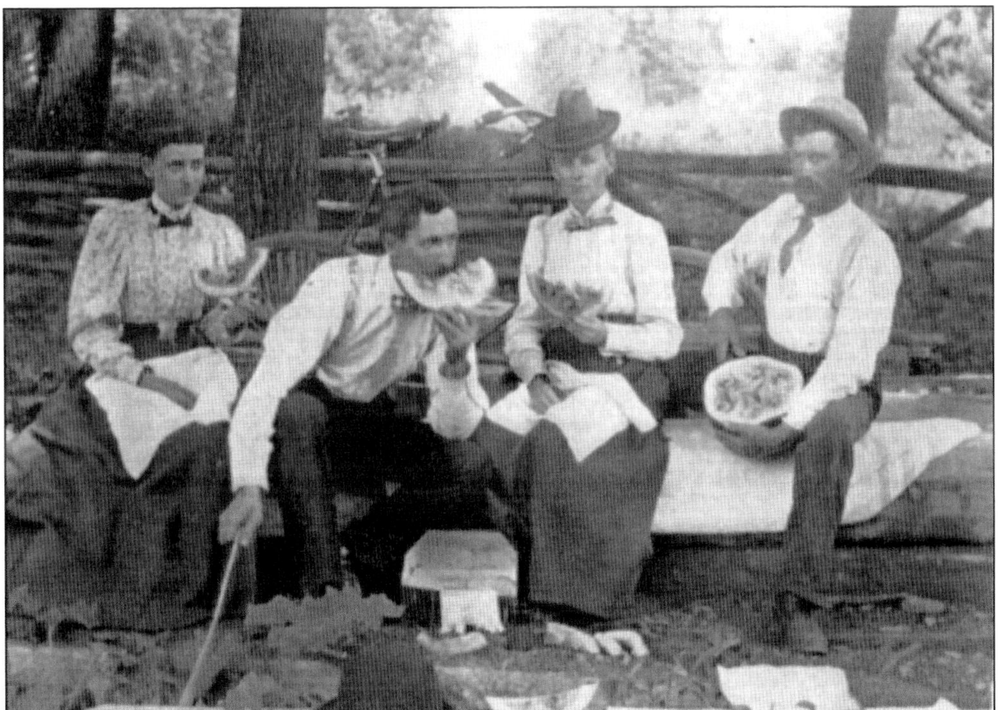

Watermelon was an enjoyable commodity in the early 1900s as a refreshing treat on a warm summer day.

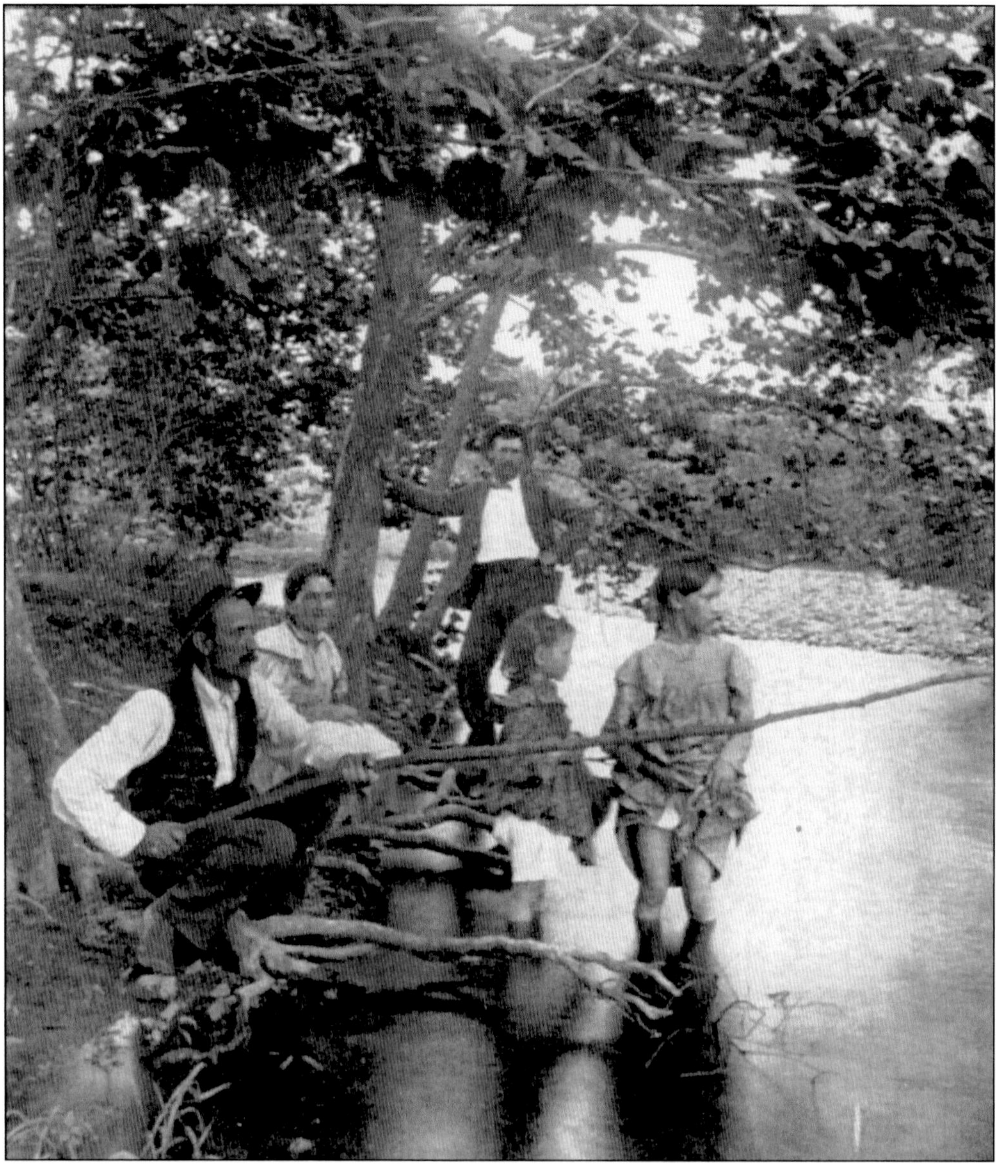

Family members of all ages enjoy fishing and just wading along the banks of the Poesten Kill.

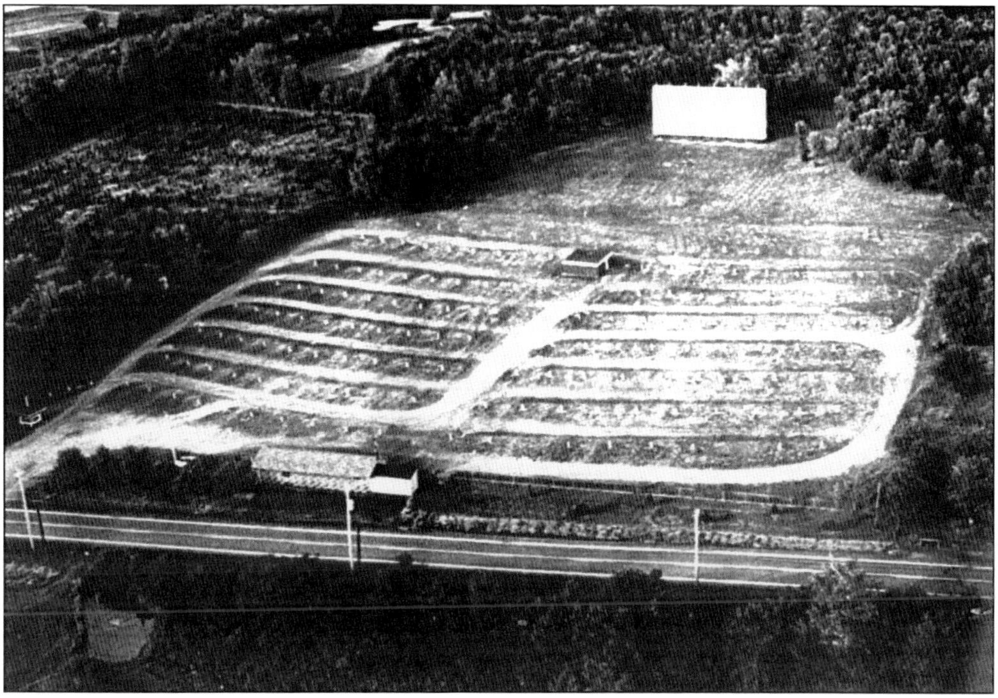

Poestenkill has 1 of only 463 existing drive-in theaters, the Hollywood drive-in, built in 1952 by James Fisher, who oversaw the operation for the next 16 years. In 1960, son Frank joined the family business and continues to run the theater today. Frank has seen many changes over the years in projection, sound, concessions, and all that goes with the business.

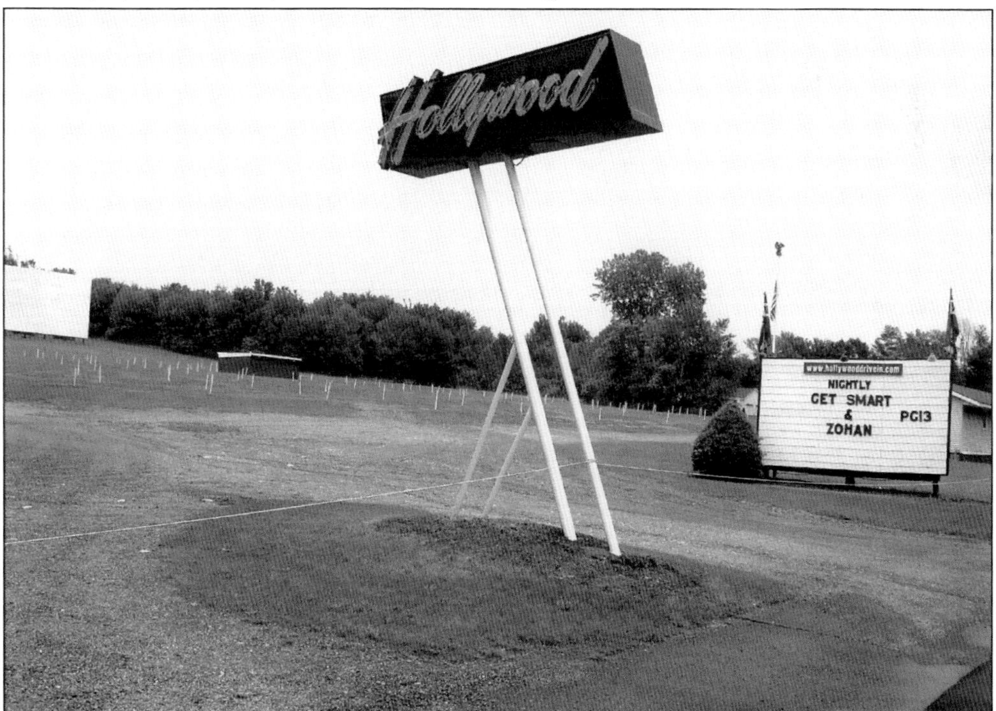

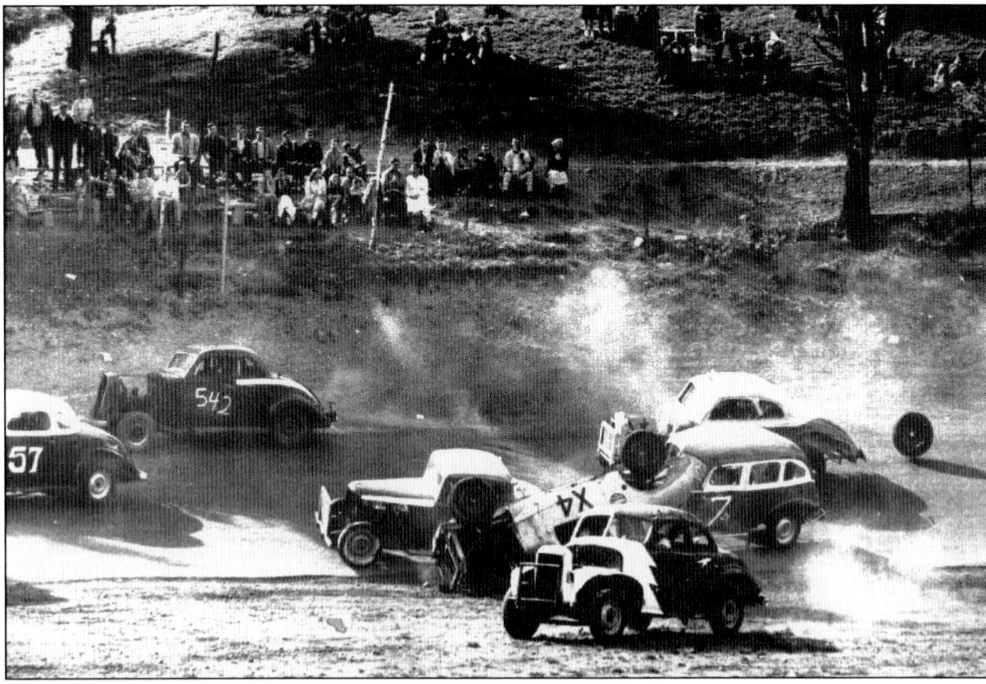


Pinebowl Speedway was opened in 1948 with a dirt track. Later the corners were paved, and about 1950, the entire track was paved. The track closed in 1966. Well-known drivers here were Link Pettit, Mike Ething, and Tommy Corellis.

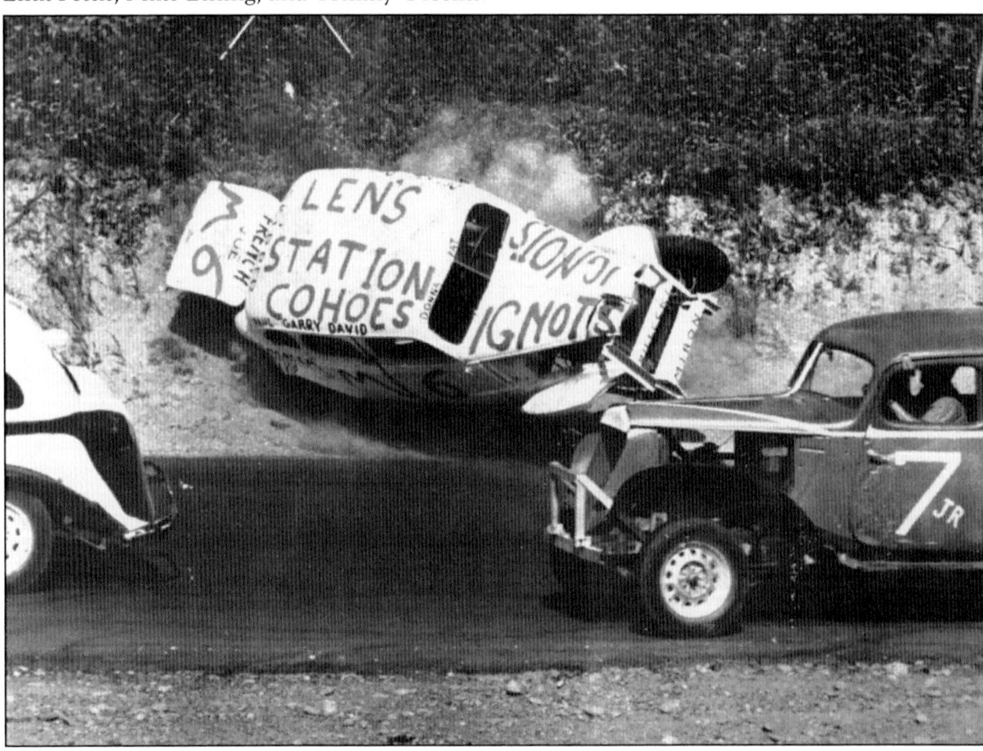


In 1957, Len Miron was paid $15 by the promoters to flip his car for the spectators.

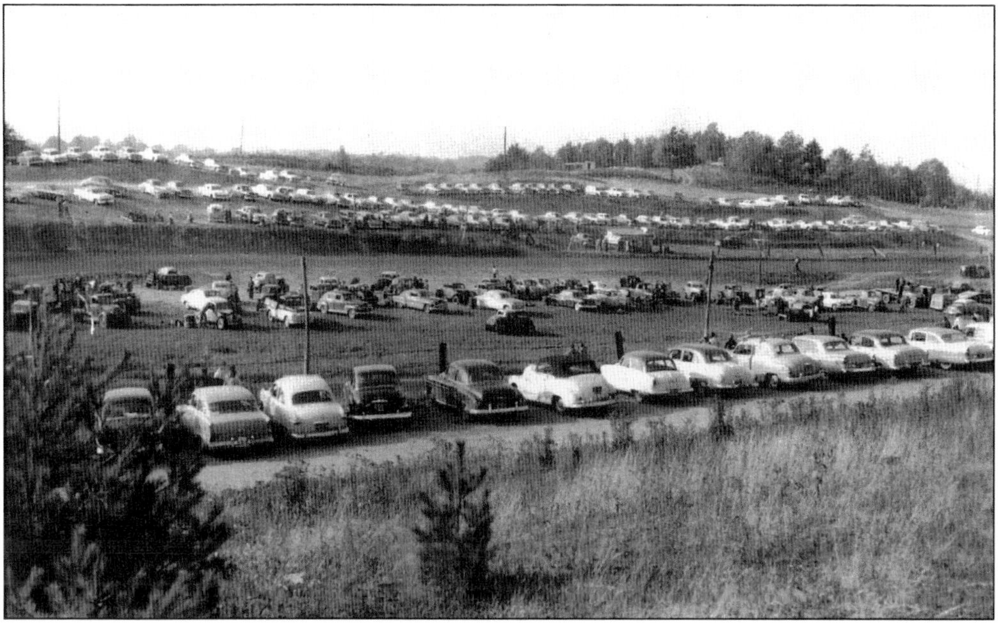

Route 66 Speedway opened in 1950 and was run by Harold Garstang. Ed Ryan took over running the track in 1960 and renamed it the Hollywood Bowl, also known as the "Hollywood Hole." The most famous driver to run this track was Mario Andretti in 1960. Johnny Kettel was the only black driver to race on this track.

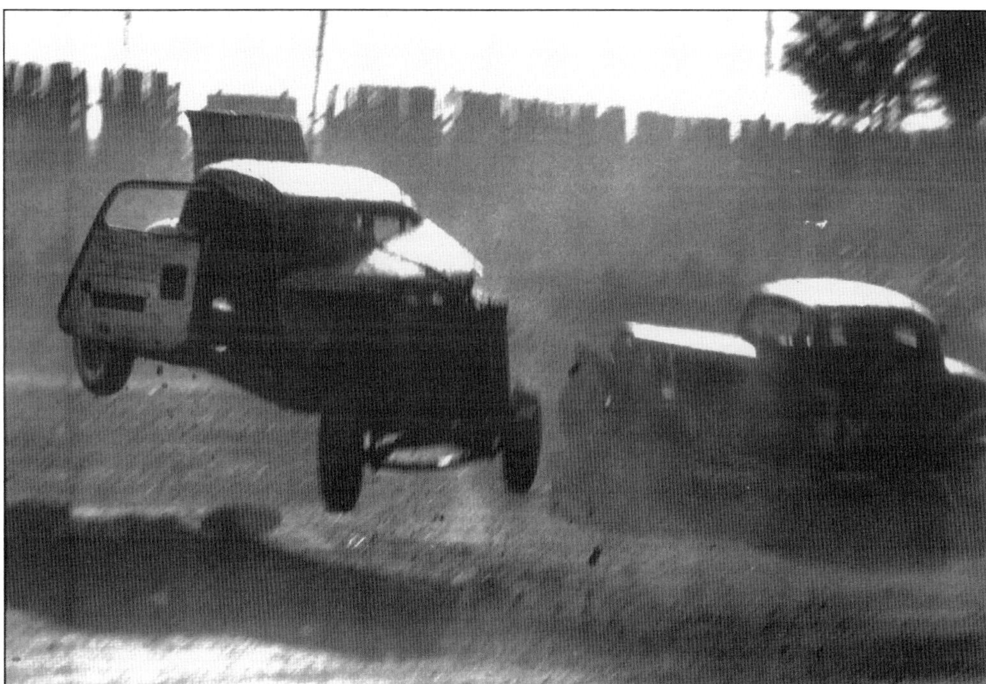

This is an action picture at the Route 66 Speedway from around the 1950s.

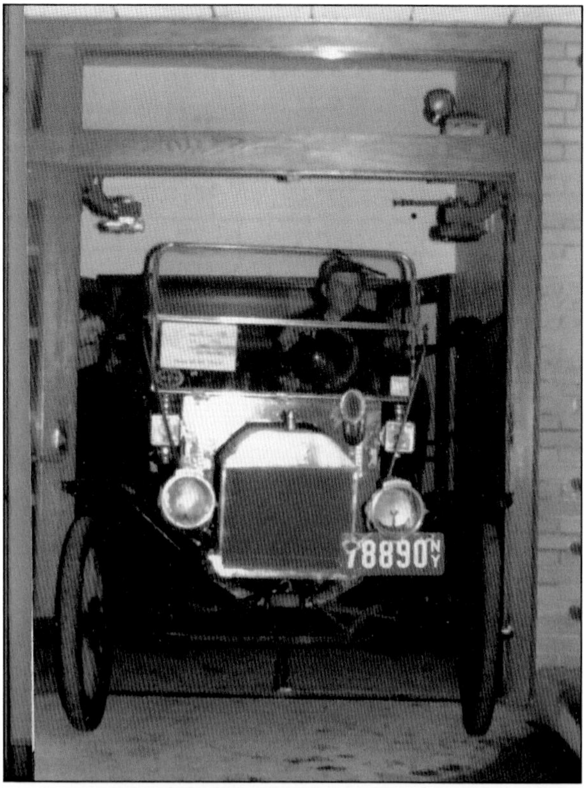


Poestenkill was one of the first towns in the nation to be recognized as an official bicentennial community by the American Revolution Bicentennial Administration. The Bicentennial Commission was formed and plans for celebrations were begun. On two occasions, the commission presented Country Living at Its Best, a replicated exhibit of rural Poestenkill. Buildings were erected and furnished, exhibits set up, and many demonstrations took place throughout the weeklong exhibit. Ernest Legenbauer's old Ford Model T (left) was brought into the school building and put on exhibit. Below are the mailboxes used in the mid-1900s in the Poestenkill Village Post Office.

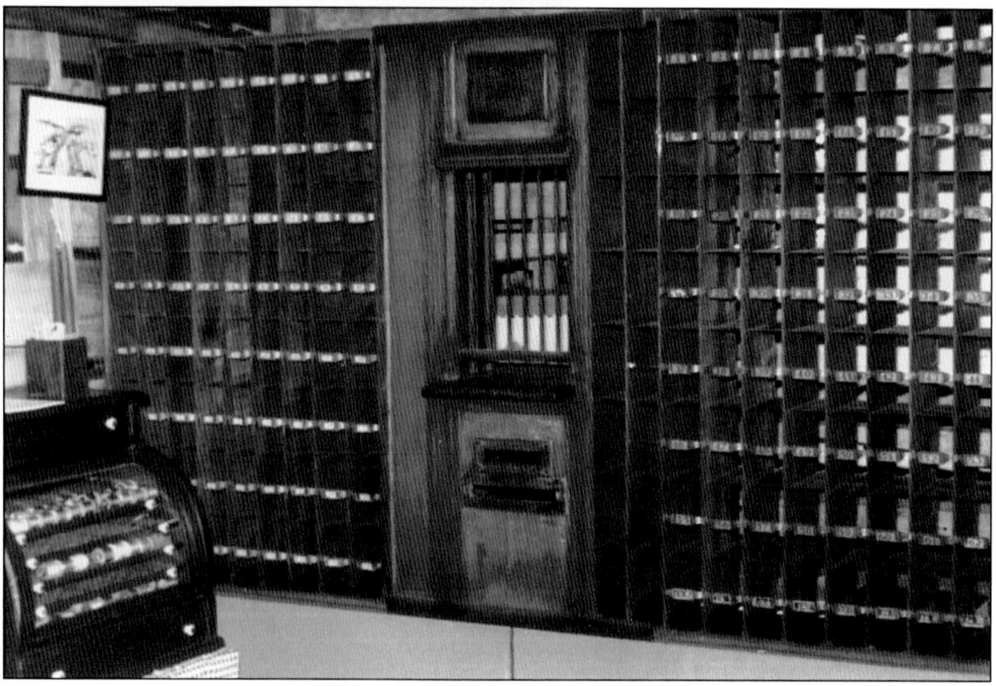

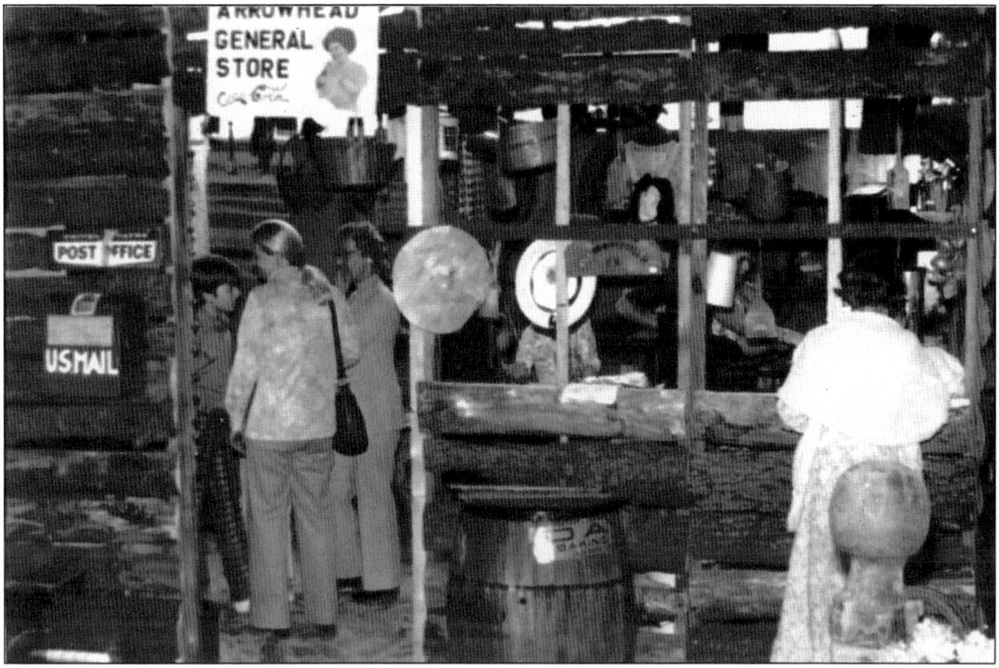


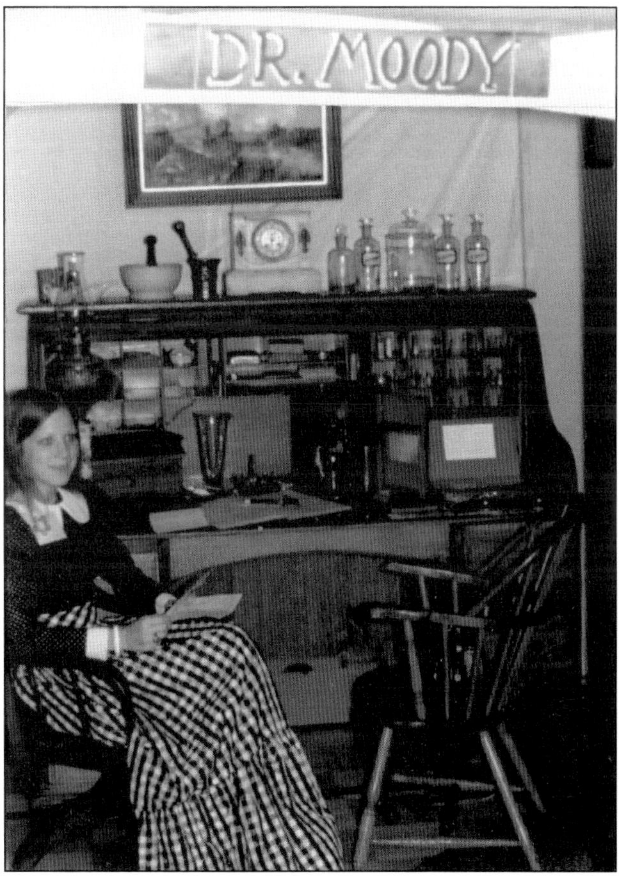


Above shows the general store that was erected and filled with early items to browse. Outside the door is an early mail drop box. At right is the office of one of Poestenkill's early doctors, Dr. Matthew Moody. Many apothecary items were displayed around the room including the old desk shown here.

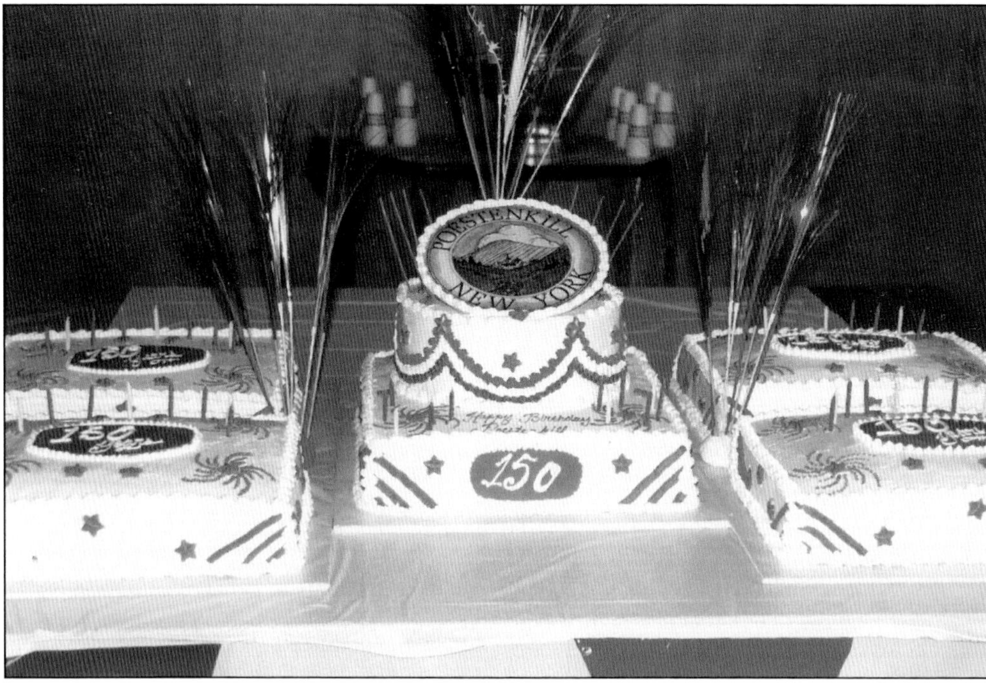


The Town of Poestenkill celebrated its sesquicentennial birthday, 150 years, in 1998. Many activities were held throughout the year. This large birthday cake was shared with the community at the April birthday party.

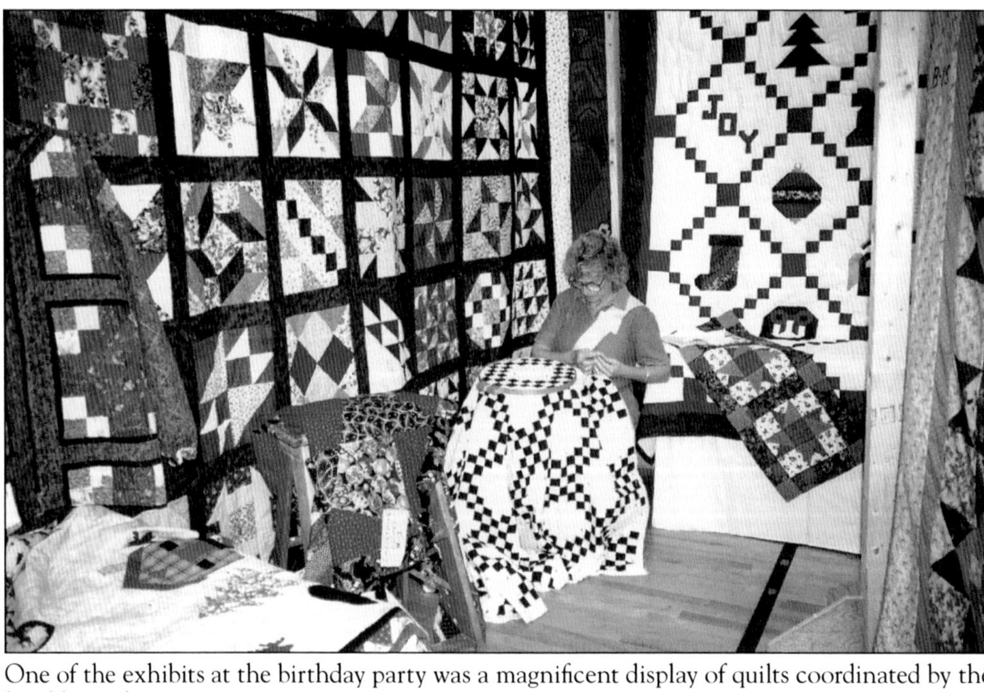


One of the exhibits at the birthday party was a magnificent display of quilts coordinated by the local home bureau organization.

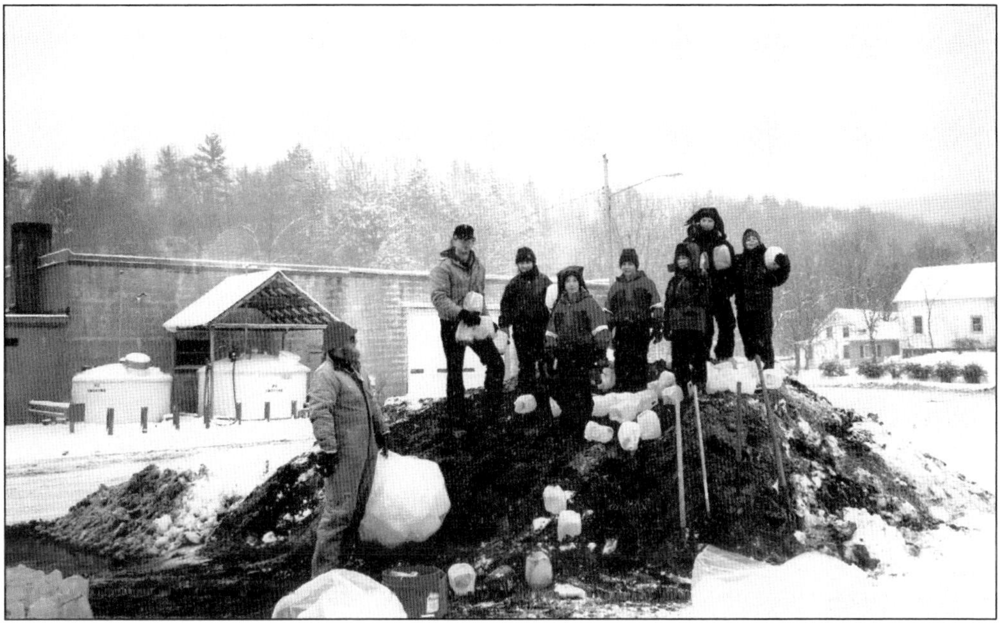

The Poestenkill Boy Scout troop filled milk jugs with dirt and then placed a candle in each jug. The candles were lit at dusk and placed along all the main roads leading to the center of the village, lighting the way to the first Family Fun Night, December 31, 1997.

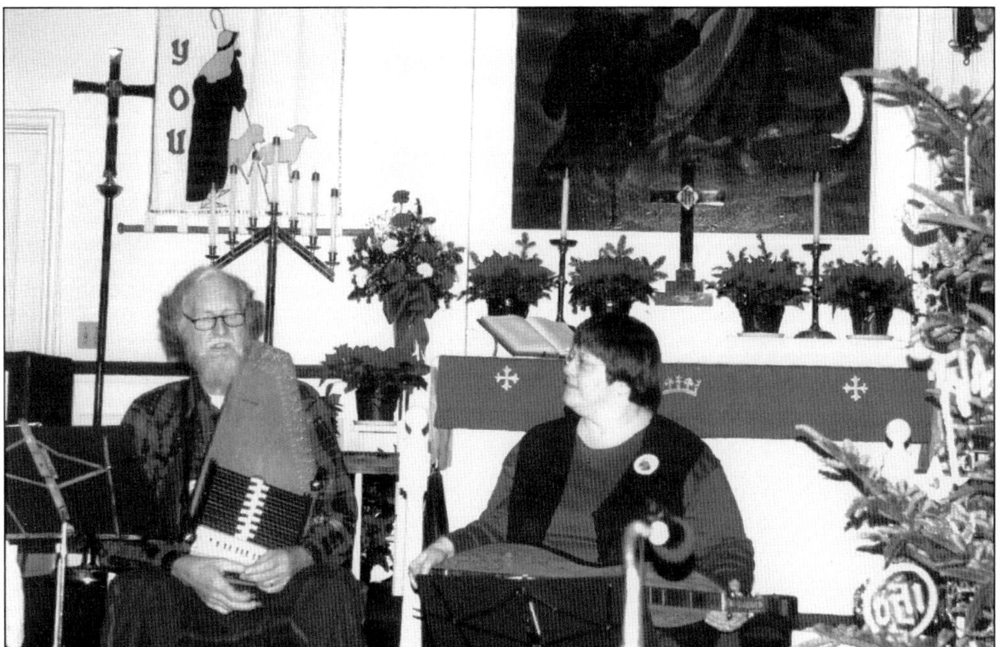

Gene and Carol Langley were among the many entertainment groups who played, sang, told stories, danced, and exhibited items to welcome in the New Year.

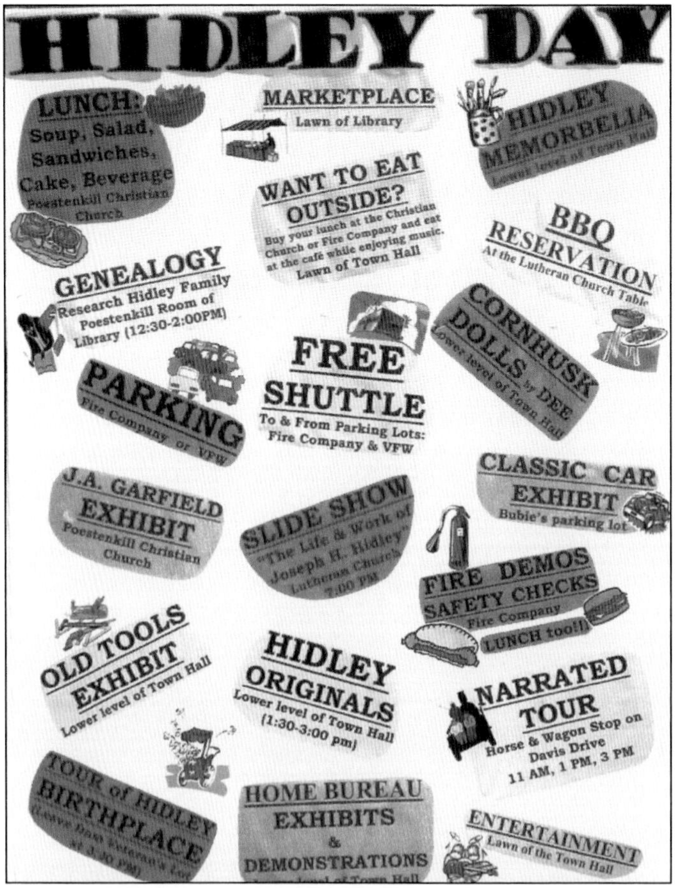


Hidley Day was celebrated by the community on September 20, 2003. This was a day full of exhibits and activities. Below is a picture of Toby Chadwick taking people on a guided, narrated tour of the village of Poestenkill. Narration was provided by Joan Zweig, who pointed out many landmarks of the past as well as told stories.

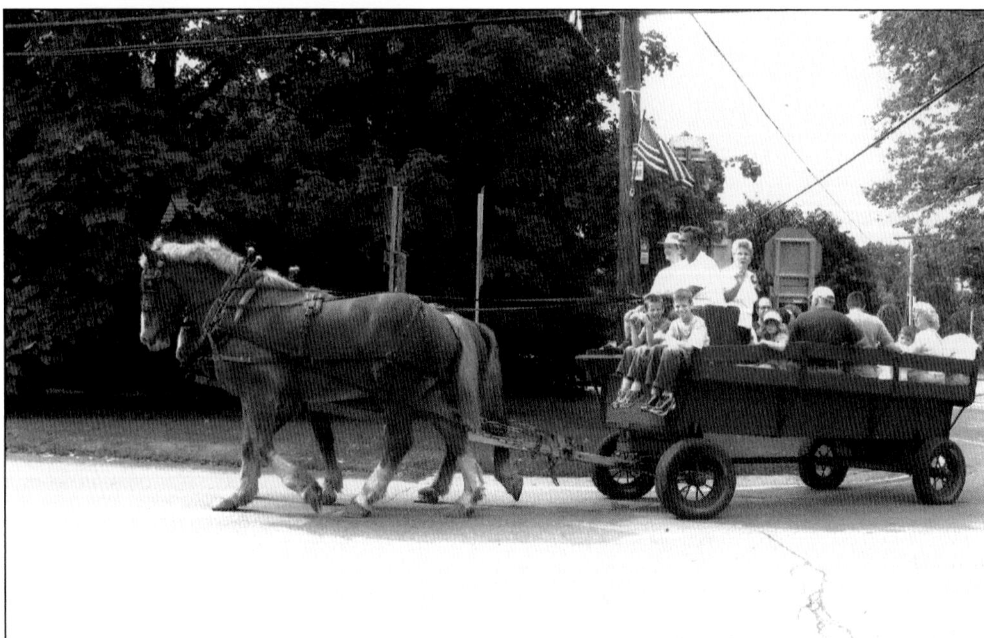

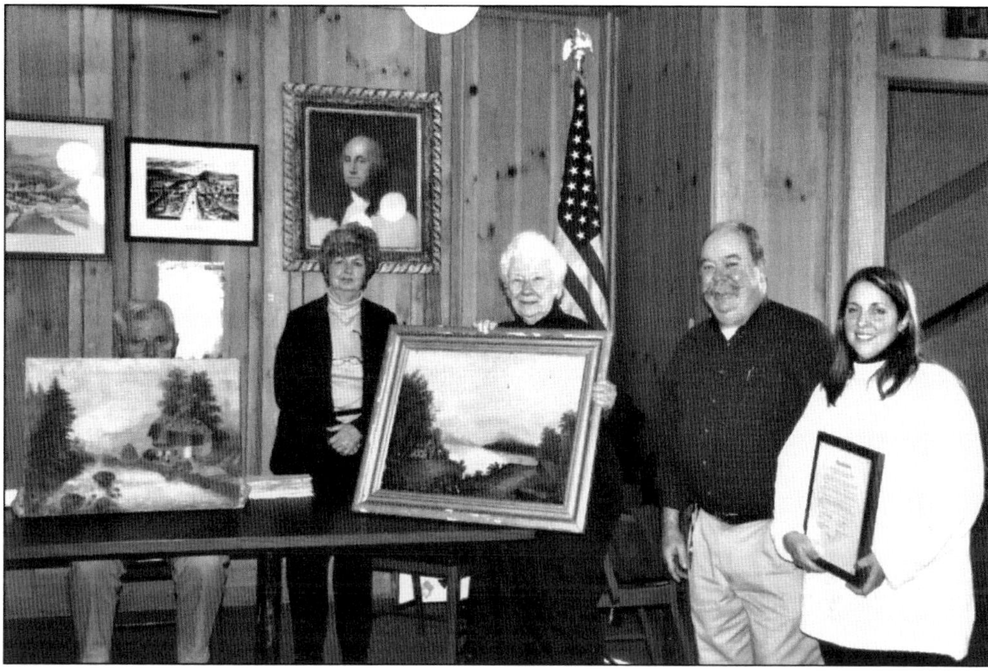

The Cox family found two canvases that were documented as being painted by Joseph Henry Hidley, a local primitive folk artist. These were donated to the town, and the town, in turn, had them restored.

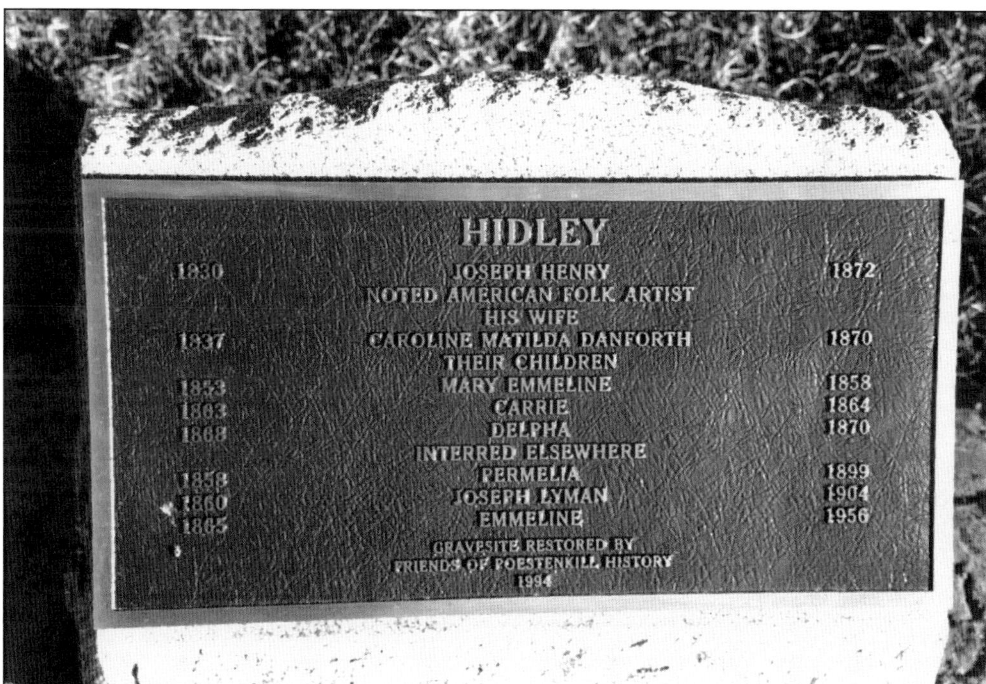


Joseph Hidley, his wife, Caroline, and some of their children are buried in the village cemetery, Hillside Cemetery. The Friends of Poestenkill History had the gravestones set upright and a bronze marker placed in front of the graves.

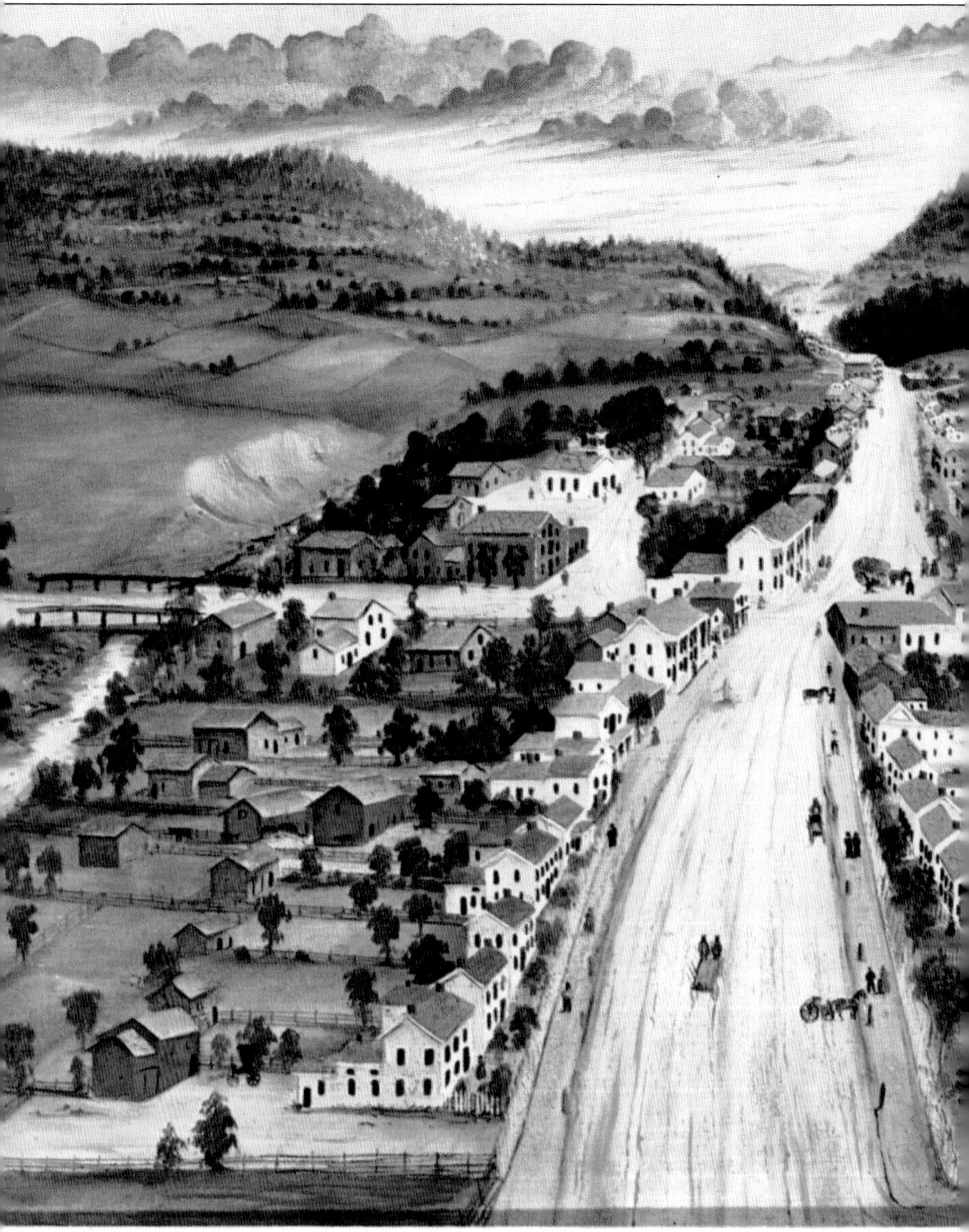

*Poestenkill, New York* BY JOSEPH H. HI

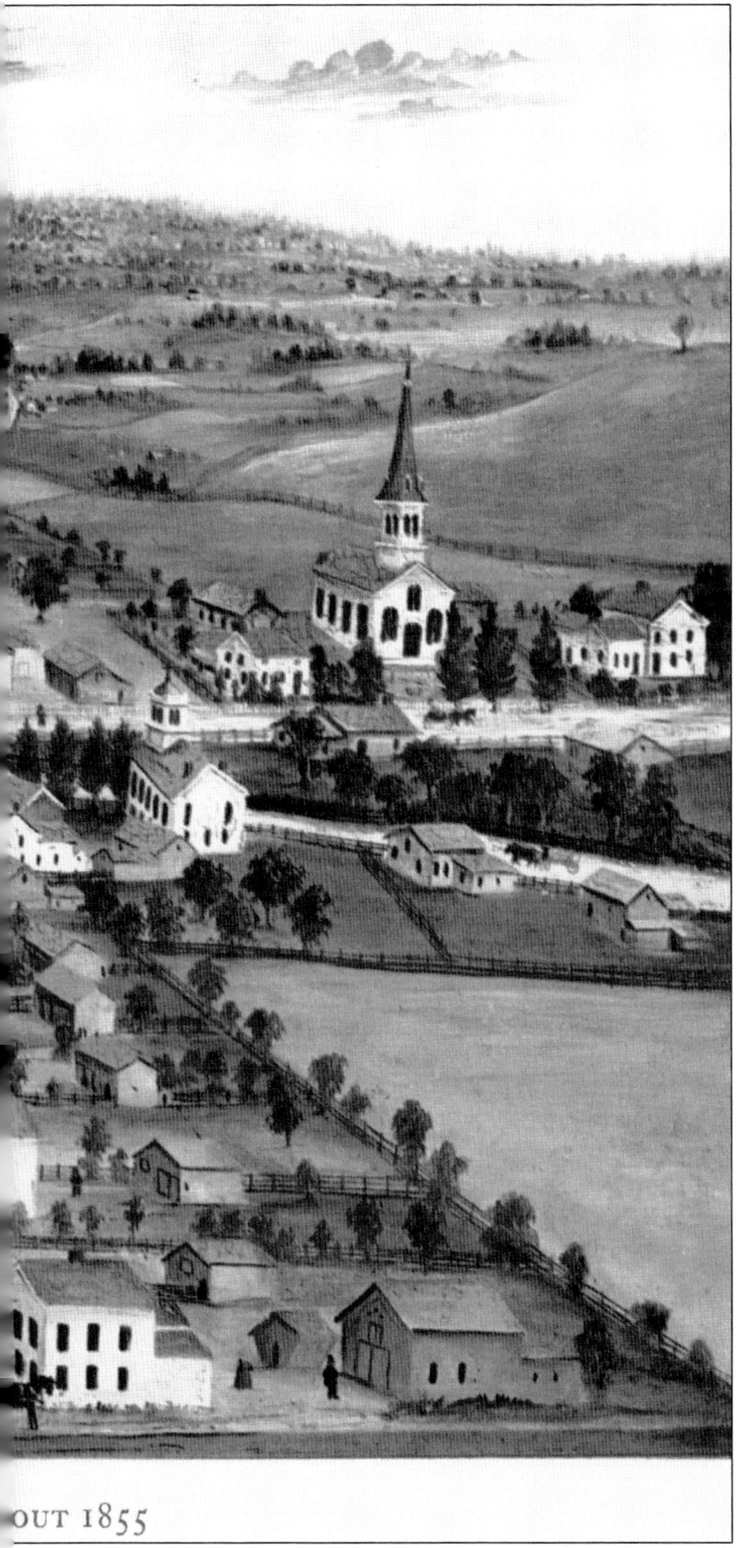


This image is titled "Crow's Eye View of Poestenkill." This is one of the several paintings done by Joseph Henry Hidley, a primitive folk artist who lived in the village of Poestenkill. Hidley used to paint scenes and still-life pictures for residents, as well as paint fire screens and decorative scenes under people's windows in their homes. He was a painter and taxidermist by profession.